The Thinkers

Studies in Postwar American Political Development

Steven Teles, *Series Editor*

Series Board Members
Jennifer Hochschild
Desmond King
Sanford Levinson
Taeku Lee
Shep Melnick
Paul Pierson
John Skrentny
Adam Sheingate
Reva Siegel
Thomas Sugrue

The Delegated Welfare State: Medicare, Markets, and the Governance of Social Policy
Kimberly J. Morgan and Andrea Louise Campbell

Rule and Ruin: The Downfall of Moderation and the Destruction of the Republican Party, from Eisenhower to the Tea Party
Geoffrey Kabaservice

Engines of Change: Party Factions in American Politics, 1868–2010
Daniel DiSalvo

Follow the Money: How Foundation Dollars Change Public School Politics
Sarah Reckhow

The Allure of Order: High Hopes, Dashed Expectations, and the Troubled Quest to Remake American Schooling
Jal Mehta

Rich People's Movements: Grassroots Campaigns to Untax the One Percent
Isaac William Martin

The Outrage Industry: Political Opinion Media and the New Incivility
Jeffrey M. Berry and Sarah Sobieraj

Artists of the Possible: Governing Networks and American Policy since 1945
Matt Grossman

Building the Federal Schoolhouse: Localism and the American Education State
Douglas S. Reed

The First Civil Right: How Liberals Built Prison America
Naomi Murakawa

How Policy Shapes Politics: Rights, Courts, Litigation, and the Struggle over Injury Compensation
Jeb Barnes and Thomas F. Burke

No Day in Court: Access to Justice and the Politics of Judicial Retrenchment
Sarah Staszak

Ideas with Consequences: The Federalist Society and the Conservative Counterrevolution
Amanda Hollis-Brusky

The Business of America Is Lobbying: How Corporations Became Politicized and Politics Became More Corporate
Lee Drutman

Below the Radar: How Silence Can Save Civil Rights
Alison L. Gash

Building a Business of Politics: The Rise of Political Consulting and the Transformation of American Democracy
Adam Sheingate

Prison Break: Why Conservatives Turned Against Mass Incarceration
David Dagan and Steven Teles

The Other Rights Revolution: Conservative Lawyers and the Remaking of American Government
Jefferson Decker

When Bad Policy Makes Good Politics:
Running the Numbers on Health Reform
Robert P. Saldin

Citizens by Degree: Higher Education Policy
and the Changing Gender Dynamics of
American Citizenship
Deondra Rose

Politics at Work: How Companies Turn
Their Workers into Lobbyists
Alexander Hertel-Fernandez

The Cities on the Hill: How Urban
Institutions Transformed National Politics
Thomas K. Ogorzalek

Framing Inequality: News Media, Public
Opinion, and the Neoliberal Turn in U.S.
Public Policy
Matt Guardino

Mobilized by Injustice: Criminal Justice
Contact, Political Participation, and Race
Hannah L. Walker

Short-Circuiting Policy: Interest Groups and
the Battle over Clean Energy and Climate
Policy in the American States
Leah Cardamore Stokes

The Rise of Political Action Committees:
Interest Group Electioneering and the
Transformation of American Politics
Emily J. Charnock

Separate but Faithful: The Christian Right's
Radical Struggle to Transform Law and
Legal Culture
Amanda Hollis-Brusky and Joshua C. Wilson

Captive Market: Accountability and State
Prison Privatization
Anna Gunderson

The Myth of Left and Right: How the
Political Spectrum Misleads and Harms
America
Hyrum Lewis and Verlan Lewis

Privatizing Justice: Arbitration and the
Decline of Public Governance in the US
Sarah Staszak

The Thinkers: The Rise of Partisan Think
Tanks and the Polarization of American
Politics
E. J. Fagan

The Thinkers

The Rise of Partisan Think Tanks and the Polarization of American Politics

E. J. FAGAN

OXFORD
UNIVERSITY PRESS

Oxford University Press is a department of the University of Oxford. It furthers the University's objective of excellence in research, scholarship, and education by publishing worldwide. Oxford is a registered trade mark of Oxford University Press in the UK and certain other countries.

Published in the United States of America by Oxford University Press
198 Madison Avenue, New York, NY 10016, United States of America.

© Oxford University Press 2024

All rights reserved. No part of this publication may be reproduced, stored in a retrieval system, or transmitted, in any form or by any means, without the prior permission in writing of Oxford University Press, or as expressly permitted by law, by license, or under terms agreed with the appropriate reproduction rights organization. Inquiries concerning reproduction outside the scope of the above should be sent to the Rights Department, Oxford University Press, at the address above.

You must not circulate this work in any other form
and you must impose this same condition on any acquirer.

Library of Congress Cataloging-in-Publication Data
Names: Fagan, E. J., author.
Title: The thinkers : the rise of partisan think tanks and the polarization of American politics / E.J. Fagan.
Description: New York : Oxford University Press, 2024. |
Series: Studies in postwar American political development |
Includes bibliographical references and index.
Identifiers: LCCN 2024009139 (print) | LCCN 2024009140 (ebook) |
ISBN 9780197759653 (hardback) | ISBN 9780197759660 (paperback) |
ISBN 9780197759684 (epub)
Subjects: LCSH: Polarization (Social sciences)—United States. |
Research institutes—Political aspects—United States. |
Political parties—United States. | United States—Politics and government.
Classification: LCC JK1726 .F35 2024 (print) | LCC JK1726 (ebook) |
DDC 324.273—dc23/eng/20240328
LC record available at https://lccn.loc.gov/2024009139
LC ebook record available at https://lccn.loc.gov/2024009140

DOI: 10.1093/oso/9780197759653.001.0001

Paperback printed by Marquis Book Printing, Canada
Hardback printed by Bridgeport National Bindery, Inc., United States of America

To Elle

CONTENTS

Acknowledgments xi
List of Abbreviations xiii

1. Introduction 1

2. The Problem with Problem-Solving 10

3. The Development of Partisan Knowledge Regimes 24

4. Privately Controlled Party Organizations 45

5. How Partisan Think Tanks Set Their Agenda 54

6. The Growth of Polarization and Partisan Think Tanks 69

7. Partisan Think Tanks and Polarization across Issues 86

8. Polarized Policy Analysis 99

9. Green Jobs and Climate Change Denial 119

10. Democracy and the Information Wars 135

Methodological Appendix to Chapters 5–7 147
Notes 167
References 171
Index 189

ACKNOWLEDGMENTS

Science is a social endeavor, and I am deeply indebted to dozens of people who helped me write this book. The biggest debt that I owe is to Bryan Jones. Choosing to pursue my Ph.D. with Bryan was the best decision that I ever made. I came up with the idea to study partisan think tanks in my very first graduate seminar, where Bryan challenged me to measure how think tanks influence policy. Over the next six years, Bryan was never afraid to push me to take big swings. It took a decade, but I think the result is a home run. Bryan is a legend.

However, Bryan was far from my first mentor. The real genesis for this book came from my time with the small think tank Global Financial Integrity, where I spent the first four years of my career in D.C. At GFI I learned how a small think tank can have a huge influence only through the production and dissemination of information. Thank you to all my amazing GFI mentors: Raymond Baker, Tom Cardamone, Clark Gascoigne, and Heather Lowe.

Bryan was backed up by an incredible faculty at the University of Texas at Austin. Sean Theriault always kept me detail oriented. Chris Wlezien always pushed me to be more rigorous. Alison Craig, Derek Epp, Wendy Hunter, Eric McDaniel, Bryan Roberts, Daron Shaw, Bat Sparrow, and countless other faculty were all incredibly generous, and I am eternally grateful.

I had the best peers in political science in Austin. Thank you, Christine Bird, Felipe Brasil, Ross Buchanan, Laura De Castro Quaglia, Maraam Dwidar, Connor Dye, Rebecca Eissler, Henry Flatt, Guy Freeman, Mark Hand, Jon Lewallen, Katie Madel, Zac McGee, Annelise Russell, JoBeth Shafran, Brooke Shannon, Trey Thomas, and Michelle Whyman. I miss our lab every day.

My colleagues at the University of Illinois–Chicago were as welcoming as anyone could ask for. Thank you, Aleka Filindra for organizing a great book conference that completely changed the book for the better. Thank you, Petia Kostadinova, Evan McKenzie, Deanndra Leuver, Chris Mooney, Andreas Feldman, Noah Kaplan,

Andrea Manning, and everyone else for your feedback and support to a young assistant professor.

Thank you to everyone else in the discipline who provided feedback on this project. Shaun Bevan, Matt Grossman, Chris Koski, Beth Leech, Peter Mortensen, Hans Noel, and Christina Wolbrecht are just a few of the brilliant scholars who generously contributed their feedback.

Finally, I need to thank my family. My parents never discouraged me from quitting my hard-won job in D.C. and moving to Texas to begin a career. My incredible wife, Elle, allowed me to work long hours and weekends for years to earn a Ph.D. You are the best thing that ever happened to me. I love you.

LIST OF ABBREVIATIONS

ACA	Patient Protection and Affordable Care Act
ACES	American Clean Energy and Security Act
AEA	American Enterprise Association
AEI	American Enterprise Institute
ARRA	American Recovery and Reinvestment Act
CAP	Center for American Progress
CBO	Congressional Budget Office
CBPP	Center on Budget and Policy Priorities
CES	Clean Energy Standard
CRS	Congressional Research Service
DLC	Democratic Leadership Council
EIA	Energy Information Agency
EPA	Environmental Protection Agency
IPCC	International Panel on Climate Change
KAS	Konrad Adenauer Stiftung
LDA	Lobbying Disclosure Act
MIP	Most Important Problem
NBER	National Bureau of Economic Research
OTA	Office of Technology Assessment
PAP	Policy Agendas Project

PPI	Progressive Policy Institute
RNC	Republican National Committee
RPS	Renewable Portfolio Standard
TCJA	Tax Cuts and Jobs Act
TPC	Tax Policy Center

1

Introduction

How the Affordable Care Act Was Created

In early 2010, the Patient Protection and Affordable Care Act (ACA), Barack Obama's signature law, was in trouble. Ever since the New Deal, Democrats had campaigned on providing universal healthcare coverage to Americans (Hacker 2010). Harry Truman called for universal healthcare as part of his Fair Deal. Lyndon Johnson created the Medicaid and Medicare programs in the 1960s but fell well short of covering every American. Bill Clinton's administration came the closest, proposing an ambitious single-payer structure like that of many other developed nations, but the effort ended in an embarrassing political and legislative disaster. The American healthcare system was a messy hodgepodge of lightly regulated employer-provided health insurance subsidized through the tax code and public single-payer programs for seniors, children, veterans, and the poorest families. But America's private, employer-based system had been established for decades. All previous attempts to reform the system ran up against opposition from stakeholders and apprehension toward change from normal Americans. When Obama's administration set out to craft major healthcare reform, many Democrats saw it as a dangerous third rail (Hacker 2011).

Rather than pursue a radical change to the American healthcare system, the Obama administration sought to create a universal healthcare framework that preserved much of the existing system, whereby most Americans were covered by private health insurance (Hacker 2011). The ACA was a vast and complicated law which included tax increases, new exchanges where individuals could purchase health insurance, regulatory changes, and a large expansion of Medicaid, the federal government's program to help states provide health insurance to poor families.

These alone would have gone a long way toward expanding insurance coverage, but they were plagued by the core problem that American healthcare reformers had struggled with for decades: adverse selection. Healthy people often don't want to buy health insurance and pay premiums until they get sick and need expensive care. But any insurance company would go bankrupt if too few of their

The Thinkers. E. J. Fagan, Oxford University Press. © Oxford University Press 2024.
DOI: 10.1093/oso/9780197759653.003.0001

plan holders were healthy. Thus, insurance companies refused to cover the care of medical conditions that the patient knew about before buying insurance from them, known as "preexisting conditions." By the mid-2000s, tens of millions of Americans were unable to buy health insurance. Previous Democratic attempts at comprehensive healthcare reform addressed the adverse selection problem by just providing everyone with government-sponsored health insurance, paid for with tax dollars, but the Obama plan would need a more creative policy alternative if it wanted to require private companies to sell affordable insurance to people with preexisting conditions.

The solution that they decided on originated in the unlikeliest of places: the Heritage Foundation. Heritage has long been the center of movement conservatism in the United States. Founded in 1973 by two conservative congressional staffers, Heritage quickly became a fixture in Republican Party policymaking. In 1989, Heritage's director of domestic policy studies Stuart Butler could see that Democrats were prepared to enact a socialized single-payer healthcare system as soon as they regained unified control of the federal government. Butler, a staunch conservative economist who had worked mostly on tax policy during his decade at the think tank, wanted to develop a conservative alternative to a socialized universal healthcare system.[1] In 1989, in a chapter of a volume he edited, Butler proposed a framework to provide universal care under the existing market-based system. Butler and coauthor Edmund Haislmaier (Butler and Haislmaier 1989) proposed a system whereby all individuals would be mandated to purchase health insurance, with tax credits for those who could not afford it. By requiring everyone to carry health insurance, Butler solved the adverse selection problem. In a lecture connected to the plan's release, Butler (1989) framed the mandate as a conservative alternative to socialized healthcare costs: "A mandate on individuals recognizes this implicit contract. Society does feel a moral obligation to insure that its citizens do not suffer from the unavailability of health care. But, on the other hand, each household has the obligation, to the extent that it is able, to avoid demands on society by protecting itself."

Butler's plan became the center of Republican alternative healthcare proposals in the 1990s. Rhode Island senator John Chafee's introduced the Health Equity and Access Improvement Act, which was built on Butler's framework (Klein 2012). The law did not pass but became the basis of Republican healthcare policy in the 1990s. Then-governor of Massachusetts Mitt Romney used the same structure to achieve near-universal healthcare in his state in the 2000s. While the ACA was more generous than the Republican plans and didn't include many conservative ideas also proposed by Butler in 1989, it owed its bones to ideas that originated at Heritage. There was no other way to get to near-universal coverage while also preserving the unique American market-based health insurance system.

Obama was able to pursue the ACA because, for the first time in a generation, Democrats won a filibuster-proof majority in the Senate in the 2008 elections.

Introduction

Their planning for healthcare reform predated the 2008 elections. Former Democratic Senate majority leader Tom Daschle, who lost his seat in 2004, had spent much of the second term of the Bush administration working as a senior fellow for the Center for American Progress (CAP), which was founded only a few years earlier.[2] While working for CAP, Daschle (2008) published *Critical: What We Can Do about the Health-Care Crisis* as a partial blueprint for what would become the Affordable Care Act (Pear 2008). *Critical* was both a political and a policy book, diagnosing the problems of the American healthcare system, explaining why past attempts at universal healthcare failed, and laying out a politically feasible reform plan that Democrats could pass in 2008 that resembled Romney's system in Massachusetts. Obama nominated Daschle to serve as secretary of health and human services, expecting him to take the lead in crafting the law. While Daschle's nomination ultimately failed, his book and ideas heavily influenced the ACA (Marmor 2014).

After a long and politically damaging year debating how to expand healthcare access, all sixty Senate Democrats finally voted to pass the ACA on Christmas Eve 2009. No Republicans supported the bill, or even signaled that they might be open to a deal. However, the Senate bill was flawed and could not feasibly become law. To secure its passage in a pre-Christmas rush, Democrats had included some embarrassing provisions, such as the "Cornhusker Kickback," which gave Senator Ben Nelson's state of Nebraska a special deal to avoid paying for the bill's expansion of Medicaid, as well as numerous other messy provisions and errors that the Senate expected to clean up in conference committee after returning from the holiday. House and Senate negotiators began hammering out the final deal.

But at the last minute, Democrats lost their 60-seat majority. Democratic senator Ted Kennedy of Massachusetts had died in August. The state's governor appointed a Democratic placeholder, with a special election to be held in January. Republican candidate Scott Brown campaigned on a promise to kill Obamacare, but Massachusetts was a safe Democratic state, so few expected a Brown victory. However, Brown pulled off a shocking upset on January 19, ending the Democratic filibuster-proof majority. The ACA appeared dead. Many top Democrats, such as White House Chief of Staff Rahm Emanuel, pushed for Democrats to throw in the towel on comprehensive healthcare reform and instead pass a more limited bill to expand children's health insurance.[3]

Progressives did not want to give up on their chance to expand healthcare access to millions. With no Republican votes, Democrats would have to use the Budget Reconciliation procedure to pass any bill, which can allow some bills to proceed through the Senate without being subject to the filibuster. However, there were a few problems. First, the Byrd Rule limited reconciliation bills to provisions directly related to revenue and spending, but the bill passed by the Senate contained numerous legal and regulatory changes that the Senate parliamentarian would not allow in a reconciliation bill. Second, Democrats hadn't used the complex procedure to pass a party-line major bill since the 1993 Omnibus Budget Appropriations Act and hadn't planned for the ACA to pass with reconciliation. Many Democrats believed that reconciliation could not even be used to amend a healthcare bill that hadn't been intended to pass under the procedure.

But within a week of Brown's victory, two staffers at the Center on Budget and Policy Priorities (CBPP), another leading Democratic-aligned think tank, began laying a blueprint for how Democrats could pass a final bill.[4] Senior Advisor for Federal Fiscal Policy James Horney, along with Paul Van de Water, wrote a private document that came to be known in D.C. as the "Horney Memo." Horney, a political scientist by training,[5] and Van de Water had decades of combined experience at the Congressional Budget Office and as congressional staff. The memo laid out a step-by-step plan for amending the Senate bill using the reconciliation process, which would be one of the most complicated processes to pass a bill in congressional history. House Democrats would first have to pass the Senate bill as written, which President Obama would sign into law. Then they would have to pass a new bill that would amend the newly signed law using reconciliation, taking care not to include any provisions that the parliamentarian would eliminate for violating the Byrd Rule. CBPP president Robert Greenstein then passed the memo to senior White House staff, who followed its instructions to the T.[6] President Obama signed both the original law and amendments enacted in March, securing the largest expansion of U.S. healthcare access since the 1960s.

These are just three stories of how partisan think tanks played an important role from the very beginning to the very end of the process that produced the largest change to U.S. healthcare policy in decades. Many others played big and small roles in between by coming up with ideas about how to change U.S. healthcare law, estimating the costs and benefits of the changes, or defending or attacking policy changes in the media. More broadly, they have played similar roles in countless big and small policy debates over the past five decades.

Indeed, partisan think tanks are some of the most powerful interest groups operating in Washington today. Organizations like the Heritage Foundation, CAP, and CBPP are important players in many of the policy debates that are fought between members of the Republican and Democratic parties. Yet U.S. partisan think tanks do little work in the electoral sphere, such as organizing campaign volunteers, funneling money to candidates and parties, or releasing campaign advertising. They do not represent constituencies, interests, or individuals. Instead, they exert power and influence only through the production and dissemination of information about public policy. How they can be so influential with so little hard political power is a puzzle, complicated by little political science research into their activities. This book aims to address that puzzle, along with the downstream consequences of their role in the American party system.

The Role of Partisan Think Tanks in American Party Politics

In most democracies, political parties control their own think tanks (Campbell and Pedersen 2014). Political parties and their elected officials need policy advice they can trust to make decisions and turn political and ideological priorities into concrete policy proposals. Within the paradigm most common outside of the United States, political parties control party think tanks either as formal party organizations or as de facto formal party organizations organized through university systems (McGann 2016). Party think tanks are deeply integrated into policymaking, helping the party to generate positions, write manifestos, staff the executive branch, and communicate their ideas to the public. The largest, such as the German Christian Democratic Party's Konrad Adenauer Stiftung Foundation, have budgets that far exceed even the largest think tanks in the United States. They are almost entirely publicly financed, with political parties controlling their operations.

The system of think tanks that has evolved to fill this role in the United States is very different (Campbell and Pedersen 2014). The U.S. government provides little public financing for political parties in any form, including to conduct policy analysis. To fill the void, U.S. political parties have turned to privately financed 501(c)(3) nonprofit organizations that they do not control. Under U.S. tax law, 501(c)(3) organizations are technically required to be nonpartisan, but in practice they work exclusively with one political party and are deeply integrated into that party's operations.

Hundreds of think tanks operate in Washington (McGann 2016). Some are small organizations employing just a few people, such as American Compass, which was set up by former Romney advisor Oren Cass to develop a policy agenda for the Republican Party post-Trump. Others are sponsored by industry, such as the American Petroleum Institute. Many have clear ideological missions that align with one party or another, such as the progressive Center for Economic and Policy Research or the single-issue conservative Tax Foundation. These think tanks are often too small to play a core role in party politics and act more like traditional interest groups. Some large think tanks like the Brookings Institution are essentially universities without students, who may in practice employ more scholars who tend to support one party over the other but aren't strategic party actors. Others, like the RAND Corporaiton, are quasi-government organizations working on contract. However, I demonstrate in Chapter 3 that four think tanks stand out from the pack, becoming de facto party organizations rather than mere interest groups. These are the Republican-aligned partisan think tanks Heritage Foundation and American Enterprise Institute (AEI) and the Democratic-aligned Center for American Progress and Center on Budget and Policy Priorities.

The biggest consequence of the emergence of partisan think tanks is that they drove the polarization of American political parties. When political scientists consider the causes of the rapid polarization that began in the late 1970s, we rarely point to information as a mechanism. Partisan think tanks did not polarize American politics by themselves. Polarization is a complex and multifaceted phenomenon, with causes as far-ranging as changes in media environments, money in politics, and cultural and geographic shifts (Barber and McCarty 2015). However, I argue that well-organized information that is integrated into the decision-making of political parties and elected officials was necessary to enable the parties to take vastly different policy positions. They can disrupt the problem-solving processes that often bring reluctant policymakers of both parties together. If partisan think tanks didn't exist, American politics would be far less polarized.

Even beyond their impact on broader trends in American politics, this book demonstrates their ubiquity in modern American policymaking. In anecdotes derived from interviews and archival documents, I show the role that partisan think tanks played in many of the most important moments in recent American political history. During almost all the episodes that defined policymaking during the era of polarization, such as the Reagan administration's redefinition of Republican Party orthodoxy to the right, Newt Gingrich's decisive first two years as Speaker of the House, and the Democratic Party's decade of progressive policymaking on healthcare and climate change during the Obama administration, partisan think tanks were at the center of decision-making.

Plan for the Book

The book contains nine chapters in addition to this introduction, divided into two halves. In the first half of the book, I examine how partisan think tanks use information to influence politics, why the system of partisan think tanks evolved, and how they choose which issues to produce information on. In the second half of the book, I explore their impact on American politics, arguing that they were an important part of the rapid polarization of the party system that began in the 1970s.

Chapter 2, "The Problem with Problem-Solving," explores how an opportunistic information producer can capitalize on the problem-solving instincts of political systems by taking advantage of windows of opportunities to accomplish preexisting goals. Agenda-setting scholars consistently find that policymaking attention is determined by what problems are most important at any given time. Expert information is crucial to problem-solving, as policymakers need to understand the salient problem and find solutions to address it. Neutral experts will provide policymakers with a range of options to consider that they believe will help to solve the problem on the agenda. However, some nonneutral experts, such as those at partisan think tanks, have their own agenda. They both see problem-solving as both an obstacle and an opportunity. If they don't insert themselves between elected officials and neutral experts, problem-solving means that their allies in government aren't attending to their priorities and may even be enacting public policy that they oppose. If they can insert themselves, problem-solving becomes an opportunity to pass something, even if it doesn't do as good a job addressing the problem as a solution that neutral experts might recommend. Partisan think tanks are especially well-positioned to play this close advisor role, even if it occasionally hurts their party in the next election.

Chapter 3, "The Development of Partisan Knowledge Regimes," asks why the U.S. system of partisan think tanks developed in the time, place, and manner that it did. The United States built up a technocratic policy advisory system composed of nonpartisan think tanks, the federal bureaucracy, and research universities as its policy agenda broadened, which helped to broaden its agenda further. Conservative intellectuals reacted to the growth of government by forming the modern conservative ideology in the 1950s in explicit opposition to the technocrats who, in their minds, enabled it. However, they watched their allies in government continue to work with nonpartisan experts to further expand the federal government for the next two decades.

The turning point for modern conservativism came when two congressional staffers founded the Heritage Foundation in 1973, allowing conservatives to field their own experts to counter the technocrats. They were innovative in changing how think tanks operate, allowing them and numerous imitators to insert themselves into policy debates more easily than traditional think tanks. A conservative ecosystem emerged to rival the nonpartisan knowledge regime centered around think tanks. Conservative politicians like Reagan and Gingrich could finally call upon conservative experts to help them make policy decisions. Heritage became their right hand, helping to craft much of the conservative policy achievements of the 1980s and 1990s.

Progressives were slow to form an equal and opposite knowledge regime. They didn't hold the same grievances with technocrats who helped to expand the federal government. Indeed, they saw neutral experts as valuable allies to help design enduring policies. Eventually, after seeing Heritage and others pull the party system to the right for three decades, progressives responded by creating a knowledge regime centered around the Center for American Progress in 2003. CAP was explicitly modeled on Heritage, although in some ways it was even more deeply integrated with the Democratic Party. Today both political parties have well-developed systems of partisan think tanks.

Chapter 4, "Privately Controlled Party Organizations," examines the roles that partisan think tanks play inside modern political parties. While many interest groups work closely with political parties, partisan think tanks often form much closer relationships with parties than even their closest interest group allies. Because U.S. political parties are composed of broad coalitions with varied, often conflicting policy goals, party leaders need advice that can balance the priorities of the coalition. Rather than represent one interest, partisan think tanks represent the coalition generally. They are particularly important for maintaining a large workforce of policymaking professionals that the party can access when in government. Newly elected presidents from both parties frequently rely on partisan think tanks during presidential transitions, for both staffing and policy planning. However, this status comes at a cost. Partisan think tanks are still interest groups with their own policy goals. Political parties may find it difficult to make policy decisions that help them win elections if those decisions clash with their ideological workforce's policy goals.

Chapter 5, "How Partisan Think Tanks Set Their Agenda," concludes the first half of the book by examining the issues that partisan think tanks publish reports on. The origin story of Heritage is very much one about agenda setting; its founders were upset that AEI failed to strategically release information criticizing policy that conservatives disagreed with while debates were ongoing. Heritage's founders designed the think tank to quickly respond to issues on the policy agenda. Using a data set of thousands of partisan think tank reports, I examine whether this story fits the agenda-setting patterns of modern think tanks. I find that Heritage does indeed aggressively tailor its agenda to the issues being considered by Congress, but AEI, CAP, and CBPP do not. Rather, these think tanks create a steady stream of reports on their party's core priorities, hoping to lay the groundwork for policy entrepreneurship when the agenda shifts toward their priorities.

The book then shifts to examine the impact of partisan think tanks on the polarization of American politics. Chapter 6, "The Growth of Polarization and Partisan Think Tanks," examines the high-level and very close relationship between polarization in Congress and partisan think tank activities. Polarization rises in near lockstep with partisan think tank activities. Other forms of neutral expertise decline, while partisan think tank influence explodes. The data suggest a clear relationship between partisan think tanks and polarization, but I conclude that the relationship is likely more complicated than the correlational result suggests.

The book turns to a deeper examination of the relationship between partisan think tanks and polarization in Chapter 7, "Partisan Think Tanks and Polarization across Issues." This chapter introduces new data on polarization broken down by 20 issues using data from the U.S. Policy Agendas Project[7] and compares it to a variety of partisan think tank activities. Policymaking in many issue areas confronts a starkly polarized information environment, while others see very little activity from partisan think tanks. The chapter finds that the issues that partisan think tanks work the most on are about twice as polarized as the issues that they do not prioritize.

Chapter 8, "Polarized Policy Analysis," examines the findings in partisan think tank reports. It compares the conclusions of reports from partisan think tanks and neutral experts, such as the Congressional Budget Office or academic centers. The chapter examines three cases: the debate over the cost of the ACA, the debate over the impact of the Tax Cuts and Jobs Act on economic growth, and the debate over the revenue generated by the Biden-Harris campaign tax plan. It finds that partisan think tanks often produce results far more favorable to their party's plans than do neutral experts, except for the Center on Budget and Policy Priorities.

Finally, the book examines a case study of polarization and partisan think tank activity in Chapter 9, "Green Jobs and Climate Change Denial." The positions of the Republican and Democratic parties on climate change diverged drastically in the late 2000s. The Republican Party, which had been the leader between the two on environmental policy to address air pollution over the previous three decades, suddenly reversed course, denying the science on climate change and refusing to support any solutions to address it. At the same time, Democrats began to propose big, comprehensive plans to reduce U.S. greenhouse gas emissions and build out renewable energy, following a broader global prioritization of the climate change issue. The chapter explores the role of partisan think tanks in both changes, finding strong evidence that partisan think tanks were key to polarizing the parties on climate change.

The book concludes with a discussion of the implications of its findings in Chapter 10, "Democracy and the Information Wars." Democracy struggles to function without some consensus on what information is valid. Without neutral experts, the Republican and Democratic parties will struggle to find compromise even when they both want to solve the problems the public tasks them with. The chapter ends with a discussion of the future of partisan think tanks and U.S. party politics.

2

The Problem with Problem-Solving

Barack Obama took office in the middle of an economic catastrophe. After a year of shaky economic news, the investment bank Lehman Brothers declared bankruptcy on September 15, 2008. Lehman's failure kicked off the most serious financial crisis since the Great Depression. By January, when Obama took the Oath of Office, the economy was losing hundreds of thousands of jobs each month. Obama had spent much of 2007–8 campaigning on renewable energy, immigration, healthcare, and Iraq and Afghanistan, but his first major legislative achievement was going to have to focus on this new problem. If he failed, his presidency would be derailed as soon as it began.

Long before taking office, Obama and leading Democrats knew that they would have to pass a large economic stimulus package early in 2009, with the goal of reducing unemployment and getting the economy back to growth. They wanted to use the opportunity to pass their preexisting priorities. Rahm Emanuel, who would become Obama's first chief of staff, famously summarized the potential of the moment in an interview with the *Wall Street Journal* shortly after the election:

> You never want a serious crisis to go to waste. And what I mean by that is an opportunity to do things that you could not do before. I think America as a whole missed the opportunity to deal with the energy crisis that came before us. For a long time, our entire energy policy came down to cheap oil. This is an opportunity to let long-term problems, be them in the health care area, energy area, fiscal area, tax area, regulatory reform era, things that we had postponed for too long, that were long-term, were immediate and must be dealt with. (*Wall Street Journal* 2008).

Two months earlier, both CAP and CBPP started working on packages of policy alternatives that could best be applied to the economic crisis that ultimately made it into the American Recovery and Reinvestment Act (ARRA) of 2009. The bill that President Obama eventually signed into law less than one month into his term in office contained $787 billion in direct spending, tax cuts, and tax expenditures.

The Thinkers. E. J. Fagan, Oxford University Press. © Oxford University Press 2024.
DOI: 10.1093/oso/9780197759653.003.0002

However, under immense time pressure, Democrats would have to figure out what to spend the money on in the months leading up to Obama's inauguration. They called on the CAP and CBPP to help them decide.

CAP focused on using the bill as a vehicle to subsidize renewable energy. They released a report titled "Green Recovery: A New Program to Create Good Jobs and Start Building a Low-Carbon Economy" (Podesta 2008) on September 8. The report was authored by the CAP's president John Podesta, who was also serving as the co-chair of Obama's transition committee. It argued that, to address the coming recession, Congress should pass a $100 billion package of direct spending, tax cuts, and loan guarantees. Specifically, it called for $50 billion in tax credits for wind power, solar power, advanced biofuels, and upgrades to the electrical grid to prepare for an influx of new renewable energy over the next decade, as well as to encourage homeowners to retrofit existing buildings to increase energy efficiency. It also argued for $46 billion in direct spending to build intercity rail lines and mass transit systems, fund grants to develop new electrical grid technology, and invest $26 billion to retrofit federal buildings to be more energy efficient. Finally, the report recommended that the government guarantee $4 billion in loans to private renewable energy and smart grid companies to encourage innovation. Podesta projected that, if passed, the proposal would create approximately 2 million jobs, many of which were for newly unemployed workers in the crashing construction and manufacturing industries, and reduce surging gas prices while jump-starting the transition to a low-carbon economy.

CBPP designed the low-income and state fiscal relief part of the crisis response.[1] The Center's president Robert Greenstein had started serving on an informal transition policy planning team in early September with about five other Democratic economic policy experts. Greenstein oversaw policy planning for the federal budgetary process. He described the process as "really intense."[2] Five days after the election, Greenstein flew to Chicago to present their recommendations to President-elect Obama and his senior staff. Greenstein presented a lengthy PowerPoint presentation to describe their recommendations in a grueling, two-hour meeting.

Shortly afterward, Greenstein received a call from Jason Furman, the Obama campaign's economic policy director and incoming deputy director of the White House National Economic Council. Furman needed help. The transition team had its hands full trying to staff the government, but the economy was beginning to enter free fall. They were going to have to pass the stimulus bill quicker than expected, but large pieces of the bill remained unwritten, including key provisions to increase aid for poor families who would be hit hardest by the recession. Furman asked Greenstein to write the first draft of the bill. CBPP went to work, crafting a plan for large increases in the child tax credit, earned income tax credit (EITC), and other low-income cash aid programs, as well as food stamps and unemployment insurance.

Given the urgency of the crisis, Congress began writing the legislation as soon as it gaveled in at the turn of the new year, but before the Inauguration on January 20. With a new Congress and Democrats not yet in control of the White House, congressional leaders needed help writing the bill. Greenstein recounts how CBPP functioned as de facto transition staff during this period:

> The Obama people, in meeting with Democrats on the Hill when they would say, we need more detail than this, they would say, "Call the Center on Budget. They're authorized, as far as we're concerned, to go over the details with you." It was very unusual. Of course, something like that ended the minute he was inaugurated. There were actually officials of the administration in office in the White House. We played that role in the interim period because we had developed those proposals for them and talked to them, and they had talked to us. They modified some things we suggested. It wasn't like they just took everything with no change. But we knew the nuts and bolts and the details and why they were designed the way they were. It was logical for them to send those Hill staff to us. At that point, that was the ultimate in being part of a transition.[3]

From the perspective of progressive policy goals, the bill was a success. The energy investments were a major contributor to the movement toward clean energy and energy efficiency in the 2010s (Lim, Tang, and Bowen 2021). States that received large clean energy and energy efficiency block grants generated more renewable energy during the decade than states that did not (Lim, Tang, and Bowen 2021). The loan guarantees helped create or sustain several companies important to the transition to renewables, most notably the electric vehicle manufacturer Tesla. The low-income provisions that CBPP designed also had a lasting effect. While they were originally written to expire after a few years,[4] Greenstein had a plan to extend them further, but he needed Republican votes. He immediately began planning for the "fiscal cliff," when several of the temporary measures introduced by ARRA were set to expire alongside large tax cuts passed under the Bush administration a decade earlier. They convinced Democrats to trade an extension of the tax cuts for the extension of the child tax credit and EITC expansion for five years. They did.

However, Democratic policymakers paid a price for their policy successes, particularly on CAP's renewable energy proposals. While it successfully generated industrial activity in the long term, there is little evidence that the "green jobs" legislation had a significant impact on the U.S. economy in the short term (Popp, Vona, and Noailly 2020). Democrats lost 63 House seats in the 2010 midterm elections, a historic loss in part caused by an ineffective federal response to a deep recession. CAP made a case to Democratic policymakers that they could have their cake and eat it too: they could do something that progressive groups sought while also solving a problem on the policy agenda. There were likely stimulus options that nonpartisan experts believed would be more effective at strictly reducing unemployment or propping up economic growth but which did not support progressive policy priorities. The nature of a stimulus bill allowed policy entrepreneurs to offer a broad set of alternatives to push public money into an economy that needed it. But even with the wide set of policy alternatives that could help the economy and labor market recover, CAP was unable to provide its Democratic allies in government with an effective solution to the most pressing problem on the agenda. It did manage to accomplish an important progressive policy goal, but at a severe cost to Democratic electoral fortunes.

Taking Advantage of the Agenda

Rahm Emanuel's wisdom is well-understood in political systems. Political parties run for office on detailed platforms about what they will promise to do when elected to office. They win, form a government, and sit down to start negotiating over the finer details of legislation. Then, inevitably, something changes. The change could be an event, such as a major economic or international crisis. It could be a scandal. A news report or idea could go viral to reframe how people think about an issue. The party in government is then forced to pivot toward solving some problem that they didn't worry about when they ran for office. However, an entrepreneurial leader like Emanuel understands that a crisis will come along and often open a window of opportunity for a party in government to get something they want.

The reason why parties can't just enact all their goals as soon as possible is due to the limitations of our human brains (Jones and Baumgartner 2005). At any given time, there is a near-infinite amount of information blasting policymakers. The world is big and complicated, and they are bound by the same cognitive limitations that we all are. We can't pay attention to more than a few things at any one moment. Because of this limitation, we process information disproportionately, ignoring most things at any given time while intensely focusing on the most important items. When some unattended problem pops up that suddenly becomes the most important item, policymakers rapidly shift their attention toward it, often dropping whatever they were working on previously.

These attention dynamics structure the policy agenda (Bevan and Jennings 2014; Jones and Baumgartner 2005). Policymakers focus on a small set of issues at any given time but are frequently forced to put down what they were working on and shift toward something else. The problems that pop up are essentially random; elected officials can't predict what will come up beyond a short horizon (Fagan 2018). Sometimes things settle down enough that parties or presidents can stop and try to enact their core priorities, but those moments are often fleeting (Lovett, Bevan, and Baumgartner 2015). Policymakers may try to carve out enough time and resources to enact their core priorities, but problems have a nasty way of forcing their attention elsewhere.

Once a problem is prioritized, policymakers search for solutions to address it (Baumgartner and Jones 2015; Fagan and McGee 2022). Most elected officials, especially high-level decision-makers like executives and party leaders, are generalists. Because they must deal with a wide variety of problems, they aren't able to acquire deep expertise in most issue areas. Instead, they perform searches for expert advice after they prioritize a problem. Huge systems grow up inside democracies to help provide expertise when needed, with countless political actors competing to supply information to decision-makers (Craft and Howlett 2012). The vast universe of available experts is a core advantage that democracies have over authoritarian systems. In addition to think tanks, policymakers may consult lobbyists (Hall and Deardorff 2006), bureaucrats (Workman, Jones, and Jochim 2009), academics (Maher et al. 2020) or their own analytical bureaucracies (Fagan and McGee 2022) when searching for expert information to solve problems.

Problem-solving is core to democratic representation. Political scientists have long observed that Americans tend to have low levels of knowledge about most policy details and thus weak preferences for specific policy outputs on most issues (Burstein 2003). However, the public has stronger opinions about solving problems, whether fixing high unemployment, reducing gas prices, or effectively responding to a natural disaster (Bevan and Jennings 2014; Jones and Baumgartner 2004). Public preferences are "double-peaked," meaning that people often seek both liberal and conservative solutions to solving a problem over doing nothing at all (Egan 2014). Politicians seek to avoid being blamed for problems that the public cares about (McConnell, Gauja, and Botterill 2008; Weaver 1986). A democratic government is thus responsive to the problems that the public deems important, even if it means dropping some of the promises that they made before the election or taking some position counter to its ideological commitments (Fagan 2018). A government that fails to solve problems fails to represent the will of the voters. If the problem is on the agenda, everyone is watching.

Policy entrepreneurs like Emanuel try to exploit the fickle nature of the agenda (Kingdon 2011). They know that at some point the government will be forced to respond to some issue on the agenda, but that there is rarely time to sit down and craft new policy solutions to address a problem that suddenly finds its way to the top of the agenda. With this understanding, government policymakers prepare for their window of opportunity. Social scientists have a set of terribly undescriptive names for this process of developing solutions to problems before they are needed, such as "garbage cans," "multiple streams," and "disjunctive decision-making." The point, however, is that an opportunistic actor can get something they want by pushing their preferred policy alternative as a solution to the day's most important problem. They want to hijack the window of opportunity to support their preexisting priorities.

There are lots of great examples of agenda hijacking, but I prefer one from my own career. Before I went to graduate school to study political science, I worked for a small nonprofit think tank called Global Financial Integrity (GFI). We wanted to enact a series of changes to strengthen anti-money-laundering laws. Our leadership and funders cared about anti-money-laundering because they believed, backed by data, that trillions of dollars were flowing from poor countries to rich countries. My boss was Raymond Baker, a retired American entrepreneur who ran businesses out of Nigeria for decades. He argued that a lot of the problems that foreign aid was trying to solve—such as slow economic growth and poverty in places like Nigeria—could instead be solved by preventing those illicit financial flows from poor to rich countries. He managed to convince a few large donors, like Norway's Ministry of Foreign Affairs, which normally fund more traditional foreign aid NGOs, to fund GFI's alternative strategy to helping developing countries.

Our most important bill was called the Corporation Transparency Act, which eliminated anonymous shell companies in the United States. The problem with the bill was that few decision-makers outside of aid organizations and developing country finance ministries cared about illicit financial flows, while powerful interest groups that would be regulated under the law strongly opposed it. Our strategy was, essentially, agenda hijacking. Money laundering is at the center of tons of issues. Criminals make money illegally and want to spend it on normal things like cars, houses, and yachts. If they didn't have access to anonymous shell companies, they would have a harder time cleaning their ill-gotten gains, and thus would, on the margins, do fewer illegal things or take more risks in laundering their money that law enforcement could track down. We offered our bill as a solution to any number of problems, including terrorism, North Korean nuclear proliferation, human trafficking, elephant poaching, and bourbon counterfeiting. I wrote dozens of op-eds that made the same basic argument about anti-money-laundering and whatever happened to be on the agenda at the time. Eventually, long after I left the organization, GFI and its allies convinced enough people that eliminating shell companies was a solution to their problem. The Corporation Transparency Act became law during the waning days of the Trump administration. I'm pretty sure that precisely no one in government who was critical to getting the law passed cared about reducing illicit financial flows from poor countries, but it will go a long way toward that goal.

There are costs to agenda hijacking. If a problem isn't solved, it usually doesn't just go away. While there can be multiple ways to solve the same problem, some work better than others. A policy entrepreneur might claim that a policymaker can have their cake and eat it too: they can solve the problem on the agenda while also doing something that they already wanted to do. Anyone familiar with motivated reasoning can understand why that argument often works. However, the ability of a plan to solve a problem is constrained by reality. A qualified expert without an exterior motive will give their opinion about how effective a solution might be at solving the problem on the agenda. A biased expert will try to sell policymakers the Brooklyn Bridge if they can. Elected officials who choose poorly may have to defend their bad choices during the next election, as Obama had to after the ARRA's lackluster response to job losses during his first two years in office.

Partisan Policy Demanders

The same tension between the policy entrepreneur and elected official exists more broadly in political parties. Political scientists usually think about political parties as office-seeking organizations (Downs 1957). Their goal is to win as many seats as they can in the next election. That might involve enacting policy changes, such as following through on promises made during elections or solving problems in advance of the next one (Froio, Bevan, and Jennings 2017), but policymaking is a means to the end of winning more seats. If effectively solving problems helps a party win more seats, the party will try to do so.

However, parties need help. American parties need money to fund campaigns. They need to staff the government. They need favorable stories in the media. They find support from a broad network of interest groups, donors, consultants, and activists known as the extended political party (Bawn et al. 2012; Schwartz 1990). Critically, members of the extended political party are not office-seeking but policy-seeking, or composed of "intense policy demanders" in the language that political scientists use. They want their allies to win elections, but only because winning elections allows them to deliver policy gains. Policy demanders understand that they need to moderate their demands a little bit in order to allow their allies to win elections, but they try to reap the maximum benefit out of their relationship with elected officials (Bawn et al. 2012). They are highly adaptive and cooperative, working with each other to share information and support strong candidates who will be loyal to their collective goals (Grossmann and Dominguez 2009; Koger, Masket, and Noel 2009, 2010; Masket 2016).

The literature usually focuses on how policy demanders exert control over political parties by intervening in nomination contests (Albert and Barney 2018; Cohen et al. 2009; Desmarais, La Raja, and Kowal 2015). They pick winners by directing money and independent expenditures, staffing campaigns, offering powerful symbolic support through endorsements, getting their supporters to vote, or pursuing favorable media coverage. In return, they demand that candidates conform as much as possible to their policy goals. Because primary electorates are much more elastic than the general electorate, they are easier to nudge toward the right candidate. However, policy demanders perform all sorts of other activities unrelated to primaries. They generate policy networks, linking activists and information producers to office-holders (Albert 2019). They often serve as staff for not only campaigns but also legislative and executive branch policy positions. Finally, they are important players in generating ideas and arguments in the opinion media, leading to the creation of modern ideologies (Noel 2014).

Large partisan think tanks are key nodes in the party network (Albert 2019). We can divide policy demanders into two groups: those that are motivated by specific policy demands on a relatively narrow set of issues and those that are motivated by a general ideological commitment across a broad range of issues. The former includes groups like oil and gas companies, chambers of commerce, environmental protection groups, labor unions, and gun rights advocates. They are often some of the most well-organized and best-resourced interest groups operating in Washington. While they are often pulled into policy fights across a range of issues, their core policy agenda can be quite narrow (Fagan, McGee, and Thomas 2019). Labor unions care about issues of concern to their members, such as collective bargaining rights, employment benefits, and working conditions. Environmental groups care about issues such as climate change, land and water conservation, and clean water. When push comes to shove, they are going to demand that their allies prioritize their issues, not those of the other groups in the coalition. They will produce information that, consciously or not, will show that their concerns are the most important issues on policy or electoral grounds.

On the other hand, many policy demanders are general ideologues. They care about the full range of conservative or liberal issues, or at least a large package of them across domains. The best example of general ideological commitment is the signs that dot my suburban neighborhood, pledging that in this house they believe "Black Lives Matter," "Women's Rights Are Human Rights," "No Human Is Illegal," "Science Is Real," and "Love Is Love." The liberal households that put up those signs have strong ideological commitments across a broad range of issues. They likely hold liberal views on other issues as well, such as redistributive social programs, worker's rights, and progressive tax policy. Many leading intellectual and media figures are general ideologues, often working to bind together disparate issues inside the party coalition (Karol 2019; Noel 2014). Like more narrow groups, they likely have quite strong preferences on ideological issues. Unlike more narrow groups, they likely have much weaker priorities in deciding which issues are more important. When it comes time to decide among relative priorities, general ideological groups are more useful to parties than narrow groups.

As with other political actors with broad interests, general ideologues are at a disadvantage in political organizing when compared with narrow interests (Olson 2003). To quote Max Weber, success in politics is the result of "slow boring of hard boards." To succeed in delivering policy gains through a system often designed to frustrate change requires a long-term investment in lobbyists, expertise, and relationship-building. Groups with intense issue priorities make up most of the lobbying environment in Washington because they can pay those costs (Fagan and Furnas 2024). It is harder for generalists to mobilize and develop the long-term infrastructure needed to represent an ideology more generally. Many ideological leaders are small shops; they might be employed by a news publication or write books on their own, but they don't hire large staffs to do the grinding work of pushing policy through the system. Think tanks can function as the organizers of general ideological policy demanders. They work across a broad range of issues, with extra emphasis on issues prioritized by the extended party network (Fagan 2021). As I document in later chapters, they develop fundraising techniques to raise money from a broad network of general ideologues, like candidates and political parties, rather than being reliant on a few patrons who can demand that they focus on their personal top issues.

For example, Workman et al. (2021) studied organizations sending in public comments on Department of Education regulations. They identified issues within the regulations, such as student loans and standardized testing requirements. Many of these regulations received intense lobbying in the comments. Representatives of state, local, and tribal school systems lobbied on requirements to qualify for Title I funds. Charter school organizations lobbied on charter school regulations. Colleges and universities lobbied on Title IX requirements relating to gender, sports, and sexual assault regulations. The groups that lobbied most consistently across domains were think tanks, because they had strong ideological opinions about all sorts of issues relating to education policy.

The Problem with Problem-Solving

Policy demanders in party networks don't like it when their allies in government just solve whatever problem hits the agenda. Most of their core policy demands are stable. Gun rights groups want more permissive regulations around guns. Evangelical churches want more restrictions on abortions. Environmental groups want more government promotion of renewable energy. But the issues that hit the agenda are somewhat random, determined by whatever crisis, media moment, or endogenous process pushes an issue to the top. The result is that most of the time, the problem on the agenda isn't the problem that policy demanders want government to focus on.

To make matters worse, effective solutions to problems can run counter to policy demander goals. If high gas prices are at the top of the agenda, environmental groups are not going to want a Democratic government to enact policy changes to increase oil production. If there is a crisis in teenage pregnancy, evangelical groups are not going to want to expand sex education and contraceptive programs. Experts might recommend both sets of policies as the most effective way to deal with the problems, but they could be seen as significant betrayals within the party network. Policy demanders don't want their allies to go rogue and listen to the experts because they can't control what solution will come out.

The problem of problem-solving is particularly fraught for economic conservatives. Laissez-faire libertarianism holds that government should, in most cases, allow society and the market to address problems without significant interference from government. When a pressing problem is on the agenda, laissez-faire libertarians would often prefer that government not address it at all. Economic conservatives in government will feel cross-pressured between the double-peaked preferences of their constituents and resistance to government intervention from their intense policy demanders. In most cases, non-conservatives will conduct an expert search and find a wide range of government programs that experts believe will help solve the problem that they are comfortable with, or even eager to enact. Economic conservatives will conduct the same expert search and find most effective solutions to the problem involve interventions into the domestic economy that the intense policy demanders in their coalition believe are an improper use of the state. They could choose to do nothing, but their constituents pressure them to do something rather than nothing, frequently causing them to betray their coalition and seek out public solutions for what they consider to be private problems.

Indeed, libertarian billionaire Peter Thiel expressed this sentiment in a famous 2009 blog post. Thiel had witnessed the aggressive government interventions by both Republican and Democratic administrations during the 2008–9 financial crisis. Upset by what he saw as yet another betrayal by his allies, he declared, "Most importantly, I no longer believe that freedom and democracy are compatible." Thiel then described his ideal response to a financial crisis (government does nothing) and blamed the responses to the Great Depression and Great Recession on people who receive support from government programs and the enfranchisement of women:

> Indeed, even more pessimistically, the trend has been going the wrong way for a long time. To return to finance, the last economic depression in the United States that did not result in massive government intervention was the collapse of 1920–21. It was sharp but short and entailed the sort of Schumpeterian "creative destruction" that could lead to a real boom. The decade that followed—the roaring 1920s—was so strong that historians have forgotten the depression that started it. The 1920s were the last decade in American history during which one could be genuinely optimistic about politics. Since 1920, the vast increase in welfare beneficiaries and the extension of the franchise to women—two constituencies that are notoriously tough for libertarians—have rendered the notion of "capitalist democracy" into an oxymoron. (Thiel 2009)

Of course, such a response to the Great Recession would have been disastrous for the party in government. Herbert Hoover's administration did little to respond to the beginning of the Great Depression, losing the presidency, 167 seats in the House of Representatives, and 28 seats in the Senate over the next six years. Even after averting the worst outcomes of the more recent financial crisis, Democrats got hammered in the 2010 midterms. "Do something" politics leads to big government. It's no coincidence that American government grew as it expanded the franchise beyond rich white men like Thiel.

Policy demanders that don't want the government to go rogue on them have two options: reduce the problem's prioritization or try to pair the problem with one of their preferred solutions. The former is more difficult in many circumstances. Some problems are prioritized endogenously, by convincing elites in the system that an existing policy image is no longer valid (Baumgartner and Jones 1993). Political actors, including policy demanders, can play an important role in maintaining or shifting policy images (Peterson 2023). However, sometimes the tide of the agenda is too strong, and no one can stop the problem from being prioritized. Focusing events, such as a natural disaster, foreign policy crisis, or scandal, will often rocket problems to the top of the agenda (Birkland 1998; DeLeo et al. 2021; Fagan 2022). Acute problems, such as a recession or a surge in gas prices, will also move an issue toward the top of the agenda. Policy demanders may be able to deflect some of these problems, but voters may demand that politicians do something about them.

In those cases, policy demanders can try to convince their allies to adopt their preferred solution. Experts may recommend one policy alternative, but demanders may be able to credibly connect the problem to some other solution. As long-term, savvy political actors, policy demanders develop ideas that can be paired to predictable problems. Their challenge is in convincing their allies in government that *their* idea is the best possible solution, not some neutral expert's idea. That challenge is not trivial. The stakes are high. Elected officials know that policy demanders are often unreliable partners in solving problems. They are unlikely to see one report or press release and dart toward some crazy idea. But sometimes they can offer a solution that does a plausible enough job of addressing the problem while also advancing their policy goals. In the ARRA case, CAP may have made a plausible case that if you are going to be injecting hundreds of billions of dollars into the economy, what you spend it on doesn't matter *that much*, so you might as well spend it on subsidizing renewable energy. If they are persuasive, policy demanders can turn the problem of problem-solving into an opportunity to get something they want out of government.

The line elected officials and parties straddle is dangerous. Drawing information from mostly neutral experts is far less risky than consulting with policy demanders. Managing this push-and-pull between the angels and the devils on opposite shoulders is a key political skill that the best political leaders must acquire.

Polarizing Problem-Solving

Problem-solving is one of the core processes that creates consensus between competing political parties, under two conditions. First, the parties must agree on

The Problem with Problem-Solving

what problems are important at any given time. Second, the parties must agree on a range of solutions that could effectively address the problem. If both conditions are met, there isn't much room left for deep conflict. The parties may disagree over who should bear the trade-offs of solving the problem or the relative importance of problems sitting near the top of the agenda. The opposition party might not want to give the governing party a win (Lee 2016). The parties will still fight over performance and personality. But generally, when parties agree on what the problem is and what solutions can address it, they can find a middle ground and compromise.

Even in today's hyperpolarized party system, the Republican and Democratic parties still routinely reach compromises around salient problems. At the beginning of the COVID-19 pandemic, when America met simultaneous public health and economic crises not seen in generations, a divided Congress quickly passed three large legislative packages in just two months. The third, a massive $2.2 trillion law called the CARES Act, provided $1,200 in cash aid to families, hundreds of billions for expanded unemployment benefits, and loans to small businesses that continued to employ workers during the shutdown. The pandemic year 2020 was one of the most polarized, contentious years in American history, but problem-solving brought the parties together to pass one of the largest impromptu spending bills ever.

Two years later, the pandemic created huge shortages in microchip supplies. Any manufacturer who needed microchips in their products—companies that produced cars, consumer electronics, home appliances, to name a few—was impacted. All-but-completed Ford F-150s sat in parking lots outside factories, waiting for chips. American companies invented the semiconductor, but the U.S. economy was now largely reliant on foreign suppliers to produce even basic microchips. U.S. policymakers had been working behind the scenes for years to come up with policy changes that would encourage new microchip manufacturing in the United States (Miller 2022), but now the window of opportunity was open. Large bipartisan majorities in both chambers passed the Creative Helpful Incentives to Produce Semiconductors Act of 2022, a massive $280 billion investment in domestic semiconductor manufacturing. Just three months later, the United States held contentious, polarized midterm elections.

These are just two examples of many that point to the centripetal power of problem-solving. When both parties agree on the problem and range of solutions, they can come to a consensus, even in today's dangerous, escalatory war between Republicans and Democrats.

However, the second necessary condition for problem-solving, agreement over solutions, is vulnerable to misinformation. The belief that enacting a solution will address a problem is fundamentally one of cause and effect. If we enact any of a list of potential policy changes, what will happen to Y outcome compared with some counterfactual? That basic question is at the heart of all policy analysis, more a question of policy engineering than of politics or ideology. In a perfect world, members of even deeply polarized parties should have the same answer to the question, just as they would have over a question about why the sky is blue or why taking an antibiotic will improve health outcomes for a sick person. The parties would then move on to fight about the politics of the decision, who bears the trade-offs, who gets credit, theoretical debates about what is right or wrong for government to do, and all the other things that make political decisions more complicated than engineering decisions.

But we don't consume information in a perfect world. When humans process information, we confront all sorts of powerful psychological biases (Knobloch-Westerwick, Mothes, and Polavin 2020). We are more willing to accept information that confirms our preexisting beliefs. Politics triggers our emotions and identities as much as it triggers the rational side of our brains. We reject information that we perceive as coming from the out-group. Policymakers aren't immune to their biases. In fact, they may even be more likely to err. The more educated and engaged we are about politics, the less we are willing to be uncertain about our beliefs and be persuaded by false confirmatory information (Zhou and Shen 2022). In the words of columnist Ezra Klein (2021), "politics makes smart people stupid (90)."

When policy demanders are trying to divert allies in government toward their preferred solutions, they are playing in the imperfect world of confirmation bias. Lobbyists spend most of their time talking to their allies (Hall and Deardorff 2006). From the perspective of the elected official, policy demanders are your people. They support you when you run for reelection. You and your staff run in their social circles. And they tell you what you want to hear. They have an advantage over neutral experts in the psychological game.

Over the long run, these interactions can lead to vastly different beliefs about how policy impacts the world. Members of each political party could earnestly agree that they want to solve a common problem but hold vastly different beliefs about the cause-and-effect relationship between that problem and policy solutions. We often think about ideological beliefs as arising from feelings about what is right or fair in politics, or strong beliefs in certain normative frameworks. However, they increasingly include views about the cause-and-effect nature of reality or what conclusions could be produced by a credible source of information. If policymakers become untethered from reality, they can begin to believe in quite extreme policy solutions while also believing that, at the end of the day, they are enacting good public policy that solves salient problems their constituents care about.

In a policy debate over solving some problem, one side might believe that the solution is significantly more costly than the other. One might believe that it will be efficacious, while the other believes that it will have little impact on the problem. While trying to solve a problem that they believe is severe enough to warrant government attention, each could honestly believe they are supporting an effective solution and that the solutions the other side are supporting are either a waste of time or actively harmful. The problem-solving process is then short-circuited, making a compromise between the two parties impossible.

When polarization increases, these types of disagreements will be routine. In any system, elected officials will hold divergent beliefs about how policy impacts the world for any number of reasons. In a polarized system, these beliefs are strongly correlated with political party affiliation. As information becomes more polarized, it takes a bigger and bigger crisis to force the parties to both recognize a problem and come to a consensus on a policy response.

3

The Development of Partisan Knowledge Regimes

Rush Limbaugh, the powerhouse right-wing talk radio host who pioneered the brand of confrontational, angry commentary that now dominates conservative media, had a recurring mantra that he called "The Four Corners of Deceit":

> We really live, folks, in two worlds. There are two worlds. We live in two universes. One universe is a lie. One universe is an entire lie. Everything run, dominated, and controlled by the left here and around the world is a lie. The other universe is where we are, and that's where reality reigns supreme and we deal with it. And seldom do these two universes ever overlap. . . . The Four Corners of Deceit: government, academia, science, and media. Those institutions are now corrupt and exist by virtue of deceit. That's how they promulgate themselves; it is how they prosper. (Roberts 2010)

In a later broadcast, Limbaugh sharpened the connection that he perceived between science and liberalism:

> One of the things that I pointed out back on this program on November 4th of 2011, a year and a half ago, is that one of the things the left in this country attempts to do is to codify elements of their ideology as science. Liberalism is science, and therefore it's irrefutable. Science is what is. Science allows for no agreement. Once science says something, then that something is, and you can't refute it and you can't disagree with it. You can, but you would be a kook. This is one of the techniques that the left has used. Global warming is nothing more than the left's political ideology. It's nothing more than one of the planks of their grand design, but they codify it as science so it's indisputable. (*The Rush Limbaugh Show* 2013a)

The Thinkers. E. J. Fagan, Oxford University Press. © Oxford University Press 2024.
DOI: 10.1093/oso/9780197759653.003.0003

Limbaugh's rhetoric toward the non-conservative information ecosystem is familiar to even the casual observer of Republican Party politics. Since the conception of the modern conservative ideology, Republicans have had an adversarial relationship with neutral experts. Expertise that clashes with conservative orthodoxy is, in their minds, just as liberal as an ideological opinion about the proper role of government or permissiveness of nontraditional moral values coming from a progressive politician or opinion writer.

However, conservative Republican policymakers still need some form of expertise to make decisions. Someone has to write the white paper, crunch some data, administer an agency, or craft a plan before conservative attitudes can be translated into public policy enactments. Indeed, they need a comprehensive system of experts to develop and exchange highly technical information, come up with ideas, and communicate those ideas to stakeholders and the public. They need to develop a professional class of experts to replace the Four Corners of Deceit. They need what sociologists John Campbell and Ove Pedersen (2014) call a "knowledge regime."

Campbell and Pedersen (2014, 3) define a knowledge regime as "the organizational and institutional machinery that generate data, research, policy recommendations and other ideas that influence public debate and policymaking." Their work focuses on national policy regimes, finding variation in the processes by which ideas enter the policy process across democracies. They conclude that the U.S. political system tends to draw information from private organizations more than other democracies do. Political parties in other systems closely rely on think tanks that they control directly or indirectly, but U.S. political parties tend to draw data, research, and policy recommendations from nonprofit organizations they do not control. As a result, U.S. policymakers hold different beliefs about how policy outputs produce policy outcomes.

When Campbell and Pedersen (2014) discuss knowledge regimes, they compare the overall information environment across countries. However, we can extend their logic to examine competing knowledge regimes within the United States. In this chapter, I identify three competing regimes: a neutral technocratic regime that was created in the early 20th century to help provide policy expertise to a growing federal government, a robust reactionary conservative regime that was created in the 1970s in response to concerns about the role of expertise that they associated with the now-grown federal government, and a smaller progressive knowledge regime that evolved a few decades later in part as a response to the conservative regime. We can trace their development over a century, eventually resulting in the status quo today, where both political parties have their own professional classes of partisan experts to rival neutral technocrats. We can also trace the critical role of think tanks in producing the partisan expert class, crucially beginning with the Heritage Foundation in 1973.

To understand the context that led to the development of knowledge regimes, we must first understand the development of federal policymaking in 20th century.

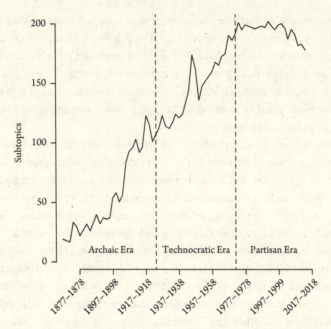

Figure 3.1 Scope of the congressional policy agenda, 1870–2018. Total subtopics addressed by Congress per two-year period. Source: Fagan, Shannon, and Jones (2023).

Knowledge regimes were developed in part in response to the growing size and scope of the federal government (Jones, Theriault, and Whyman 2019). When government entered more issue areas, it required more expertise to help it process information. Figure 3.1 shows the growing size and scope of the federal government, beginning in 1870. The y-axis shows the total issues addressed by congressional hearings during a two-year Congress, using the Policy Agendas Project subtopic coding system (Fagan, Shannon, and Jones 2023). During the late 19th century, Congress held hearings on only a few dozen issues. Around the turn of the century, the congressional agenda tripled in size, to around a hundred subtopics. The political system responded by creating the technocratic knowledge regime, helping the federal government double in size again to its modern scope. At the height of this expansion, partisans organized their own knowledge regimes to compete with the existing technocratic regime.

The Technocratic Knowledge Regime (1920s–1970s)

We begin our history in the early 20th century. By the end of the Progressive Era, the federal government had begun to take on many of its modern policymaking functions. The federal bureaucracy was being built up following the creation of the federal civil service in 1871. It began to enter issue areas as far-ranging as antitrust, agriculture, transportation, communication, and food safety. The New Deal brought new large federal spending programs in economic development and the safety net. The federal government needed to access expertise on a wide range of issues to help develop, monitor, and maintain its new policy agenda.

The political system's response was to build up a knowledge regime centered around technocratic expertise. Three new important sources of information emerged: a growing system of academic research universities, a robust professional bureaucracy, and a small group of large technocratic think tanks (Baumgartner and Jones 2015). Backhouse (2005, 370) describes this system as "based on the premise that disinterested social scientific inquiry could contribute to better policymaking." It had roots in the scientific management movement brought to American industry by Fredrick Taylor and Henry Ford (Cooke 1915; Wilsok 1973). Policymakers designed modern bureaucracies and civil service systems using scientific management principles and a strong expectation that they would employ science and technocratic expertise for decision-making (Wilsok 1973). Political science, sociology, and other social science research was routinely used by legislators, bureaucrats, and courts to inform policymaking (Applebaum 2020; Erickson and Simon 1998). These practices created a system whereby professional experts routinely provided policy analysis, and that policy analysis was central to policy design and evaluation.

Once established, the technocratic knowledge regime was critical to continued expansion of the scope of the federal government's policy agenda (Figure 3.2). From the late 1950s through the 1970s, a period called "the Great Broadening" by Jones, Theriault, and Whyman (2019) saw the federal government enter many policy areas that were previously reserved for the states or left to the free market. The federal government created dozens of new agencies and departments, including the Departments of Energy, Housing and Urban Development, and Health, Education and Welfare, and the Environmental Protection Agency. It began to protect the civil rights of racial minorities and women. Congress created countless programs, such as the Interstate Highway System, Medicare, Medicaid, Pell Grants, and the National Flood Insurance Program. Policy analysis from nonpartisan, technocratic sources was essential to policymaking during this period (Backhouse 2005), aiding cooperation between the parties.

The first nonpartisan, technocratic think tanks began to be established in the 1920s through the 1940s, forming a key cog in the knowledge regime. Before the Second World War, the federal government lacked much of the policymaking capacity necessary to design and implement the New Deal. As the political parties were weak ideologues, these think tanks were able to build consensus based on their reputations for scientific rigor and policy advice unbiased by self-interest (Weaver 1989).

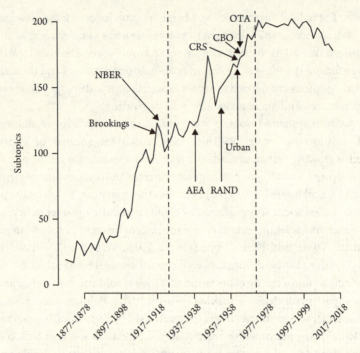

Figure 3.2 Think tank and analytical bureaucracy formation. The Congressional Research Service was founded in 1914 but took its modern form in 1970 following the Legislative Reorganization Act of 1970. Abbreviations: AEA (American Enterprise Association), AEI (American Enterprise Institute), Brookings (Brookings Institution), CBO (Congressional Budget Office), CRS (Congressional Research Service), NBER (National Bureau of Economic Research), OTA (Office of Technology Assessment), RAND (RAND Corporation), Urban (Urban Institute).

Think tanks created during the 20th century were established under two models, each of which was intended to encourage rigorous research and analysis. Many established in the first half of the century, such as the Brookings Institution, American Enterprise Association (AEA), and National Bureau of Economic Research (NBER), used a "university without students" model, where the organization hired experienced researchers and conferred a form of tenure and academic freedom (McGann 2016; Weidenbaum 2011). These think tanks generally employed scholars with either academic or public service backgrounds who sought to produce information useful for policymakers. They functioned much like other academic institutions. Individual researchers worked on their own or in small ad hoc teams, without much direction from the organization. Hiring decisions were made based on academic merit.

These new think tanks became essential to bridge the gap between scientific research produced by academics and policymakers (Stone 1996). Academics produce a tremendous volume of information, but rarely in a format that is actionable for policymakers. They are neither incentivized to work closely with policymakers nor experts at translating academic research into policy recommendations. Brookings and others began to fill that gap, offering solutions to problems that the political system was tasked with solving.

After the Second World War, several large think tanks, including the RAND Corporation and Urban Institute, were established using a "contract" model. Within this framework, clients—usually the federal government—would commission individual research projects just as they would order a new aircraft carrier or fleet of postal vehicles (McGann 2016; Weaver 1989). Through this mechanism, contract think tanks often functioned as a direct extension of the federal government's policy analysis capacity. Indeed, the RAND Corporation was established for this express purpose. During the Second World War, the U.S. military built up the first significant policy analysis capacity inside the federal government. After the end of the war, the air force set up RAND to absorb much of this capacity rather than allow it to melt away into the private sector (RAND Corporation n.d.a). While RAND was initially focused on defense policy, it also provided analysis on a range of other issues. Contract think tanks tend to employ Ph.D. researchers and apply rigorous research standards (McGann 2016). Today, 53% of the RAND workforce holds a doctorate and about 33% work on defense or homeland security policy (RAND Corporation n.d.b). In addition to contract work, RAND scholars have made several significant social scientific contributions. Most notably, RAND scholars developed game theory to model decision-making during the early Cold War and understand the geopolitics of nuclear weapons (Backhouse 2005). Both models encouraged serious scientific inquiry and created organizations that were trusted by members of both parties as authoritative voices on public policy.

The growing federal bureaucracy also evolved into a critical source of expertise during this era. Federal bureaucrats develop deep expertise in the policy area that they administer (Gailmard and Patty 2012). Few think tanks can provide the technical expertise that bureaucracies can offer, putting them at the center of problem definition, crisis management, policy design, and evaluation (Shafran 2021; Workman, Jones, and Jochim 2009; Workman, Shafran, and Bark 2017). When policymakers approached a new problem during the technocratic era, they often tasked bureaucracies with designing new programs to deal with it.

As the agenda peaked, Congress established its own robust analytical bureaucracies to produce nonpartisan information (Baumgartner and Jones 2015). In 1970, Congress changed the name of a small office in the Library of Congress, the Legislative Reference Service, to the Congressional Research Service (CRS), increasing its budget and autonomy (Rothstein 1990). CRS became an important bipartisan source of expert information for oversight and legislation on a wide variety of issues (Fagan and McGee 2022). Two years later, Congress established the Office of Technology Assessment (OTA) to produce reports on issues relating to emerging technology and science. Congress established the Congressional Budget

Office (CBO) to provide high-quality cost analyses and budgetary projections. All three analytical bureaucracies were established as nonpartisan, independent organizations, maintaining that status regardless of who controlled Congress (Binder 2017).

Once established, the technocratic knowledge regime was used by both Republicans and Democrats. All of the new programs were established by bipartisan coalitions and informed by experts, and many were led by Republican presidents or congressional leadership (Grossmann 2014; Jones, Theriault, and Whyman 2019). The period was historically unpolarized and characterized by high levels of bipartisan consensus (Poole and Rosenthal 1984). Networks of party leaders in the legislative and executive branches worked together repeatedly to design and evaluate new federal programs and agencies (Grossmann 2014).

Even Richard Nixon, who swept into office in 1968 in opposition to the civil rights laws passed that decade, frustrated conservatives by following the advice of technocrats. After taking the United States off the gold standard in 1971, Nixon famously remarked, "I am now a Keynesian in economics," referencing the famous quote from Milton Friedman, "We are all Keynesian now" (TIME 1965). Indeed, the Nixon administration employed many mainstream Keynesian economists and valued their expertise (Williams 1998).

The result was that the expansion of the federal government agenda continued at the same pace under both Republican and Democratic administrations (Jones, Theriault, and Whyman 2019). Eisenhower, Nixon, and Ford all added significant new programs and agencies to the federal government. Republican leaders in Congress helped to pass the Civil Rights Act, Elementary and Secondary Education Act, Medicare and Medicaid, and numerous other programs that conservatives hated (Grossmann 2014). One notable exception was Barry Goldwater, whose 1964 presidential campaign featured a fierce defense of extreme laissez-faire capitalism and opposition to the end of Jim Crow. But Goldwater lost in a historic landslide, failing to change the existing Republican Party establishment.

Conservative Reaction (1970s–1990s)

As the federal government expanded, intellectual leaders began to craft a new ideology. While conservatism as a concept can trace its roots back to Edmund Burke, the modern synthesis of laissez-faire economics, traditional white Christian social values, and a hawkish foreign policy emerged in the early to mid-20th century (Noel 2014). Friedrich Hayek and other Austrian economists began to develop a critique of Keynesian macroeconomic policy in the 1930s and 1940s (Backhouse 2005). Milton Friedman developed supply-side economics and monetarism in the 1950s and 1960s. Ayn Rand, Robert Nozick, and others began to develop a libertarian political theory to support laissez-faire capitalism (Noel 2014). William F. Buckley and other conservatives first published the *National Review* in 1955, bringing in hawkish anticommunist foreign policy and traditional white Christian social values. Buckley was the most important coalition merchant of the group, tying it all together (Noel 2014).

However, their efforts were not working. While Republicans professed a belief in their ideology, conservatives watched the federal government continue to grow and grow (Figure 3.3). Government was now bigger, more intrusive, and, in their eyes, more dangerous than when Hayek, Friedman, and Buckley started writing. They felt betrayed by their allies in government, assisted and enabled by technocrats. According to Stahl (2016, 9), conservatives identified technocrats as fundamentally anticonservative: "More often than not, those who subscribed to such [technocratic] innovations were inclined to advocate for the expansion of the welfare state as an ameliorative for the downsides of corporate industrial capitalism."

Indeed, critiques of the technocratic knowledge regime were present at the very beginning of modern conservatism. Noel (2014) finds that the seminal moment which crystallized the conservative ideology was the publication of Buckley's *God and Men at Yale* in 1951. In the book that launched his career, Buckley argued

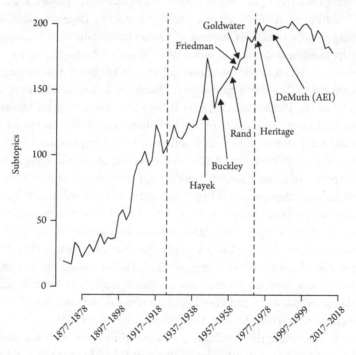

Figure 3.3 Conservatism reactions to the growth of government. Author dates correspond to their most important popular publication: *The Road to Serfdom* (Hayek 1944), *God and Men at Yale* (Buckley 1954), *Atlas Shrugged* (Rand 1957), *Capitalism and Freedom* (Friedman 1962). Other than Buckley, all authors were active well before the publication of each work.

that the Yale faculty's support of a secular worldview, racial equality, cultural relativism, Keynesian macroeconomics, and government intervention into domestic policy was inherently unconservative. Instead of technocratic or unbiased, Buckley framed the university as liberal, while conservatism represented an opposite but equally valid worldview which deserved equivalent representation in academia. Thus, it required a conservative counterweight. Soon after his book was published, he founded the *National Review* to continue to develop the intellectual foundations of modern ideological conservatism.

Before Buckley, even the nominally conservative American Economic Association (AEA) was compelled to conform to the technocratic knowledge regime. AEA was founded by a group of New York City businessmen in 1938 with a mission to achieve "greater public knowledge and understanding of the social and economic advantages accruing to the American people through the maintenance of the system of free, competitive enterprise" (AEI n.d.). It produced rigorous research like the then-established Brookings Institution, including important scholarly contributions in antitrust and labor law (Stahl 2016). AEA's reports produced conclusions a little bit more friendly to ideological conservatism than organizations like Brookings but were still broadly considered in line with rigorous academic research (Stahl 2016). AEA's fundraising tended to rely on large corporate donors, overlapping heavily with the Chamber of Commerce (Stahl 2016). Despite their free-market mission and mild conservative leanings, AEA was for the most part a participant in the technocratic consensus and was not integrated into the Republican Party (Stahl 2016). This status quo began to change under the presidency of William Baroody Sr. in the 1960s. Baroody, who changed the name of the organization to the American Enterprise Institute for Public Policy, worked with Barry Goldwater's 1964 presidential campaign to craft a conservative policy platform (Stahl 2016). Baroody clashed with Buckley and other Goldwater advisors, who thought Baroody and AEI's policy recommendations were insufficiently conservative (Stahl 2016). AEI's culture and ethos were still largely grounded in the technocratic knowledge regime, awkwardly positioning it between the current mainstream consensus and the newly insurgent conservatives (Stahl 2016). It also suffered from its reliance on cautious and technocratic corporate donors rather than conservative foundations or individuals (Stahl 2016). AEI was not successful at influencing the policy process in a conservative direction, outside of a few key issues, until much later. Republicans, led by Richard Nixon and Gerald Ford, continued to expand the scope of the federal government into the 1970s (Jones, Theriault, and Whyman 2019).

The critical juncture that established a new regime came with the creation of the Heritage Foundation in 1973 by two former Republican staffers, Ed Feulner and Paul Weyrich, and heir to the brewing company fortune Joseph Coors, who were unhappy with the Republican Party's embrace of federal government programs as solutions for domestic policy problems (Edwards 1997). Heritage rapidly changed the structure of new think tanks in the United States as well as the

The Development of Partisan Knowledge Regimes 33

relationship between think tanks and elected officials and political parties. Heritage, and the numerous organizations founded or modified in its image, would provide a means through which ideological conservatives could ultimately capture the Republican Party.

Heritage produced several important innovations in think tank operations. First, it built an organizational structure whereby researchers and support staff act strategically and in coordination, rather than following the prior model of working independently with only ad hoc teamwork. One former senior Heritage Foundation manager described the difference between the university model and the new model as the difference between a "condominium" and a "tight neighborhood."[1] In the former, researchers are related only by proximity, while the latter can foster collaboration to produce knowledge outputs greater than the sum of their parts. Heritage management exercised more control over the organization's policy agenda by producing conservative research in advance of policy debates.

Indeed, this structural change is at the heart of the organization's founding legend.[2] According to Edwards (1997, 3–4), in 1971 Congress debated whether to fund research and development for a supersonic commercial airliner. Conservatives opposed the spending as an unnecessary and wasteful government entry into a free-market function. The measure failed by just a few votes. A few days later, Heritage's two principal founders, Weyrich and Feulner, met for breakfast in the House of Representatives cafeteria. Weyrich was angry at AEI, which had published a study on the pros and cons of federal funding of supersonic commercial jets a few days after the vote. Weyrich asked Baroody why he did not release the study before the vote. Baroody replied, "We didn't want to try to affect the outcome of the vote." Feulner and Weyrich decided that conservatives needed a new organization that would anticipate the congressional policy agenda and act to influence it.

Second, Heritage aggressively marketed its research. While most think tanks are more adept than academics at putting their research in front of policymakers, Heritage invested far more resources into marketing than other think tanks (McGann 2016; Rich 2005). They were the first think tank to have a congressional liaison office, allowing them to learn what Republican leaders expected the policy agenda to focus on in the near future.[3] While other think tanks were producing long technical reports appropriate for an academic or specialist setting, Heritage edited their reports so they could pass "the briefcase test"—documents should be small enough to fit in a briefcase and read in the time it took to transit from congressional offices to the D.C. National Airport (Rich 2005). Aggressive marketing and brevity gave Heritage an advantage over its competition in convincing allied policymakers to rely on their policy analysis when making decisions.

In the days before email, rapid communication presented a logistical challenge. One former Heritage staffer spoke fondly of "report days" in Heritage's basement.[4] He would often write a brief on short notice, late at night on a typewriter, if an agenda item was imminent in Congress. In the morning, he would give the report to a group of interns in the basement, which contained a large, expensive Xerox machine. At the time, far cheaper copying options existed, such as screen printing, yet only the Xerox machine could save time by collating copies of the report. Every intern at Heritage would wait on the far end of the Xerox machine, collecting reports. Once they had collected a handful, they would run to deliver them by hand to each House and Senate office, as well as slip a copy under each door at the National Press Club. Thus Heritage could quickly rebut arguments or join a national policy conversation long before the days of email and social media.

Also, Heritage developed a more diverse fundraising strategy. Instead of relying on large foundations or government contracts, they borrowed a grassroots strategy from Republican electoral politics by raising money from a broad group of individual conservative donors (Abelson 2004). Because individual donors tend to be more ideological than large funders like the Ford Foundation, which themselves had technocratic traditions and frameworks, these new think tanks used a diversified fundraising strategy to produce more conservative information than university-based models like AEI (Rich 2005). It also allows the organization considerable autonomy from donors. Feulner (2000, 71), who was president of the Heritage Foundation from 1977 to 2013, wrote, "The importance of [having a diverse donor base] was made clear to us some years ago when a corporate CEO, taking exception to our policy in favor of free trade, ripped up a check for a six-figure contribution. Such short-term losses are significant, of course, but by accepting them, we strengthen the allegiance of our more numerous small donors." Members tended to trust that information more than information patronized by corporations, because they were receiving conservative ideas rather than self-interested ones.[5]

Collectively, these innovations created a new model for think tanks. Most modern think tanks in the United States now adopt what McGann (2016) classifies as an "advocacy" model,[6] in which they act more like interest groups than like universities. This model was ultimately adopted by a wide range of think tanks, including other conservative think tanks such as the Cato and Manhattan institutes, later progressive think tanks like Demos and the Economic Policy Institute, and numerous think tanks representing more traditional interests, such as the progressive pro-Israel group J Street (Medvetz 2014).

Heritage was enormously successful in influencing the Republican Party. The organization quickly became closely connected to Reagan and the conservative faction of the party coalition. It supported Reagan's challenge against Ford, whom Heritage saw as insufficiently conservative, in the 1976 Republican nomination contest (Edwards 1997). After Reagan won the 1980 election, Heritage played a key role in his transition (Brown 2011; Jones and Williams 2008). Heritage had spent much of 1979 and 1980 preparing a 3,000-page, 30-pound document titled *Mandate for Leadership*, laying out a plan for the first year of the Reagan presidency (Edwards 1997). The document contained more than 2,000 policy recommendations for the executive and legislative branches in close cooperation with Reagan's transition

The Development of Partisan Knowledge Regimes 35

team. Reagan passed out copies of *Mandate* at his first cabinet meeting (Edwards 1997). *Mandate*, and subsequent support from Heritage, allowed Reagan to move quickly and achieve many conservative policy goals, including a $749 billion tax cut, a large increase in defense spending, cuts to social welfare spending, and the Urban Jobs and Enterprise Zone Act of 1981 (Edwards 1997). Heritage later claimed that the Reagan administration implemented 60% of *Mandate*'s policy recommendations in his first term (Edwards 1997). Few interest groups can claim such a record of success at influencing American public policy.

Other conservative think tanks followed in Heritage's footsteps. The 1970s and early 1980s saw an explosion in the number of think tanks in Washington (Bertelli and Wenger 2009). Many were highly ideological, conservative advocacy think tanks modeled after Heritage (McGann 2016). Charles Koch and two libertarian conservatives founded the Charles Koch Foundation, later renamed the Cato Institute, in 1974. William Casey, a former Nixon appointee and future Reagan CIA director, founded the Manhattan Institute in 1977. Manhattan most notably employed Charles Murray, whose *Losing Ground* and *The Bell Curve* provided much of the conservative case underlying the backlash to federal welfare policy and the mid-1990s reform (Heckman 1995; O'Connor 2001). More recently, conservative policy entrepreneurs, including Charles Koch, founded numerous think tanks in individual states, connecting them together to share information and resources with the State Policy Network (Hertel-Fernandez 2019; Hertel-Fernandez, Skocpol, and Lynch 2016).

Even AEI, with its deep cultural roots in a more academic model, began to change. AEI fired William Baroody Jr., who had inherited the organization's presidency from his father, in 1986, hiring the much more conservative Chris DeMuth to lead the organization. While DeMuth retained AEI's university model, he significantly changed its operations following Heritage's success. AEI hired many conservative full-time resident scholars after decades of focusing on visiting or adjunct university professors, including Murray (Stahl 2016). They released a policy agenda for the second term of the Reagan presidency modeled on *Mandate* (Medvetz 2014), and they began to raise money from wealthy conservative ideologues rather than relying on corporate donors (Stahl 2016). DeMuth began to work more closely with grassroots conservatives rather than just business groups (Stahl 2016). The move paid off, with AEI working closely with both Bush administrations (Stahl 2016).

Collectively, these organizations created an alternative conservative knowledge regime. Conservatives framed the mainstream media, universities, Keynesian economics, and nonpartisan institutions as inherently liberal rather than unbiased or mainstream. They sought to elevate academic research that arrived at conservative conclusions to equal footing with what they considered to be liberal research.[7] When surveyed in the late 1990s, Republican legislative staff reported that they preferred information that they knew conformed to their ideological beliefs over information that was unbiased, while Democrats and journalists reported the opposite

(Rich 2005). While there were few large progressive think tanks active in 1997, when Rich performed his surveys, Democrats tended to rate them lower in credibility than nonpartisan think tanks like Brookings, RAND, and NBER. More recent data suggest that Republican legislative staff are less likely than their Democrat counterparts to cite material from high quality scientific journals (Furnas, LaPira, and Wang 2024).

The change in Republican Party knowledge regimes is clearly illustrated by a comparison of the Eisenhower, Nixon, and Ford administrations with the Reagan and Bush administrations. In *Honest Numbers*, economist Walter Williams (1998) recounts the rise and decline of economic policy analysis in the Executive Office of the President. Williams describes Eisenhower as an "organizational genius" who encouraged a rigorous and competitive flow of sound policy analysis (60). Nixon and Ford joined Lyndon Johnson in presiding over a "golden age of executive branch policy analysis" (56), where bureaucratic agencies and scientific expertise were central to their policymaking processes. Reagan, on the other hand, kicked off what Williams describes as "the anti-analytic presidency" (148), where professional policy analysts in the federal government were treated as the enemy rather than a source of expertise. Finally, Williams argues that George H. W. Bush somewhat surprisingly continued Reagan's distrust and devaluing of nonpartisan expertise. Bush did not emerge out of the ideological conservative faction of the Republican Party that boosted both Reagan and the Heritage Foundation. Instead, Bush had high-level experience in the Nixon and Ford administrations. Indeed, Williams notes that Bush brought in respected academics to advise him on domestic policy, including Harvard professor Roger Porter and Stanford economist Michael Boskin (155). However, his administration rarely incorporated rigorous policy analysis into its decision-making. He attributes this to Bush's disinterest in domestic policy as well as intra-administration conflict over ideological policy decisions. Reagan may have been so successful at transitioning the Republican Party away from the nonpartisan knowledge regime that even a president more committed to effective policymaking like Bush could not reestablish it.

One contemporary illustration of conservative attitudes toward science and technocracy is Conservapedia. This website was founded by Andrew Schlafly, son of the famous conservative activist Phyllis Schlafly, in 2006. Schlafly founded the site in response to his belief that Wikipedia moderators were tilting an article on a debate over teaching evolution in Kansas schools away from creationism (Zeller 2007). The site's self-described ethos rejects positivism as a concept for an encyclopedia to strive for, insisting instead that all facts are inherently biased: "Conservapedia strives to keep its articles concise, informative, family-friendly, and true to the facts, which often back up conservative ideas more than liberal ones. Rather than claim a neutral point of view and then insert bias, Conservapedia is clear that it seeks to give due credit to conservatism and Christianity. Schlafly said in regard to the point of view issue, 'It's impossible for an encyclopedia to be neutral'" (Conservapedia n.d.).

According to Schlafly's logic, facts can only be liberal or conservative. Therefore, disagreement with conservatives necessitates alternative facts. In one entry that best exemplifies this ethos and its conflict with the technocratic knowledge regime, Conservapedia defines "econometrics" as "a field of economics that uses statistics to analyze economic data for patterns. It is frequently used by liberal influences in economic think tanks, like the Brookings Institution, to justify increased government deficit spending in order to weaken America's currency advantage in world trade." In these two sentences, the conservative ethos regarding positivism is clear. The first sentence correctly defines econometrics in positivist terms. The second sentence notes that positivism is used to justify policy outcomes that conservatives disagree with and that liberals use positivism, and specifically points to activities of a nonpartisan think tank as an example of the relationship between anticonservative policy change and positivism.

Republican politicians express the same sentiment. In another example, former senator Rick Santorum addressed the Values Voter summit in 2012: "We will never have the media on our side, ever, in this country. We will never have the elite smart people on our side, because they believe they should have the power to tell you what to do. So our colleges and universities, they're not going to be on our side. The conservative movement will always be—and that's why we founded Patriot Voices—the basic premise of America and American values will always be sustained through two institutions, the church and the family" (*Politico* Staff 2012). Santorum makes it clear that science, academic institutions, and the media are inherently and inevitably anticonservative, and so alternative institutions are necessary to promote conservative policy preferences.

In a final example, columnist Ron Suskind (2004) recounts a 2002 conversation with an anonymous George W. Bush White House official in which the official explicitly argued against positivism:

> The aide said that guys like me were "in what we call the reality-based community," which he defined as people who "believe that solutions emerge from your judicious study of discernible reality." I nodded and murmured something about enlightenment principles and empiricism. He cut me off. "That's not the way the world really works anymore," he continued. "We're an empire now, and when we act, we create our own reality. And while you're studying that reality—judiciously, as you will—we'll act again, creating other new realities, which you can study too, and that's how things will sort out."

The anonymous official perhaps best summarizes the goal of the conservative reaction to the technocratic era. Conservatives saw that a rigorous, neutral community of experts came to conclusions about public policy that they did not agree with. They sought to build their own reality and convince the Republican Party to adopt it. They did so by creating a knowledge regime centered around partisan think tanks as an alternative to the existing knowledge regime centered around government agencies, universities, and nonpartisan think tanks.

Progressive Counterreaction (2000s–present)

Progressive Democrats were slow to respond to the trend of advocacy-oriented think tanks with their clear ideological missions and deep integration into political parties. For the most part, Democrats continued to value rigorous, nonpartisan research produced by universities and nonpartisan organizations (Grossmann and Hopkins 2016; Rich 2005). It took two more decades for progressives to create their own equal and opposite reaction to Heritage.

The first significant Democratic-aligned advocacy think tank was the Center on Budget and Policy Priorities, which was founded by Robert Greenstein in 1981.[8] Greenstein had just served as the Food Nutrition Service administrator in the Carter administration but was out of government following Reagan's election. During Carter's presidency, new policies added millions of new recipients to food aid programs. Greenstein and others expected the Reagan administration to try to claw back those gains. The Food Nutrition Service had produced a lot of high-quality reports on the effectiveness of food aid programs, persuading even top Republicans like Senator Bob Dole, then the chair of the Senate Agriculture Committee, to support generous funding for food aid. Greenstein expected that Reagan's administration, which had already promised to enact the deep cuts to food aid programs recommended by Heritage, to stop producing the same analysis. The Field Foundation gave Greenstein a $50,000 grant to establish a temporary organization to produce analysis on food aid programs, called the Project for Food Assistance. Greenstein produced a report rebutting many of the claims about food assistance programs made by Reagan. The report got significant media attention, allowing Greenstein to attract enough grant money to form a permanent organization in 1982.

CBPP was a small operation through most of the 1980s, initially employing just six staff members.[9] Still, they quickly expanded past food assistance programs to issues relating to progressive tax policy, a range of low-income assistance programs, and healthcare. They developed a strong reputation and culture for rigorous data analysis. They worked closely with members of Congress and the Clinton administration. Unlike Heritage, CBPP did not stand in opposition to technocrats in the bureaucracy and academia, but rather sought to play a more traditional think tank role of bridging the gap between the more technical experts and policymakers. Indeed, they often hired experts from nonpartisan organizations like the Congressional Budget Office. They played an insider role more than the other three think tanks, eschewing big public events in favor of private meetings with Democratic policymakers. Greenstein served in a minor role on the Clinton transition team in 1992 and was set to become deputy director of the Office of Management and Budget after the 1994 midterms. However, after huge Republican victories in the 1994 midterm elections, Greenstein elected to stay outside of government to defend redistributive programs that were now under threat.

The moderate wing of the Democratic Party also created their own think tank during this period. In 1985, a group of moderate Democratic elected officials founded the Democratic Leadership Council (DLC) to move the party toward the center. The DLC was the chief party organization supporting the New Democrats, a moderate faction of the party that included Bill Clinton. As part of their efforts, they founded the Progressive Policy Institute (PPI), a centrist think tank, in 1989. Despite its name and association with the Democratic Party, PPI often supported quite conservative policy proposals. For example, during the 1996 welfare reform debate, PPI supported welfare work requirements and time limits and criticized progressive plans to expand aid to the poor (Medvetz 2014). They often clashed with more progressive think tanks like CBPP, but they were "scarcely audible over the din of their conservative competitors" (207). PPI defined much of the Democratic Party's policy agenda during the 1990s.

Democratic elites led by former Clinton chief of staff John Podesta thought the DLC had pushed the Democratic Party too far to the center (Dreyfuss 2004; Savage 2008). In the 1990s and early 2000s, liberal Democrats lost policy fights not only on welfare but also on marriage equality, tax cuts for the wealthy, and the Iraq War. To move the party to the left, they founded the Center for American Progress, which would provide a left-of-center counterweight to AEI and Heritage, with more of a thumb on the progressive scale in the information they produced than organizations like CBPP. Podesta was supported by a $30 million grant from a group of Democratic Party megadonors known as the Democracy Alliance, led by George Soros, Peter Lewis, and Herb and Marion Sandler. CAP was immediately the largest Democratic-aligned think tank in the United States, with revenue averaging between $40 million and $50 million during the 2010s and 2020s.[10] Unlike Heritage, which began as an outsider group looking to capture the Republican Party, CAP was much more explicitly allied with the Democratic Party from the outset. For example, Bob Boorstin, a CAP researcher focused on national security, described his mission as explicitly aiding the Democratic Party: "My job is to take the thirty-five-point gap and shrink it, so that we're viewed as credible again [on foreign policy].... It's vital that we Democrats demonstrate through our ideas that we are not a bunch of wimps" (Scherer 2008). Furthermore, Podesta described CAP's mission as an intraparty organization focused on representing the party's mainstream, which felt tugged on by both centrists and more extreme left-wing groups (Dreyfuss 2004). At the same time, the organization was designed as a modern update of the Heritage advocacy model. Indeed, the CAP founders informally consulted with Heritage management about how to best organize their think tank.[11]

In addition to producing policy analysis, CAP built its apparatus to engage actively in policy debates in the media and the halls of Congress. CAP was one of the first think tanks to set up an independently financed companion 501(c)(4) lobbying organization, the Center for American Progress Action Fund. The companion organization allowed its employees, many of whom were simultaneously employed by the 501(c)(3) organization, to lobby and engage in electoral politics. Heritage would follow up a few years later by creating their own 501(c)(4) companion organization named Heritage Action. Jennifer Palmieri, CAP's first communication director, who would later hold communication director titles for Hillary Clinton's 2016 campaign and the Obama White House, sent CAP experts out to engage in television news debates. Shortly after CAP was founded, a talk show booker stated, "For conservatives, we can call Heritage or AEI. Now we have a place to get liberals" (Dreyfuss 2004).

CAP was quickly integrated into the Democratic Party. CAP presidents Podesta and Neera Tanden chaired the Obama and Clinton transition committees. For the Obama administration, CAP followed the lead of Heritage's *Mandate* by preparing a similar document, *Change for America: A Progressive Blueprint for the 44th President*, to lay out an agenda for the executive branch (Scherer 2008). Like *Mandate*, many of the authors of *Change* were later nominated to agencies in order to implement their own recommendations, including the solicitor general, secretary of health and human services, director of the National Economic Council, and director of the Office of Management and Budget. Tanden also served on the 2016 Democratic platform committee.

More recently, CAP helped define the healthcare plan adopted by the 2020 Democratic platform. In February 2018, it released "Medicare Extra for All" (CAP Health Policy Team 2018), a detailed plan which would allow individuals and businesses to buy in to a public insurance plan administered by the Center on Medicare and Medicaid Services. Both elite media and progressive activists understood the new CAP plan as a major ideological shift within the Democratic Party, signaling that mainstream Democrats were embracing more expansive universal care than they had previously (see Bruenig 2018; Friedman 2018; Klein 2019; Kliff 2018). The basic structure of CAP's plan resembles healthcare plans later introduced by the Joe Biden campaign, as well as Pete Buttigieg and Amy Klobuchar during the 2020 Democratic nomination contest. The 2020 platform included language that pointed toward a version of the plan, although details are vague.[12]

While CBPP grew steadily in the 1990s, it began to explode in size around the same time that CAP entered the scene. In 2005, CBPP spent $9.3 million.[13] By 2006, its budget had increased to $16 million, and by 2021 to $53 million.[14] It continued to play an important role inside Democratic Party politics, but unlike CAP, it maintained its brand of rigorous analysis. With an increased budget, Greenstein was able to hire more midlevel Democratic policy staff and experienced insiders with knowledge of both policy and congressional processes.

Other progressive think tanks began to grow rapidly in the 2000s (Table 3.1). The budget of New America, a center-left foundation established in 1999, grew from $4 million in 2004 to $40 million in 2021, thanks in large part to donations from Google chairman Eric Schmidt (Cohen 2018).[15] The budget of the Economic Policy Institute, a small progressive think tank founded in 1986 that works closely with organized labor, grew to $16 million in 2021. Most recently, the Roosevelt Institute, which grew out of the nonprofit associated with the Roosevelt Presidency Library, led by progressive activist and political scientist Felicia Wong and economist Joseph Stiglitz, grew from just a few staff members to a $14 million organization in 2021. These think tanks and others formed the basis of a robust and varied progressive knowledge regime that rivaled conservative think tanks.

The knowledge regime established by Democratic think tanks maintained a legacy technocratic ethos. Democratic think tanks produce more rigorous research that is more likely to be written by Ph.D. researchers than do Republican think tanks (Furnas, LaPira, and Wang 2024; Grossman and Hopkins 2016). In surveys, congressional staff tend to report that they value impartial expertise over ideological policy analysis, while Republicans report the opposite (Rich 2005). Democratic congressional staff are more likely to trust a think tank report associated with scientific organizations (Furnas et al. 2023). The new Democratic knowledge regime tended to organize and package high-quality research that supported

Table 3.1 **Selected Partisan-Aligned Think Tanks Expenditures, 501(c)(3) Only**

Think Tank	2005	2013	2021
Republican			
Heritage Foundation	$36 million	$80 million	$86 million
American Enterprise Institute	$34 million	$45 million	$51 million
Hudson Institute	$7 million	$13 million	$23 million
Manhattan Institute	$10 million	$14 million	$16 million
Democratic			
Center for American Progress	$16 million	$41 million	$50 million
Center on Budget and Policy Priorities	$15 million	$27 million	$49 million
New America	$6 million	$19 million	$37 million
Economic Policy Institute	$5 million	$6 million	$10 million
Roosevelt Institute	$2 million	$9 million	$12 million

Note: Expenditures reported in IRS Form 990s contained in ProPublica's Non-Profit Explorer Database. Many think tanks also operate companion 501(c)(4) lobbying organizations.

progressive policy priorities rather than commission new research to support its goals. Grossmann and Hopkins (2016) attribute the Democratic preference for more rigorous policy information and deference to scientific consensus to a dominant technocratic ethos among party actors.

However, unlike Republican Party elites, Democratic Party elites never held policy preferences in deep conflict with the technocratic policy regime. On most issues, Democrats broadly agree with the scientific consensus because they seek to use policy outputs to change policy outcomes in the real world. Without rigorous policy design, they will fail to accomplish their goals. One senior Democratic think tank official describes this as the difference between "vision" think tank reports and "practical" think tank reports.[16] Conservatives whose goals revolve around decreasing the size and scope of government activity have the luxury of focusing on visions for public policy, but don't need to focus on the policy outcomes that a particular policy output could cause. Progressives use policy outputs as an instrument to achieve policy outcomes, so they must write more practical reports.

Summary

The Republican Party adopted their new knowledge regime in the 1970s because elites inside the party coalition disagreed with the policy preferences supported by nonpartisan technocrats under the status quo. Their goal was to change the preferences of elected officials in the party who they believed were insufficiently conservative in practice due to a reliance on the nonpartisan knowledge regime. Conservative activists within the party had developed a deep distrust for the regime and incorporated opposition to it into their ideology. Conservatives were still only a faction within the Republican Party, so the new knowledge regime was unable to gain policymaking traction with the Nixon-Ford administrations and Republican leadership in Congress. When Reagan and later Gingrich took over leadership of the party, they incorporated this vein of conservatism into the heart of Republican policymaking.

The Democratic Party adopted their own alternative knowledge regime for different reasons. While conservatives sought to change deeply held elite beliefs about public policy, such as replacing mainstream Keynesian economics with Austrian or Monetarist ideas, progressive activists in the Democratic Party sought to solve an organizational problem. They believed that the nonpartisan policy regime was insufficiently supplying the plans, policy information, and arguments necessary to achieve progressive policy goals. They did not have strong ideological objections to major policy conclusions produced by the nonpartisan knowledge regime. Thus, their new structures were complementary to it rather than intended to fundamentally replace it.

We can conclude that parties adopt new knowledge regimes when the status quo knowledge regime fails to meet elite goals. Had Democratic elites developed deep ideological beliefs in conflict with the nonpartisan knowledge regime, they would likely have eventually adopted a distinct new model like the one adopted by Republicans. However, the nonpartisan knowledge regime was not initially built as a partisan one. Both parties participated in it from the beginning.

It is important to remember that partisan knowledge regimes are the product of political entrepreneurship and are not self-generating. The Republican Party developed conflicts with the nonpartisan knowledge regime two decades before it developed its alternative. Buckley's *God and Men at Yale*, published in 1951, clearly articulated a critique of academia that would become a centerpiece of conservative ideology. In an act of entrepreneurship, Buckley established the *National Review* four years later, but it was insufficient to supplant the nonpartisan knowledge regime. The magazine provided an intellectual basis for ideological conservatism (Noel 2014), but it did not succeed in creating organized political action that could effectively counterbalance the weight of the academy, government agencies, and large nonpartisan think tanks. Republican officials still relied on the policy information and proposals generated by the nonpartisan knowledge regime. When Feulner and his colleagues established the Heritage Foundation in 1973, they created a model that could substantially replace the functions of a knowledge regime in ways that the *National Review* could not. Other conservative organizations imitated the model to build out a true alternative knowledge regime. Had conservative entrepreneurs acted earlier, they may have been able to develop the alternative knowledge regime sooner. Similarly, the Democratic Party's shift to its new knowledge regime was the result of entrepreneurship by Democratic Party elites.

In both cases, the entrepreneurship was led by a partnership between well-connected party staffers and big donors. Feulner and Weyrich were Republican congressional staff. Feulner was particularly influential as executive director of the Republican Study Committee. Podesta was Bill Clinton's chief of staff. In both cases, large party-connected donors played an important role in launching the new knowledge regime. Early on, the Heritage Foundation was resourced by Joseph Coors, heir to his family's brewing fortune. Other Republican-aligned think tanks were funded by wealthy factions in the party. Similarly, CAP began with large donations from notable Democratic donors and progressive foundations.

The expansion of political party activity into knowledge regimes either coincided with or was followed by a vast expansion in the scope of party activity. For most of modern American history, political parties primarily organized electoral activity. They recruited and resourced candidates to run for office under their label, coordinated campaign activity, and occasionally released a platform. Beginning in the 1970s, political parties began to expand to other activities, including organizing factions within the legal profession (Teles 2008), partisan media (Levendusky 2013), networks of for-profit campaign consulting firms (Miller 2017, 2019), and networks of lobbyists (Furnas, Heaney, and LaPira 2019). By taking up the function of knowledge regimes, political parties expanded into two roles. First, they began to control policy advisory systems, which translate information from basic science, academia, and other sources into actionable policy advice (Howlett 2019). Second, they increased their role in executive branch staffing. Presidents have always brought in allies as executive branch officials, but partisan knowledge regimes allowed the parties to reach farther and deeper into the bureaucracy. Where nonpartisan experts, who might disagree with the party's policy preferences, may have received presidential appointments, parties could now access a deep well of likeminded specialists. Partisan think tanks provided the new class of partisan policy professionals with permanent homes, stable organization, and expanded networks.

4

Privately Controlled Party Organizations

After graduating from Yale Law School in 1997, Neera Tanden began her career in Democratic Party policy development (Wadler 2000). She worked in the office of First Lady Hillary Clinton as a policy aid, before departing to serve as policy director on Clinton's first Senate campaign. In an early profile in the *New York Times*, Tanden was called "the Wonk behind Mrs. Clinton," attributing her interest in public policy to growing up in an immigrant household on food stamps and Section 8 housing vouchers (Wadler 2000). She worked in Clinton's Senate office until John Podesta, former chief of staff in under Bill Clinton, hired her to work at the newly created Center for American Progress as senior vice president for domestic policy.

Over the next two decades, Tanden moved seamlessly between policy jobs at CAP, the Democratic Party's political apparatus, and senior staff appointments in government. During the Bush administration, she served as issues director for the Democratic Congressional Campaign Committee, returned to Hillary Clinton's Senate office as legislative director (McArdle 2003), and eventually returned full time to CAP. She became policy director for Hillary Clinton's 2008 Senate campaign and was known as a loyal defender of Clinton. During the height of the 2008 campaign, Tanden allegedly punched Faiz Shakir, the founding editor of the CAP's *ThinkProgress* blog, for asking Clinton about her vote in favor of the Iraq War in 2003 (Williamson and Vogel 2019). Tanden then finished the Bush years as policy director for both Clinton's and, after he won the nomination, Barack Obama's presidential campaigns. Obama appointed her to senior advisor to Secretary of Health and Human Services Kathleen Sebelius in 2009, where she helped craft the Affordable Care Act (Berman 2016). She later returned to the CAP, where she became president in 2011. She stayed at the CAP for the remainder of the 2010s, serving on the 2016 Democratic Party Platform Committee (Lee 2016) and on Hillary Clinton's transition team (Karni 2016). After Joe Biden won the presidency in 2020, he nominated her as the powerful director of the Office of Management and Budget. Her nomination failed after senators objected to years of tweets attacking both Republican senators and Bernie Sanders. Ultimately, Biden brought her into a nonconfirmed appointment as a senior advisor and staff secretary to the president,

The Thinkers. E. J. Fagan, Oxford University Press. © Oxford University Press 2024.
DOI: 10.1093/oso/9780197759653.003.0004

eventually appointing her director of the White House Domestic Policy Council in 2023.

Tanden is just one representative of the professional class of partisan foot soldiers who move between developing policy ideas at partisan think tanks and working for the party in political roles or in government. A ProPublica study found that other than the Trump campaign, the Heritage Foundation was the most common former employer of Trump administration appointees, while the AEI was third most common (Figure 4.1). Other Republican-aligned interest groups, like the U.S. Chamber of Commerce, National Right to Life, and National Rifle Association, saw many fewer employees hired by the Trump administration. Partisan think tanks can develop closer relationships than even inner-circle interest groups in the party coalition.

Political parties need people like Tanden and the many Heritage and AEI staff hired by the Trump administration to provide policy planning and advice across a range of issues but who are not beholden to a particular lobby or policy demander. Other democracies often solve this problem by giving political parties control over publicly financed think tanks, which function much like other office-seeking formal party organizations. The United States instead requires political parties to look

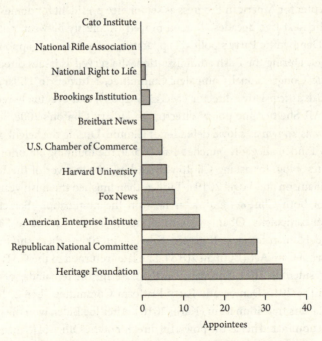

Figure 4.1 Trump administration appointees from select political organizations. Data from ProPublica's TrumpTown Project (Kravitz et al. 2018). The Trump administration hired 147 former employees of the 2016 Trump presidential campaign, which are omitted from this figure.

toward privately controlled, policy-seeking 501(c)(3) organizations to perform the same function. However, these partnerships can be a devil's bargain. Instead of supporting the party's core electoral mission, policy-seeking organizations seek to change the party's policy positions. Partisan think tanks shift the party's policymaking away from trying to solve pressing problems concerning voters and toward fulfilling the policy goals of the party's policy demanders.

More broadly, political parties need long-term organizations dedicated to public policy. American scholars often think about party organizations as dedicated primarily to electoral politics, such as raising money, running advertisements, nominating candidates, managing voter data, and recruiting candidates, but not policy-related tasks, which scholars tend to assign to a different class of nonparty organizations. This conceptualization is understandable, given that American campaign finance law pushes formal party organizations toward these types of activities. In other democratic systems, parties commonly maintain a full-time policy apparatus to do policy work—staffing the government, developing plans and promises, defending the party's position in public debates, and providing trusted policy advice to party leaders. These activities are almost always housed in party-controlled, publicly financed think tanks (McGann 2016).

U.S. political parties have instead come to rely on privately financed think tanks to do the same critical tasks. While these think tanks have distinct advantages for political parties over asking traditional interest groups to fill the same role, American partisan think tanks are still interest groups, with their own policy goals that are different from the party's.

Parties Need Generalist Organizations

There is no shortage of policy expertise in Washington, D.C. If you walk down any street in the business district, you can throw a stone and hit the headquarters of a lobbying firm, public interest group, or trade association. Most see producing information to support the goals of friendly policymakers as their primary route to influencing public policy (Hall and Deardorff 2006). They often employ experienced former members of Congress, experienced staff, or former top bureaucrats to produce high-quality, often technical policy analysis (LaPira and Thomas 2017). As the policy agenda expanded, every conceivable informational niche was filled by interest groups (Jones, Theriault, and Whyman 2019; Leech et al. 2005). Information in politics is oversupplied. (Jones and Baumgartner 2005).

While many interest groups work with members of both parties, others form long-term alliances with just one (Bawn et al. 2012). Democrats ally with organized labor, environmental interest groups, constituency groups representing racial or ethnic minorities, anti-gun groups, and a wide variety of smaller groups that make up its diverse coalition. Republicans ally with a narrower collection of conservative Christian groups, pro-gun groups, economic libertarian organizations, and oil, gas, coal, and other businesses. These interest groups both compete to control the political party in nominations processes and also provide important resources to candidates and parties to help them win elections (Cohen et al. 2009). Collectively, the interest groups form the backbone of an extended network of party activists, who work together to prevent their allies in government from deviating from their policy goals (Bawn et al. 2012; Grossmann and Dominguez 2009; Koger, Masket, and Noel 2009, 2010). If political parties need an expert, they can probably find one in their extended party network. So why do they need big generalist think tanks?

Think tanks solve the core problem within the extended party network: issue prioritization. Each member of the extended party network cares intensely about one set of issues, only occasionally expanding to issues on the periphery (Fagan, McGee, and Thomas 2019). But policymaking often involves tough choices, sacrificing one priority for another. Experts from a traditional interest group will always advise their allies in government to prioritize *their issue* at the expense of others and will feel betrayed if their allies make the opposite choice. If serving as staff within the government, they will be unwilling to sacrifice their issue for some broader compromise. Some will serve in government, and many more will be consulted on major policy decisions, but they are bad policy advisors. On the other hand, generalist think tanks can aggregate the various interests of a party coalition. Because they work across issues, they serve as an interest group representing progressives, conservatives, or some other ideology rather than an interest or constituency. They can connect interest groups within the party network, facilitating cooperation (Albert 2019). They are often the best strategic planners in the party system (Fraussen and Halpin 2017). They can make sacrifices for the greater progressive or conservative mission that organizations with members may not be able to. Congressional leaders will often bring them into meetings with their caucus to explain a deal or complex policy alternative.[1]

In one example, former CBPP president Robert Greenstein recalls a meeting with several other Democratic interest groups at the White House after Obama's 2012 reelection. The purpose of the meeting was to discuss with the president what their priorities should be for the second term:

> The afternoon before the meeting, [AFL-CIO President Richard] Trumpka had organized a phone meeting of the people who would be going in. I had a conflict and couldn't make it and I didn't know what had been discussed at the meeting. I only later learned that apparently Trumpka had laid out some things and said we all should agree on X. I'll open and I'll say, we all favor X. I didn't know that was coming. He goes first and he said, Mr. President, we all agree anything in Social Security and Medicare totally off the table, don't touch anything.

Each person got two or three or four minutes [to] speak to the president. They got to me and I said, "Look, I mainly want to talk about a key decision that you face on Medicaid and where I think you need to immediately reverse a policy that's in your budget proposal. Before I get there, I do just feel constrained to say that I actually don't agree that you can't touch anything in Social Security and Medicare. You'll have some tough budget negotiations coming up and for example, I don't think you should take off the table the concept of increasing the income-related premiums for affluent people in Medicare as a way to help pay for something else. That seems like a very reasonable policy to consider for me." I then went to my Medicaid part. Trumpka was furious, livid. I heard about that for days. I would have done it anyway.[2]

In this case, CBPP was no less a progressive organization than the labor, environmental, and constituency groups that were in the room but was able to provide better policy advice than they. Because they neither represent a defined constituency nor are reliant on a few patrons for funding, they can make choices between priorities. They still want to further progressive policy goals, but more holistically. Their role is less a policy demander and more a consigliere.

People Are Policy

Their close relationship with political parties is particularly apparent when the party is out of government. The Democratic and Republican parties have thousands of specialized staffers who make policy in executive branch agencies and congressional committees when their party is in charge. When their party loses an election, they are out of the job until the next time they win. Many will get jobs in the private sector, often working in lobbying or industry. In many cases, they won't be available to return to government. They may develop conflicts of interest in their new jobs or might just enjoy the higher pay and job security that isn't tied to who wins an election. Even those who can return to government may not be able to conduct significant policy planning while out of government, participate in electoral politics, or defend the party in the media. Partisan think tanks provide a home for the party's future policy talent.

Similarly, partisan think tanks play a key role in the transition between opposition and government (Brown 2012). New presidents must fill thousands of highly specialized executive branch policy jobs quickly, most of which are at the staff level. They need staff who are competent, on board with their policy agenda, and loyal. Partisan think tanks have always played an important role in providing staff to executive branch organizations, both in the form of their own employees and by connecting networks of partisans with party leaders.

Heritage founder Ed Feulner frequently repeated the maxim "People are policy"[3] and made it a central part of Heritage's strategy in its first decade (Edwards 1997). In addition to hundreds of policy recommendations for the Reagan administration in *Mandate for Leadership* (see Chapter 3), Heritage helped the Reagan transition staff the government. In *The Power of Ideas*, Lee Edwards's (1997, 50) history of the Heritage Foundation, the author claims that "several dozen" *Mandate* authors were offered jobs in the Reagan administration, ranging from cabinet secretaries to more junior policy positions. They created a job bank for conservative policy workers, claiming to connect "more than two hundred" staff to jobs per year during Reagan's administration (51). Edwards points out that Heritage was not the only think tank to place staff in the Reagan administration, claiming, somewhat passive-aggressively, that AEI placed 27 senior staff members over eight years (52). Heritage began to regularly publish a directory of conservative policy experts, many editions of which are still available at university libraries. More recently, they announced Project 2025, a $22 million organization aimed at staffing a potential 2025 Republican administration, which commentators called a "conservative LinkedIn" (Swan and Haberman 2023). Heritage announced that 50 conservative interest groups, mostly far-right social conservative groups and state-based think tanks, would partner with them on the project.

CAP has played an even more obvious role in Democratic presidential transitions (Brown 2012). Like Heritage, CAP saw the 2008 Obama transition as a way for the young organization to influence public policy and cement its position in the Democratic Party. It produced *Change for America*, a book of policy recommendations modeled on *Mandate*. At least 16 *Change* co-authors were appointed to top positions in the Obama administration (Brown 2012). Aside from Tanden, who served on Hillary Clinton's transition committee in 2016, CAP president Podesta was co-chair of Obama's transition. Six other current or former CAP staffers would serve on the Obama transition team, including Associate Personnel Director Patrick Gaspard, who would become president of CAP after Tanden left for the Biden administration. CAP arguably established a stronger influence over the Obama administration's staffing than even Heritage had over the Reagan administration. However, CAP was conspicuously absent from the Biden transition team, with Biden handing the co-chair jobs to three former politicians and senior Obama White House staff Jeffrey Zients and Anita Dunn.

True to its behind-the-scenes reputation, CBPP never played the kind of formal role on a presidential transition that CAP and Heritage did. Jared Bernstein, a CBPP senior fellow and former staffer during Biden's vice presidency, served on the advisory committee. Greenstein served in a minor policy-planning role during the 1992 Clinton transition and a larger role during the 2008 Obama transition, helping to design the American Recovery and Reinvestment Act (see Chapter 1).

By placing people throughout the White House and federal agencies, these think tanks achieved immense influence over public policy. Presidents could fill many of these positions with career civil servants, former elected officials, academics, lobbyists, business leaders, or other subject-matter expects. Indeed, presidential transitions before Heritage did exactly that. Working out of Brookings Institution offices (Dews 2016), John F. Kennedy's transition team included the preeminent political scientist studying the presidency at that time, Richard Neustadt, and Nobel Prize–winning economist Paul Samuelsson, along with several members of the Kennedy family. They famously hired a team of academics, business leaders, and technocrats, among them Ford CEO Robert McNamara, to run federal agencies (Halberstam 1992). Today new presidents reach into their party's think tank world to find reliable conservative or progressive staff. The result is a net more ideological slate of appointees who make more conservative or progressive policy.

The Problem of Private Control

Privately funded organizations have different goals than an organization controlled by political parties. Political parties are naturally office-seeking organizations. When making public policy decisions, they usually land on positions that help them maximize their electoral fortunes. Our most basic models of party competition suggest that office-seeking parties will choose positions that target the median voter and support a moderate ideological reputation (Downs 1957). When public opinion veers away from a policy position, the party will face pressure to adopt one closer to the public's preferences. Voters both punish parties that adopt extreme policy positions and make smaller thermostatic adjustments when the overall policy environment veers away from their preferences (Jennings 2009; Wlezien 1995). Furthermore, voters want to see parties in government address the most pressing problems on the agenda at any given time and will blame parties that pursue other goals while significant problems remain unsolved (see Chapter 2). Policymaking is just an instrument for office-seeking parties to win elections. If the electoral winds shift, they will adjust to the new incentives. Formal party organizations, like the Republican and Democratic national committees, are by extension office-seeking organizations.

In most other democracies, party think tanks are formal party organizations, funded directly or indirectly by tax dollars (Campbell and Pedersen 2014). For example, Germany's Konrad Adenauer Stiftung (KAS), the think tank affiliated with the Christian Democratic Party and European People's Party, raised €222 million in 2022 (Konrad Adenauer Stiftung n.d.). They are also largely publicly financed; KAS received €214 million in grants from the German federal government in the same year.[4] KAS's board of directors is directly elected by its party's members of Parliament, and most are current MPs who served as ministers when in government (Konrad Adenauer Stiftung n.d.) In contrast, the Heritage Foundation's board of trustees had only one former government official, Reagan's attorney general Edwin

Meese. Most board members were senior business or finance leaders, presumably to assist with fundraising (Heritage Foundation n.d.).

Because of their formal affiliation, party think tanks tend to take on a lower profile in their country's politics (Braml 2006). Party think tank systems also tend to have weak privately funded think tank ecosystems (Braml 2006), perhaps because they struggle to compete with the party think tanks. Because they are controlled by the political party, they function like other formal party organizations, supporting their office-seeking goals.

In the United States, privately funded think tanks have taken on the party think tank role. In their comparative study of knowledge regimes in the United States, France, Germany, and Denmark, Campbell and Pedersen (2014) find that some U.S. think tanks perform many of the same functions as party think tanks in the other countries by bringing ideas from broader knowledge regimes into party positions. Albert (2019) finds that they are critical actors in the party network, transmitting ideas from outside research sources to both officeholders and interest groups in the party network. Fagan (2019) finds that they tend to produce information on the party's core priorities. Policy entrepreneurs in U.S. political parties in essence exploit the need for organizations to fill the party think tank role to carve out a role for private organizations.

But U.S. partisan think tanks are not office-seeking organizations. They have policy goals and see their party winning elections as merely instrumental to achieving them. Because they are generalist organizations, their policy goals are to move public policy overall, or at least on issues prioritized by the party coalition, in a more conservative or progressive direction. They can balance priorities within the party coalition, but necessarily not in service of winning elections. They always want their allies in government to be more progressive or conservative, not to tack to the center to win a few more votes. If that means a few more allies in government lose next November, so be it. If their elected bosses try to take positions that they disagree with, they will feel deeply betrayed and will let their feelings be known. From their perspective, all the campaigning, fundraising, and electoral battles were for the purpose of doing progressive or conservative work in government, not just holding office.

This misalignment of goals creates a problem for elected officials and their parties. Elected officials may bring their own policy staff into government with them, or hire staff from Congress or state offices. But policy-oriented staff who ultimately care about winning elections will be in short supply, with formal party organizations able to supply only staff with experience in electoral politics. Congress has steadily cut its policy workforce over the past few decades, concurrent with the rise of partisan think tanks (see Chapter 6). Nonpartisan experts like bureaucrats, academics, or nonpartisan think tanks are only a partial solution to the problem, as they can be relied on to give sound advice but not necessarily advice with politics in mind. Instead, most of the thousands of people appointed to the federal government, plus all the policy advice given by partisan think tank experts outside of government, are motivated to achieve some policy goals. Elected officials will find it difficult to chart a path forward in a direction that their policy workforce disagrees with.

The net result of the privileged role that partisan think tanks have carved out within U.S. political parties is increased influence for ideologues in the extended party network. They are party organizations without being formal party organizations. But they also have the explicit goal of shifting their party's positions away from where they would be all else being equal. The alliance they form is uneasy, but it's the best the party can do absent the public support enjoyed by parties in most other democracies. It's costly for parties, as their policymaking activities are constrained by the personnel and advice available to them.

5

How Partisan Think Tanks Set Their Agenda

In 2017 Republicans regained unified control of government following the election of Donald Trump. The first major item on their legislative agenda was to repeal Barack Obama's signature legislative achievement, the Patient Protection and Affordable Care Act. Republicans had spent much of the past six years promising to repeal the law. The ACA expanded access to healthcare in a variety of ways, such as expanding Medicaid to the working poor, creating a subsidized marketplace for individuals, and preventing insurance from being priced based on most preexisting conditions. The law's fate seemed sealed when Trump won the 2016 election. Republican leaders in Congress pushed repeal to the top of their agenda.

The CBPP aggressively shifted its agenda toward defending the ACA (Figure 5.1). The law, and healthcare policy more broadly, had always been an important part of CBPP's policy agenda. The Center published about 50 reports each year mentioning the law as it was being proposed, enacted, and implemented from 2009 until 2016. As soon as Trump was declared the winner of the 2016 election, it was clear that the law was under threat. CBPP began meeting with other progressive groups to organize in defense of the law that same week.[1] Seeing a fight coming, CBPP immediately began hiring top healthcare policy experts from the outgoing Obama administration, including Aviva Aron-Dine, a former official in the Department of Health and Human Services, who would go on to serve in a senior role in the Biden White House. Aron-Dine would lead CBPP's healthcare policy analysis during the ACA repeal debate. Over the next year, CBPP published 155 reports mentioning the law, by far the most of any year since it was enacted in 2010.

CBPP used a wide range of arguments to support the ACA, including those related to healthcare and to the law's broader impact on segments of society. Because Republicans had unified control of government, they often focused on the impact of repeal on core Republican constituencies. In one CBPP report, the author argued that repeal would have a disproportionate effect on veterans:

The Thinkers. E. J. Fagan, Oxford University Press. © Oxford University Press 2024.
DOI: 10.1093/oso/9780197759653.003.0005

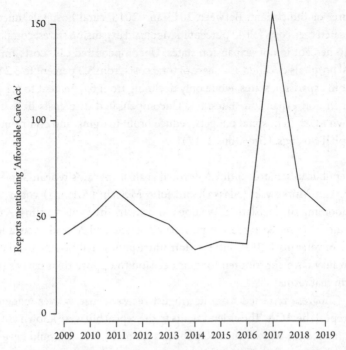

Figure 5.1 Number of Center on Budget and Policy Priorities reports mentioning "Affordable Care Act." Author's counts of reports published on the CBPP website.

> Before those major ACA coverage expansions took effect, 89 percent of uninsured veterans would have been eligible for them based on their income (either the Medicaid expansion that states could adopt or the premium tax credits that help families buy marketplace coverage). Largely because veterans took advantage of these options, their uninsured rate dropped from 11.9 percent in 2013 to 6.8 percent in 2015, according to an Urban Institute analysis of the CDC's National Health Interview Survey (NHIS). States that adopted the Medicaid expansion have experienced the greatest gains. Since health reform took effect, fewer veterans report unmet health needs due to the cost of care, and fewer report trouble paying medical bills. (Cross-Call 2017)

CBPP also published reports arguing that repeal would have a disproportionately negative impact on rural hospitals, possibly leading to widespread hospital closures:

> Health coverage gains in states that expanded Medicaid to low-income adults have substantially improved rural hospitals' finances. First, the Medicaid expansion significantly reduced rural hospitals' uncompensated care costs—services for which hospitals are not reimbursed by an

insurer or the patient. Between 2013 and 2015, rural hospitals' uncompensated care costs fell 43 percent in Medicaid expansion states, compared to 16 percent in non-expansion states. Uncompensated care costs among rural hospitals declined as a share of total costs from 5.3 percent to 3.2 percent in expansion states, while only declining from 6.8 percent to 6.1 percent in non-expansion states. . . . Uncompensated care costs have been shown to strain hospital budgets, reduce profit margins, and contribute to hospital closings. (Broaddus 2017)

Three Republican senators ultimately voted against the law's repeal: Susan Collins (Maine), Lisa Murkowski (Alaska), and John McCain (Arizona) voted against it in July, dooming the legislation. We don't know why they voted against repeal, but Collins and Murkowski represent poor, rural states, and McCain was a longtime advocate for veterans. CBPP's effort to introduce policy analysis into the public conversation may have contributed to their decision to oppose their party's signature legislation that term.

After Congress returned from its August recess, conservatives made one last push to repeal the ACA. The amendments to the repeal bill were known as Graham-Cassidy, named for its two chief Republican sponsors, which would have allowed states to opt out of many of the ACA's insurance regulations and altered its Medicaid expansion. If passed, the amendment would de facto repeal Obamacare's insurance requirements in states controlled by Republicans and redistribute much of the money allocated in blue states for Medicaid expansion toward red states that had not adopted it. The amendment looked to have a real chance of passing.

Enter Jimmy Kimmel, a popular late-night television host. Kimmel had hosted *Jimmy Kimmel Live* on ABC since 2003. Unlike Stephen Colbert, John Oliver, and other hosts, Kimmel was not known for political comedy. His career started in sports talk radio before hosting Comedy Central shows *Win Ben Stein's Money*, a trivia game show, and *The Man Show*, a parody of a late-night show (Gray 2016). On ABC, he was better known for edgy pranks and parody music videos than political satire or commentary. But in late April 2017, when Republicans were moving the first version of ACA repeal through Congress, his newborn child had to have open-heart surgery. Barely holding back tears, Kimmel told the emotional story on his show a week later. He ended the story with this message for his viewers watching the ACA repeal debate: "We were brought up to believe that we live in the greatest country in the world. Until a few years ago, millions and millions of us had no access to health insurance at all. You know, before 2014, if you were born with congenital heart disease, like my son was, there's a good chance you'd never be able to get health insurance, because you had a preexisting condition. . . . No parent should ever have to decide if they can afford to save their child's life. It just shouldn't happen. Not here" (Abad-Santos 2017). Shortly after, Republican senator Bill Cassidy, a medical doctor and leader on healthcare issues among Senate Republicans, came on Kimmel's show and declared that any healthcare bill they support would have to pass the "Jimmy Kimmel Test": "The Jimmy Kimmel Test, I think, should be that no family should be denied medical care, emergency or otherwise, because they can't afford it" (Kliff 2017). Over the summer Cassidy repeatedly used the term when discussing ACA repeal. When he advocated for the Graham-Cassidy amendment, the senator claimed that in addition to passing the Jimmy Kimmel Test, the bill would provide health coverage for everyone, prevent discrimination against people with preexisting conditions, lower premiums for middle-class Americans, and prohibit lifetime limits on insurance benefits (Scott 2017).

Recently hired Aron-Dine wrote a memo arguing that Graham-Cassidy would do none of the things that Cassidy was claiming.[2] The memo made its way to Kimmel's producers, prompting an impassioned September 19, 2017, monologue:

> So last week, Bill Cassidy and Senator Lindsey Graham proposed a new bill and it does in fact pass the Jimmy Kimmel Test. But a different test. With this one your child with a pre-existing condition will get the care he needs if his father is Jimmy Kimmel. Otherwise, you might be screwed. I don't know what happened to Bill Cassidy when he was on this publicity tour, he listed his demands for a health care bill very clearly. These were his words. He said he wants coverage for all. No discrimination based on pre-existing conditions. Lower premiums for middle class families and no lifetime caps. Guess what? The new bill does none of those things.... Not only did it fail the Jimmy Kimmel Test, he failed the Bill Cassidy Test....
>
> Listen. Health care is complicated. It's boring. I don't want to talk about it. And that's what these guys are relying on. This guy, Bill Cassidy, just lied right to my face.... I never imagined that I would get involved in something like this. This is not my area of expertise. My area of expertise is eating pizza and that's about it.... So instead of jamming this horrible bill down our throats, go pitch in and be a part of [bipartisan negotiations]. I'm sure they could use a guy with your medical background. If not, stop using my name. I don't want my name on it. There's a new Jimmy Kimmel Test. It is called a lie detector test. You're welcome to stop by the studio and take it any time. (Scott 2017)

Kimmel's monologue went viral. It was both emotional and, thanks to CBPP's memo, grounded in policy specifics. The next day, swing Republican senators started coming out against the bill (Kim, Haberkorn, and Everett 2017). Graham-Cassidy, the final serious attempt to repeal the ACA, died less than a week later, in large part thanks to the Center's decision to prioritize the issue as soon as it was clear that it would hit the congressional policy agenda.

Partisan Think Tanks and Agenda Setting

A think tank's ability to deftly shift its focus toward issues that are on the agenda is often cited as one of the reasons why think tanks are more effective at influencing public policy than similar information producers such as academia. Indeed, the Heritage Foundation's origin story, as detailed in Chapter 3, is fundamentally an agenda-setting story. Heritage's founders were upset that AEI released a report criticizing a policy change only after it was enacted, thus minimizing their policy impact. Heritage was structured from the beginning to be capable of responding quickly to the agenda. Think tanks founded in its image did the same. This nimble approach is costly: it requires think tanks to invest in excess capacity to provide credible policy expertise on whatever issue is salient at the time, or at least to divert resources from other priorities. Whether or not they pay those costs is a largely untested proposition; we do not know the extent to which partisan think tanks try to tailor their activities to the problems demanding attention from Congress.

There are many reasons why a partisan think tank might wish to closely align the information it produces with the policy agenda. First, partisan think tanks might want to give their allies access to arguments to use in public debates over policy, or directly participate in those debates by acting as spokespeople (Rich 2005). Busy reporters or producers on a deadline often use partisan think tank reports or personnel as shortcuts to identify representatives of both sides of a partisan policy debate (McDonald 2014; Rich and Weaver 2000). Partisan think tanks can shift the outcomes of debates to their side by helping proponents win the public debate. Their elected allies can take more aggressive positions knowing that they will have some policy analysis backing them up. Partisan think tanks need not change their allies' underlying support for policy, but rather activate latent preferences already held.

Second, information that is most proximate to the window of opportunity for policy change is likely to be most effective at impacting preferences. If partisan think tank policy recommendations are tailored or framed for the specific circumstances of the moment, think tanks can more easily satisfy demand for information from policymakers when they conduct searches for expert information. Information that is older may give general guidance but is less actionable. Partisan think tanks can rebut arguments that they disagree with or find threatening only after those arguments are made. Furthermore, policymakers frequently use the availability heuristic to make decisions (Jones 2001). Because policymaking attention is divided among many issues, information released well before the window of opportunity might be ignored or forgotten.

Finally, partisan think tanks that work across multiple issues may potentially impact more areas of policy than those that specialize in a narrowly defined set. Windows of opportunity on any one issue are relatively rare. A partisan think tank with a narrow issue portfolio will have fewer opportunities to impact public policy than one with a broader portfolio. Partisan think tanks that see policy entrepreneurship as an opportunity to attach policy solutions to problems will more aggressively discuss problems on the agenda, even if the solutions they propose don't change much with it.

There are also reasons why an agenda-setting strategy might be ineffective. Information that is rushed is likely to be less rigorous and thus less persuasive. Less rigorous information may lack credibility with policymakers, reducing its impact (Furnas, LaPira, and Wang 2024). Some partisan think tanks mitigate this problem by producing more rigorous, detailed reports in advance, then republishing quicker reports tied to the agenda.[3] Even if think tanks can maintain high standards on deadlines, they will find much more competition from other information producers during windows of opportunity.

Think tanks that take a more slow-and-steady strategy may be able to develop long-term relationships with policymakers that they can cash in during moments of opportunity. Beliefs about policy are usually sticky. If policymakers are convinced to think about an issue the way the partisan think tank does, other groups that are activated during windows of opportunity will struggle to change their minds. Partisan think tanks are particularly well-suited to a slow-and-steady strategy as close, long-term political allies of their party.

Data and Methods

To observe partisan think tank policy agendas in relation to the congressional and public agenda, I use white papers published on their websites from 2001 to 2016.[4] Producing, publishing, and disseminating white papers is in many ways the core activity of any think tank. Many think tanks, even advocacy think tanks like Heritage, present themselves as pseudo-academic institutions. They call their employees scholars, encourage donors to fund endowed chairs, publish journals and books, and hold seminars. AEI even gives its scholars a version of tenure and academic freedom. White papers are their answer to the academic journal article, although without peer review. We can observe the issues that think tanks work on by observing the policy content of the white papers they publish on their website.

To measure the distribution of attention to issues in partisan think tank reports, I collected data on the policy content of the posted white papers. I coded each output for its policy content using the Policy Agendas Project (PAP) topic coding system. PAP is a collaboration among dozens of scholars across countries to categorize the issue content of policy outputs using a system that allows for valid comparisons across time and context. The PAP system assigns each policy output to one of 20 major topic areas, such as energy or defense policy, and one of 221 subtopic areas, such as nuclear energy and weapon sales. The U.S. PAP has coded over a dozen data sets of policy outputs over a long time series, allowing us to relate U.S. think

Table 5.1 **Comparative Agendas Project Major Topics and Think Tank Examples**

Major Topic Area	Example
Macroeconomics	"A Territorial Tax System Would Create Jobs and Raise Wages for U.S. Workers"—Heritage
Civil Rights	"The Unintended Consequences of Section 5 of the Voting Rights Act"—AEI
Healthcare	"Health Reform Law Makes Clear That Subsidies Will Be Available in States with Federally Operated Exchanges"—CBPP
Agriculture	"Food Safety: Background, Analysis and Recommendations"—AEI
Labor	"Real Family Values: Raising the Federal Minimum Wage"—CAP
Education	"The Future of Teacher Compensation"—CAP
Environment	"Impact of the Waxman-Markey Climate Change Legislation on the States"—Heritage
Energy	"Electricity Pricing to U.S. Manufacturing Plants, 1963–2000"—AEI
Immigration	"The Senate Immigration Bill Rewards Lawbreaking: Why the DREAM Act Is a Nightmare"—Heritage
Transportation	"It's Time for States to Invest in Infrastructure"—CBPP
Law and Crime	"Changing Priorities: State Criminal Justice Reforms and Investments in Education"—CBPP
Social Welfare	"Would Private Accounts Provide a Higher Rate of Return Than Social Security?"—CBPP
Housing	"Retrofitting Foreclosed Homes: A Matter of Public Trust"—CAP
Commerce	"Is There a Way to Create a Transatlantic Securities Market?"—AEI
Defense	"Afghanistan: Zero Troops Should Not Be an Option"—Heritage
Science and Communication	"Bundles of Trouble: The FCC's Telephone Competition Rules"—Heritage
Trade	"Global Value Chains and the Continuing Case for Free Trade"—AEI
Foreign Affairs	"A Plan B with Teeth for Darfur"—CAP
Government Operations	"Federal Pay Is Out of Line with Private Sector Pay"—Heritage
Public Lands	"A Continued Push for Reform Is Needed on Public Lands' Energy Leasing"—CAP

tank outputs to the activities of political parties, Congress, and the public. Table 5.1 shows the 20 PAP major topic areas,[5] along with examples of partisan think tank white papers coded under each. Each output was assigned to a single topic area. If an output contained policy content in multiple topic areas (for example, a report on the fiscal health of Medicaid and Social Security), it was assigned to a single topic area based upon the rules of the PAP codebook.

We can see the distribution of attention to policy by think tanks in Figure 5.2. All 20 issues received reports, but there is tremendous variation in attention among issues. The macroeconomics category, which includes reports on taxes, budgets, unemployment, inflation, monetary, and industrial policy, received more attention than any other issue. There is also a tremendous amount of attention to foreign affairs, which includes topics like foreign aid, human rights, and international organizations, as well as defense, which includes reports on topics like war, homeland security, nonproliferation, and procurement. Rounding out the top four is healthcare, which includes reports on pharmaceuticals, health insurance, and healthcare research. These four issues represent the biggest policy debates of the period: the war on terror and wars in Iraq and Afghanistan, the 2008 financial crisis and Great Recession, and 2010s enactment of and reaction to the ACA. Partisan think tanks were active participants in all these debates.

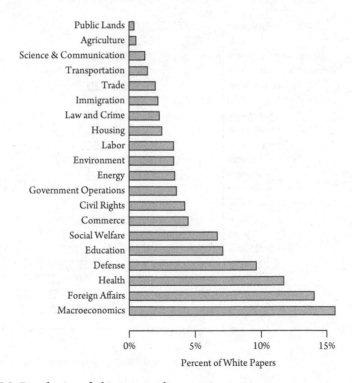

Figure 5.2 Distribution of white paper policy attention.

However, it is helpful to compare partisan think tank agendas to some baseline demand for information from Congress. To account for demand, we can compare partisan think tank attention to reports published by Congress's internal think tank, the Congressional Research Service (Fagan and McGee 2022). The CRS is in many ways a competitor to partisan think tanks, providing sober, nonpartisan policy analysis in the interest of the legislature rather than private interests. Because, until recently, members of Congress could request that CRS address a topic anonymously, CRS reports allow us to measure the demand for information on an issue by members of Congress.

A comparison of relative partisan think tank attention reveals the issues that are overrepresented relative to demand (Figure 5.3). Social welfare policy, which includes huge federal programs such as food aid, Social Security, and the earned income tax credit, now holds the top spot. Macroeconomics and education policy follow. These issues, along with all other issues involved in long-standing policy debates over redistributing wealth and government intervening in the battles of labor versus capital, all see more relative partisan think tank attention when compared with CRS reports. Some issues see much less attention. Partisan think tanks devote barely any attention to public lands, which includes forestry and national parks, to Native American affairs, or to agriculture, which includes agricultural subsidies,

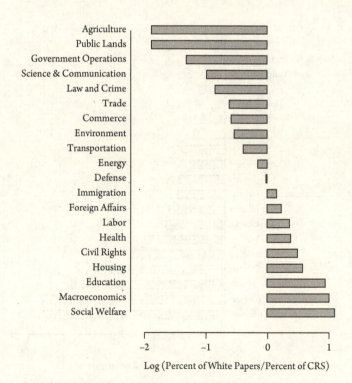

Figure 5.3 Distribution of white paper policy attention relative to CRS reports.

food safety and inspection, and the regulation of fisheries. Because there are few long-standing partisan debates over these issues, partisan think tanks may see little value in producing reports on them. Policymakers may also prefer the more objective policy analysis they receive from nonpartisan experts, especially if the issue intersects with their own local political considerations.

We can also look at how the issues discussed by individual think tanks align with demand for nonpartisan information from CRS (Figure 5.4). Three of the four think tanks on average release more reports on an issue if the CRS publishes more reports on it. The exception is the CBPP, which essentially ignores foreign policy, government operations, and several other key areas while focusing intensely on social and tax policy. We see that Heritage's agenda aligns closely with the CRS, with slightly more attention to foreign affairs, defense, macroeconomics, and healthcare than CRS and much less on science, technology and communication, environmental policy, and government operations. AEI has a portfolio similar to Heritage's, although they tend to ignore defense issues and publish more reports on commerce, science, antitrust issues, and education. CAP works broadly across most issues but gives extra attention to education, civil rights, healthcare, and foreign affairs.

Of course, these are just cross-sectional averages over 16 years. To test if partisan think tanks tailor the issues they release reports on to the issues that are on the congressional and public agendas, we need to examine this relationship dynamically. To do so, I use what is called an error correction model. This model treats each issue as a panel, observed once per year over 16 years. The dependent variable is the change in attention to each issue in each year. The independent variables are the change in attention to policy in CRS reports and others, along with its long-term effect.

Dynamic Agenda Setting

We can examine the relationship between the policy agenda of Congress and the public and partisan think tanks with models predicting the change (Δ) in attention to each issue in each year (Table 5.2). First, we should look at how partisan think tanks respond to the same inputs that Congress does. When a problem grows dramatically worse in a moment in time, voters will often list it as the "most important problem" (MIP) facing America and demand that their representatives attend to it. Congress tends to respond by holding hearings and legislating on those MIPs (Jones and Baumgartner 2004). Partisan think tanks can also observe that problems are getting worse and generating public concern and may respond by publishing reports on related solutions. However, MIP is an imperfect measure of public concern (Wlezien 2005). Some issues, like macroeconomics and foreign policy, often rise to the status of "most important" and thus are routinely named by respondents in surveys. Other issues may become more important but rarely rise to the level of most important. We can approach this analytic challenge by examining

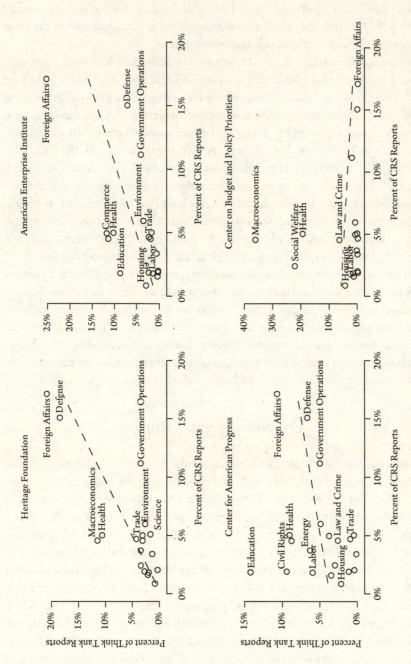

Figure 5.4 Issue attention in think tank reports compared to CRS reports. Overlapping observation labels suppressed for clarity.

Table 5.2 **Panel Estimation of Issue Salience and Δ Issue Attention in Think Tank Reports$_{it}$**

Independent Variable	Think Tank Reports			
	AEIi$_t$	CAP$_{it}$	CBPP$_{it}$	Heritage$_{it}$
Think Tank Reports$_{it-1}$	−0.12*	−0.46***	−0.63***	−0.36***
	(0.06)	(0.11)	(0.11)	(0.09)
ΔCRS Reports$_{it}$	−0.19	−0.2	−0.1	0.27*
	(0.15)	(0.2)	(0.21)	(0.13)
CRS Reports$_{it-1}$	0.04	0.01	−0.42***	0.34***
	(0.06)	(0.10)	(0.09)	(0.09)
ΔMIP$_{it}$	−0.03	0.01	0.60**	0.15*
	(0.07)	(0.10)	(0.23)	(0.06)
MIP$_{it-1}$	0.01	0.06	0.54***	0.07*
	(0.03)	(0.04)	(0.11)	(0.03)
r^2	0.08	0.29	0.4	0.22
n	300	2201	300	d300

* p<.05 ** p<.01 *** p<.001. Panel-corrected standard errors in parentheses.
[1] n = 220 for CAP because the organization was not founded until 2004.

wthe relationship between partisan think tank reports and short-term changes in the demand for nonpartisan information. Congress requests more information on issues that become salient (Fagan and McGee 2022). Thus we can observe the policy content of CRS reports, which are generated from congressional demand for information, to measure short-term changes in issue salience.

Table 5.3 shows the relationship between short-term attention to policy in each think tank's reports and issue salience. We see huge variation in the strategies used by think tanks in response to both short-term and long-term increase in issue salience. Both AEI and CAP do little to align their agendas to issue salience. Each year, they do not respond to short-term changes in public concern, ΔMIP_{it}, or demand for expert information, $\Delta CRS\ Reports_{it}$, by publishing more reports on the same issues. They also do not tend to publish more reports on the topics that tend to receive more public concern, MIP_{it-1}, and demand for expert information, $CRS\ Reports_{it-1}$, over the long term. On the other hand, the Heritage Foundation aggressively sets its agenda to respond to issue salience. As public concern on an issue increases, Heritage publishes reports on the same issue (p<0.05). Similarly, they publish more reports while CRS publishes fewer reports on an issue (p<0.05). They also tailor their agenda over the long term to focus on more salient issues. Unlike CAP and

Table 5.3 **Panel Estimation of the Congressional Agenda and Δ Issue Attention in Think Tank Reports$_{it}$**

Independent Variable	Think Tank Reports			
	AEIi$_t$	*CAP$_{it}$*	*CBPP$_{it}$*	*Heritage$_{it}$*
Think Tank Reports$_{it-1}$	−0.14**	−0.43***	−0.42***	−0.18**
	(0.05)	(0.10)	(0.10)	(0.05)
Δ Roll Call Votes$_{it}$	−0.11	0.1	0.23	0.18*
	(0.07)	(0.14)	(0.15)	(0.07)
Roll Call Votes$_{it-1}$	−0.1	−0.1	0.17**	−0.04
	(0.05)	(0.1)	(0.06)	(0.05)
Δ Hearings$_{it}$	0.2	0.41	−0.0004	0.05
	(0.16)	(0.36)	(0.30)	(0.16)
Hearings$_{it-1}$	0.18	0.06	−0.34*	0.20*
	(0.10)	(0.13)	(0.17)	(0.10)
r^2	0.08	0.3	0.27	0.14
n	300	220	300	300

* p<.05 ** p<.01 *** p<.001. Panel-corrected standard errors in parentheses.
n = 220 for CAP because the organization was not founded until 2004.

AEI, Heritage tends to publish reports on issues that generally generate more public concern (p<0.05) and especially those that generate demand for reports from CRS (p<0.001). Finally, CBPP uses a strategy somewhere in between the other think tanks. CBPP does not publish more reports on issues that receive more demand from CRS but does adjust its agenda in response to short-term changes in public concern (p<0.01), and it also tends to work on issues that generate more public concern over the long term (p<0.001).

Next, we can look more directly at the relationship between issues that partisan think tanks publish reports on and the congressional policy agenda. The lowest-friction action that Congress can conduct is a hearing (Jones, Larsen-Price, and Wilkerson 2009). Unlike when legislating, members of Congress can quickly pull together a hearing in response to an emerging problem. Congress uses hearings to gather information and highlight important issues or arguments. Increasingly, Congress has focused on using a hearing less to consider bills and more as a platform to communicate their concerns to the bureaucracy (Jones, Theriault, and Whyman 2019; Lewallen, Theriault, and Jones 2016; Workman 2015). Hearings are thus highly responsive to public concerns (Jones, Larsen-Price, and Wilkerson 2009). Partisan think tanks may choose to produce information in response to salient issues raised by hearings if they attempt to impact the early stages of the legislative process.

In contrast to the low-friction, early-stage hearings, Congress can address a problem by passing laws. Legislating is by nature a complicated, high-friction endeavor. Members who seek to push a law through Congress must overcome multiple veto players in their own chamber, the opposite chamber, and the White House. When an issue is prioritized, opportunities open up for ambitious legislators and outside interest groups to weigh in and accomplish their policy goals. Partisan think tanks may try to impact this process by releasing reports aimed at the later stages of the policy process, either by trying to kill a bill they don't like, supporting a bill they do like, or modifying a bill that is expected to advance with their own proposals.

Table 5.3 shows the relationship between partisan think tank agendas and the congressional agenda. There is little evidence that any of the partisan think tanks aggressively respond to hearings. No think tank significantly increases its short-term policy attention when Δ $Hearings_{it}$ increases. Heritage's policy agenda has a positive and significant long-term relationship with hearings, $Hearings_{it-1}$, indicating that it tends to focus on issues that receive more hearings overall but does not target its agenda toward hearings. The partisan think tanks do not appear to see the early stages of the legislative process as important or worthy of high report volume. On the other hand, Heritage does respond to changes in the issue content of roll call votes, Δ $Roll$ $Call$ $Votes_{it}$, by publishing more reports on the issue ($p<0.05$). The other think tanks do not.

Taken together, these data insights paint a clear picture. The Heritage Foundation aggressively shifts its policy agenda to respond to short-term shifts in the congressional policy agenda. The other three think tanks do not. Heritage seeks to provide arguments and policy analysis for use by its allies in public debates, likely seeking to allow its co-partisan allies to take positions farther to the right than they could if they relied only on nonpartisan expertise. This behavior is similar to the behavior observed by Rich (2005), which makes sense given that the other think tanks featured much less prominently in Rich's analysis (conducted in the late 1990s) than did Heritage. A massive think tank, Heritage functions as an all-purpose fire hose of ideologically conservative information, ready to provide information for whatever debates members of Congress choose to enter. The other think tanks do not adjust their policy agendas to respond to the congressional agenda. While this result does not rule out that their information can activate the latent preferences of policymakers who hold more ideological preferences than they can justify in public debates, it does suggest that those think tanks focus on more long-term strategies.

Summary

The agenda claims made in Heritage's founding story are clearly supported by the evidence. The leading partisan think tank aggressively responds to the congressional agenda by publishing white papers on issues that Congress is actively considering. This allows Heritage to opportunistically attach its conservative policy solutions to any issue that Congress may consider. When a crisis happens, Heritage leverages an opportunity. This strategy also allows Heritage to support a "cover" model, where it gives conservative Republicans the resources they need to take the policy positions they already prefer but do not otherwise believe would survive public debate. Heritage adjusts its policy agenda both year to year, addressing hot issues, and over the long term, providing information roughly in proportion to the long-term policy agenda of congressional hearings.

There is less evidence that the other three major partisan think tanks adopt similar strategies. None deftly adjusts the information it releases to meet the agenda in Congress. Only the CBPP aligns its long-term information to the agenda of Congress, and only to issues at the roll call stage. These think tanks may release a few extra reports here and there, but those releases are either poorly timed when compared with Congress or are too infrequent to represent a significant shift in policy agenda. As a result, they have much less capacity to push their side to take more extreme positions in hot public debates. Rather, they selectively emphasize partisan priorities using a legislative subsidy model. When those issues eventually come up on the agenda, the think tanks will be ready to provide policy information to their co-partisans. However, they will largely lie in wait for that moment to come, hoping the agenda finds them.

6

The Growth of Polarization and Partisan Think Tanks

When the Heritage Foundation arrived on the American political scene in the early 1970s, party politics were much different than they would be in the 2020s. The Republican and Democratic parties faced off against each other in intense elections but had few major disagreements on most aspects of public policy. A generation of lawmakers in both parties worked together to pass Medicare and Medicaid; the Civil Rights Act and Voting Rights Act; the Elementary and Secondary Education Act; marginal tax rate reductions; the Environmental Protection Agency and Interstate Highway System; deregulation of the trucking, energy, communications, and airline industries; and dozens of other landmark laws (Grossmann 2014; Jones, Theriault, and Whyman 2019). The most intense policy disagreements between the political parties were on classic issues of labor versus capital, which dated back to the 19th century (Gerring 2001). The two parties had not yet diverged on issues that would define their modern-day politics, such as women's rights (Wolbrecht 2000) and environmental policy (Karol 2019). The era featured the lowest levels of polarization in American history.

The consensus policy environment of the 1970s is unrecognizable today. The 2020s Republican and Democratic parties disagree on almost every salient issue, and they rarely work together to establish new programs absent a crisis. At the same time, Heritage and the partisan think tanks founded in its image play an increasingly prominent role in party politics. It is easy to draw a theoretical connection between partisan think tanks and polarization. Partisan think tanks are staffed and funded by ideologues who want to pull their co-partisans toward the left or right. If they are successful, the system should become more polarized. Indeed, I find a very strong empirical link between partisan think tanks and polarization over time.

The Thinkers. E. J. Fagan, Oxford University Press. © Oxford University Press 2024.
DOI: 10.1093/oso/9780197759653.003.0006

Research on Polarization

Dozens of scholars spanning multiple decades have contributed to the literature on polarization in Congress. Polarization, or the distance between the policy preferences of political parties, began to increase in 1978. Poole and Rosenthal (1984) first observed the effects of increased polarization as early as 1984, when they found that same-state senators who share a party affiliation tend to vote very similarly, but same-state senators who differ in party affiliation tend to vote very differently. They inferred that the geographic forces pushing senators to represent the local median voter's preferences over national party preferences were breaking down. They also observed that while senators were increasingly polarized, their elections were also competitive. In most races, either party had an opportunity to win any given race. They speculated post hoc that activists and interest groups operating on the party's extremes were the cause of the shift toward polarization, although they did not test their intuition.

Since then, scholars have searched for causal explanations of the shift toward polarization in Congress. While literature offers multiple and varied explanations for increased polarization, scholars do agree on one basic order of events: elected officials polarized long before the public did. Median voter theory (Downs 1957; Holcombe 1980), and some related electoral-based theories of congressional behavior (Mayhew 1974), predict that elected officials and parties will support policy that is close to the median voter's preferences in order to compete in elections. Thus, a shift in preferences, such as the shift that occurs when a legislature polarizes, should follow a shift in the distribution of opinion in the electorate. However, scholars find clear evidence that the mass public polarized much later than its elected officials (Dimock et al. 2014; Fiorina 2017; Fiorina, Abrams, and Pope 2011). While there was some ideological shift by the electorate during the early period of polarization, it was confined to only a few issues, such as gay rights and abortion (Fiorina, Abrams, and Pope 2011). The electorate began to sort into coherent ideological groups only around 2010 (Dimock et al. 2014). Therefore, polarization before the recent period could not have been caused by a shift in public opinion in the general electorate.

Similarly, there is little evidence that changes in districts or primary elections caused the shift (Abramowitz, Alexander, and Gunning 2006; Barber and McCarty 2015; Hirano et al. 2010; Layman, Carsey, and Horowitz 2006; McCarty, Poole, and Rosenthal 2006; McGhee et al. 2014). Although the mass electorate did not become more polarized until long after elites did, a combination of redistricting and primary elections could have caused members to adopt more extreme policy positions to respond to changes in the preferences of the median voter in their district or primary electorate. However, research consistently rejects both explanations (Barber and McCarty 2015; Layman, Carsey, and Horowitz 2006). Republican representatives in more gerrymandered districts are as conservative as their colleagues in more competitive districts, and Democratic representatives are only slightly more liberal (Barber and McCarty 2015; McCarty, Poole, and Rosenthal 2006). Increased gerrymandering is related to polarization only to the extent that it has created more Republican representatives, who tend to be more ideologically extreme than their Democratic colleagues (McCarty, Poole, and Rosenthal 2009). There is also little evidence that changes in primary elections have an impact on polarization (Barber and McCarty 2015; Hirano et al. 2010; McGhee et al. 2014). These factors could not have caused the polarization of elites that began in the 1970s.

The consensus literature thus concludes that elites were not polarized by the electorate or political geography. While these studies leave open the possibility that the very recent and sharp increases in polarization are related to changing districts or electorates, historically these factors are not related to polarization in Congress. Indeed, the direction of causation likely runs in the other direction: elites likely transferred their preferences to the public through cue-taking and conflict extension mechanisms (Layman and Carsey 2002; Zaller 1992). The election of Barack Obama also likely played a role in the polarization of the electorate in the 2010s, as voters sorted more heavily on racial lines (Sides, Tesler, and Vavreck 2018).

If the public did not push elites to polarize, then why did elites become more extreme? One explanation argues that geographic sorting made the party positions more coherent (Jacobson 2015; Rohde 1991; Theriault 2003). When Lyndon Johnson signed the Civil Rights Act of 1964, he famously declared that, in doing so, he had signed away the South for the Democratic Party for a generation. Segregation and other civil rights issues were the most important sources of intraparty disagreement dividing the Democratic Party. Absent a key wedge issue, legislative party leaders were able to demand more unity of their caucuses (Rohde 1991). Southern whites increasingly became Republican, putting pressure on their elected officials to leave a Democratic Party that was becoming more progressive on racial issues. Johnson was eventually proven correct, but he was off by a generation. While Richard Nixon and Ronald Reagan were successful at winning Southern states in presidential elections, Democrats remained competitive in the South well into the 1990s. While these post–Civil Rights Act Southern Democrats were generally more conservative than their colleagues, both grew more progressive at similar rates (Jones, Theriault, and Whyman 2019). Geographic sorting did in fact make the parties more ideologically coherent, but it fails to explain why polarization began to increase in 1978 rather than the late 1990s. It also fails to explain contemporaneous ideological shifts on other issues such as environmental policy (Karol 2019) or ideology shifting on average toward the extremes due to adaptation (Theriault 2006).

Another explanation for elite polarization is increased partisan competition (Lee 2009, 2016; Theriault 2008, 2013). The parties not only have increasingly disagreed on ideological policy positions, but each has used the legislative process to fight the other party. Lee (2009) observes that party disagreement in the 1990s and 2000s grew sharp not only on traditionally ideological issues but also on issues with no obvious conflict between conservatives and progressives, such as anticorruption or "good governance" issues or uncontroversial spending issues such as the NASA budget. Lee argues that parties strategically use these issues as bases for attack, as illustrated by the example of condemning anticorruption actions on the executive branch only when it is held by the opposition. Lee (2016) argues that parties increasingly used these strategies when control of the chambers of Congress became less certain as the Democratic New Deal coalition slowly disintegrated. Indeed, Theriault (2013) finds that Newt Gingrich and other members of the House Republican caucus elected after 1978 quickly adopted partisan warfare tactics, pushing their colleagues to become more extreme. He also finds that changes in congressional procedures caused much of the early polarization in roll call voting, rather than votes on final passage (Theriault 2008). While increased partisan competition can explain the shift away from bipartisan cooperation and toward more intraparty teamsmanship, it does not adequately explain substantive changes in party positions over time and is thus necessary but insufficient to explain why elites polarized.

Scholars have identified several other factors external to the parties which contributed to polarization. Rising inequality and the entrance of billionaire donors may have tilted Republican Party politicians to the right (Hertel-Fernandez 2019; McCarty, Poole, and Rosenthal 2009; Page, Seawright, and Lacombe 2019). Highly ideological small donors may have pushed candidates toward the extremes (Barber 2016). Polarization and increased partisan warfare may have resulted in moderate candidates opting out of running for office (Thomsen 2014, 2017). Partisan media or cable news may have created more partisan warfare (Zelizer 2006). While many of these factors are convincing theoretical explanations for polarization, none to date has been shown to persuasively explain polarization over the entire period (Barber and McCarty 2015).

Finally, the parties themselves may have caused their own shift toward polarization. If party actors change their preferences for policy, they may be able to transmit those new preferences to the behavior of elected officials. By the early 1960s, each political party had developed a coherent progressive or conservative ideology (Noel 2014). If by some mechanism these ideologues transmitted their preferences to elected officials, they could be responsible for polarization. Jones, Theriault, and Whyman (2019) argue that the rapid expansion of the scope of the federal government policy agenda created an opening for conservative ideologues to capture the Republican Party. In both parties, ground-level party actors, such as convention delegates, changed their preferences long before elected officials did (Schickler 2016; Wolbrecht 2002). Party platforms themselves tended to use similar language to talk about policy until 1980, when they sharply diverged more quickly than polarization in roll call voting (Wood and Jordan 2017). Legislative party leaders in Congress have some ability to exert agenda control, which can increase polarization if their preferences are to the left or right of the median voter (Cox and McCubbins

1993). Party actors may also be able to exert control of party nominations, ensuring member replacement with friendly candidates (Bawn et al. 2012).

A party-level explanation for polarization is appealing for two reasons. First, the parties polarized at different times (Theriault 2008). The Republican Party moved earlier and farther to the left than the Democratic Party. Therefore, the most important cause of polarization should affect the parties unequally and at different times. Second, over the long term legislative parties, rather than individual factions of the party, moved to the left and right (Barber and McCarty 2015). Therefore, the most important cause of polarization affected the entire party rather than individual members or factions of members.

The multiplicity of explanations for polarization suggests that no one independent variable caused its rise; rather, causes varied throughout the past four decades. The systems determining policy preferences for members of Congress and political parties are complex and defy monocausal analysis. Indeed, many of these proposed causes are themselves interrelated. In this chapter, I focus on one powerful cause of polarization over time: the increased influence of highly ideological and well-organized information producers at partisan think tanks. However, we should acknowledge the complexity of the polarization story and understand that the monocausal analysis that I perform is one interrelated piece of a larger story.

Elites, Partisan Think Tanks, and Polarization

Legislators have preferences for policy outputs that are revealed by roll call voting in Congress. These preferences are informed and to some degree determined by information (see Chapter 2). Partisan think tanks can modify these preferences by reframing the issue, activating latent preferences, or using elite persuasion. If successful, they will move their co-partisan's preferences to the left or right. As they do so, the ideological distance between the political parties will increase. Thus, if we observe greater influence of partisan think tanks in Congress and on broader American politics at one point in time, we should observe greater polarization at a future point in time.

To measure the dependent variable, polarization in Congress over time, I used the difference of party means as measured by the first dimension of DW-NOMINATE data from Lewis, Poole, and Rosenthal (2019). These data use a scaling procedure to represent each legislator's roll call voting behavior on a spatial map. They are the data most often used to measure polarization in Congress. As the distance between the average legislator in each party grows larger, polarization increases. To measure the activity of partisan think tanks over time, I compared three different outputs by partisan think tanks with this measure of polarization. If partisan think tank outputs cause polarization, their activity will increase before polarization. I had no a priori expectations for the size of the lag. All data are measured at the Congress unit of analysis, as DW-NOMINATE[1] is measured by Congress rather than annually.

First, I examine partisan think tank testimony before congressional hearings. As they become more influential, partisan think tanks will be called to testify more often. Members of Congress use hearings to gather information on emerging policy problems, to build external and internal support for policy proposals, or to interrogate bureaucrats (Bawn 1997; Lewallen, Theriault, and Jones 2016; Shafran 2015; Workman 2015; Workman, Shafran, and Bark 2017). If partisan think tanks are considered more valuable information sources, they will be called to testify more often. While hearings are public, the vast majority receive little to no media attention. Thus partisan think tanks are more likely to use hearings to engage in elite persuasion and framing rather than activating latent preferences. To measure the number of times that partisan think tanks testified before Congress, I identified each instance of testimony recorded in the ProQuest Congressional database using keyword searches, aggregating by Congress. This process yielded 856 witnesses between the 93rd and 114th Congresses. Because the total number of congressional hearings varies over time, I then divided the number of witnesses by the total number of hearings.

Second, I measure think tank size over time. As think tanks become bigger, they produce and disseminate more information. Ideally, I would measure the overall expenditures of each think tank. These data are extractable from IRS Form 990s, which are publicly available only back to 2001 in the ProPublica Non-Profit Explorer database. Given that the unit of analysis is necessarily one Congress, this yields only eight observations between 2001 and 2016, and are thus not sufficient to test a time-series hypothesis. As a further difficulty, this method cannot examine the periods where polarization first began increasing (the late 1970s) or dramatically accelerated (the mid-1990s). However, I was able to reconstruct the real revenue of the Heritage Foundation going back to its creation in 1973 using a variety of archival sources.[2] While I would prefer to measure the size of all four think tanks over the whole period, the Heritage Foundation is the largest and most influential of the group, and thus data pertaining to it are relevant even in isolation (Weidenbaum 2011). However, this limitation in the data set decreases the representativeness of any results using these data.

Finally, I measured think tank newspaper citations over time. Partisan think tanks often represent the progressive or conservative side in media debates (Groseclose and Milyo 2005; Rich and Weaver 2000). Their research tends to attract more frequent media attention than academic research, due both to aggressive marketing by think tanks themselves (McGann 2016; Rich 2005) and to their ability to exploit journalist equivalency norms when reporting politics (Boykoff and Boykoff 2004; Haas 2007). While both mass publics and elites receive much of their policy information through the media (Wolfe 2012), these activities are more likely than direct outreach or congressional hearings to be aimed at a broader public. If these activities cause polarization in Congress, polarization should increase shortly after partisan think tanks are cited more frequently in the media. Using keyword searches, I identified each story where a think tank was cited by name in a *New York Times, Washington Post*, Reuters, or Associated Press story in LexisNexis's database between 1977 and 2016.[3] This process yielded 20,635 citations over the period.[4] I aggregated citations annually.

Partisan Think Tanks and Polarization in Congress

Figure 6.1 shows the overall trend of polarization in Congress between 1973 and 2016.[5] Between 1933, when Franklin Delano Roosevelt assembled the New Deal coalition, and 1978, the average difference in party means for both chambers remained between 0.50 and 0.60. It began to increase slowly, but steadily, from 1978 through 1996. During this period, policymaking was still quite bipartisan. Democrats controlled the House of Representatives during the entire period, while the Senate and presidency were split between the two parties. Even though polarization was increasing, Congress passed major bipartisan reforms against entrenched interests in the trucking, airline, natural gas, and telephone industries (Jones, Theriault, and Whyman 2019). Under divided government, Congress passed some

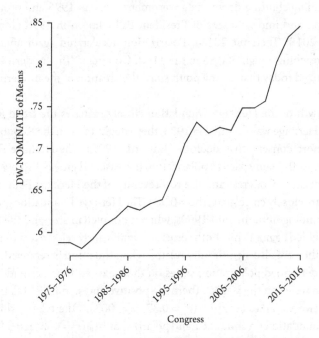

Figure 6.1 Polarization of Congress, 1973–2016. *DW-NOMINATE* difference of party means, average of both chambers, *VoteView.* Source: Lewis, Poole, and Rosenthal (2019).

of the most significant tax and budget legislation in American history, an issue area of historic partisan disagreement (Gerring 2001). These laws included the largest tax cut ever in 1981, a massive bipartisan tax reform in 1986 that reduced rates by closing loopholes and reducing inefficiencies (Birnbaum and Murray 1988), a major Social Security reform, and two significant deficit reduction deals that featured both spending cuts and tax increases (Mayhew 2005). On environmental policy, Congress passed the Superfund Act and Clean Air Act, as well as numerous laws to regulate and clean up toxic waste (Karol 2019; Mayhew 2005). Major environmental groups were strongly nonpartisan, endorsing a presidential candidate during the 1988 race only because of the strong Texas oil connections of George H. W. Bush (Karol 2019). Congress established the Department of Education and the federal job training system, sanctioned the apartheid government in South Africa over the president's veto, passed the Americans with Disabilities Act, and enacted two major immigration reforms (Mayhew 2005). While the parties disagreed on many issues, they were able to come together to solve problems effectively.

This period ended in 1995, when Republicans took control of both chambers of Congress following the 1994 midterm elections. Polarization sharply increased from 0.69 during the 103rd Congress to 0.73 during the 105th, plateauing for most of the late 1990s and 2000s. During this period, members of Congress increasingly broke established norms for conduct in Congress (Theriault 2013). Gingrich, the newly elected Speaker of the House, used aggressive tactics against the Democratic Party, including shutting down the government twice in 1995 and promoting the investigation and impeachment of President Bill Clinton in 1998 (Mason 2018; Rosenfeld 2018; Theriault 2013). Polarization accelerated again after the 2010 elections, reaching a high of 0.85 in the 114th Congress.[6] The modern Congress is more polarized today than at any point since the creation of the modern two-party system.

The growth of the Heritage Foundation closely matches the trend in polarization. After Heritage was founded in 1973, they sought to push the Republican Party toward a more conservative ideology (Edwards 1997). The Heritage Foundation grew at almost the same pace as polarization increased. Figure 6.2 shows the trends for polarization in Congress and the real revenue of the Heritage Foundation. The two series are closely correlated (rho = 0.98). The Heritage Foundation grew steadily from its founding until the mid-1990s, when it doubled in size, and the late 2000s, when it doubled again. While both series are significantly related to a trend variable (p<.001), they are also significantly related when the trend is removed. Figure 6.3 shows the detrended polarization series on the y-axis and the detrended Heritage Foundation series on the x-axis.[7] There is a positive and significant relationship between the two variables at time t ($r^2 = 0.37$, p = .003).[8] The relationship between Heritage Foundation revenue at t-1 and polarization at t ($r^2 = 0.29$, p = 0.012) is also significant, while the reverse is not ($r^2 = 0.13$, p = 0.139), suggesting that Heritage revenue increased before polarization, although relationship at time t is stronger.

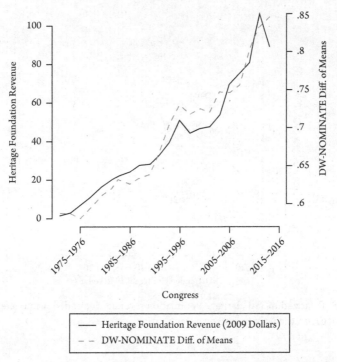

Figure 6.2 Polarization and Heritage Foundation revenue. *DW-NOMINATE* difference of party means, average of both chambers, *VoteView*. Source: Lewis, Poole, and Rosenthal (2019), author's archival estimates.

These results provide persuasive evidence of a nonspurious relationship between the two variables, and slightly less persuasive evidence that the relationship is lagged.

Next I turn to witnesses. Unlike the revenue series, these data encompass all four partisan think tanks in the sample. Figure 6.4 shows partisan witnesses per congressional hearing and the average difference of DW-NOMINATE party means. These data display a pattern similar to the revenue data, but with important differences. Like revenue, partisan think tank witnesses start out slow. During the early period, only the American Enterprise Institute and Heritage Foundation existed, as the two Democratic-aligned think tanks were not founded until 1981 and 2003. They slowly increase in influence through the early period of polarization, before making a big spike after Republicans take over Congress in 1996. During the 104th Congress, researchers at both Republican-aligned think tanks testified heavily to support the passage of policy promises contained in the Contract for America (Gayner 1995). Many of these promises were based on proposals authored at the think tanks, including severe cuts to congressional staff and legislative support organizations, the 1996 welfare reform law, cuts to the discretionary budget of the federal government, and a change in the structure of the federal tax code for dual filers to eliminate the "marriage penalty" (Gayner 1995; Stahl 2016). After these promises were

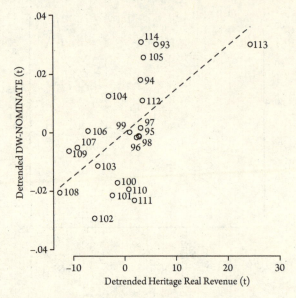

Figure 6.3 Polarization and Heritage Foundation revenue, detrended. Values are the residuals of each variable regressed on a trend variable.

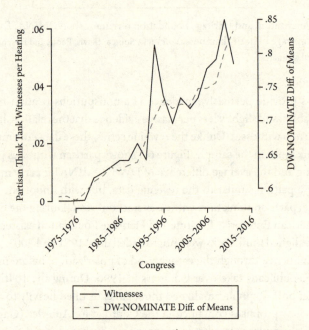

Figure 6.4 Polarization and partisan think tank witnesses. *DW-NOMINATE* difference of party means, average of both chambers, *VoteView*. Source: Lewis, Poole, and Rosenthal (2021), author estimates using ProQuest Congressional.

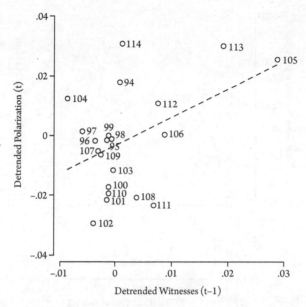

Figure 6.5 Polarization and partisan think tank witnesses, detrended. Values are the residuals of each variable regressed on a trend variable.

considered, the witness series reverts to the polarization trend in the following Congress. It begins increasing again in the late 2000s, in part due to a substantial increase in the rate of Democratic-aligned think tank witnesses. The series drops off considerably during the 114th Congress. This may be due to the 114th's status as a historically unproductive Congress in terms of legislation.

There is stronger evidence to conclude that the rate of partisan think tank testimony increased before polarization when compared with revenue. Figure 6.5 compares the detrended polarization series with detrended witness testimony. There is a positive and significant relationship between the rate of partisan think tank testimony at *t-1* and polarization at *t* ($r^2 = 0.21$, $p = 0.035$), but no relationship between the variables at time *t* ($r^2 = 0.01$, $p = 0.746$). This relationship is consistent with a process whereby partisan think tank witnesses cause polarization to increase rather than the reverse, but the relationship could also be mutually reinforcing. It also suggests that partisan think tanks engage in successful elite persuasion strategies, as hearings are largely attended by and directed to elites rather than the larger public.

Finally, I explore newspaper citations of partisan think tanks. Similarly, increased media citation of partisan think tanks may indicate that more conservative or liberal views are becoming mainstream and may thus be an indicator of their success rather than a cause of it. Figure 6.6 shows the number of citations of partisan think tanks in the *New York Times, Washington Post,* Associated Press, and Reuters from 1977 to 2016. While both are increasing over the time period and thus correlated ($p<.001$),

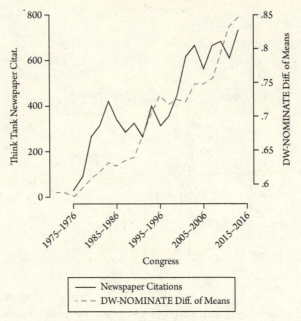

Figure 6.6 Partisan think tank newspaper citations and polarization. *DW-NOMINATE* difference of party means, average of both chambers, *VoteView.* Source: Lewis, Poole, and Rosenthal (2021), author estimates using Factiva.

there is little relationship at *t* once the series are detrended (p = 0.409), and no significant relationship at times *t-1* through *t-6*. There is a significant relationship between polarization at time *t* and newspaper citations at time *t-5* (p = 0.005), but overall, the relationship is more likely to be a product of similar trends than causal. These data suggest that the role of think tanks in activating latent preferences through media debates is less strongly linked to polarization than are the other strategies, although their media presence did increase considerably during the time series.

Partisan Think Tanks and Cuts to Congressional Capacity

In addition to a dramatic increase in the influence of partisan think tanks, another important and related event happened in the realm of information processing in Congress in 1996. Fulfilling a promise made in the Contract for America, Republicans in Congress severely cut the budgets of congressional committees and professional staff, thus curbing analytical bureaucracies (Baumgartner and Jones 2015; Glastris and Edwards 2014). These cuts had the effect of significantly

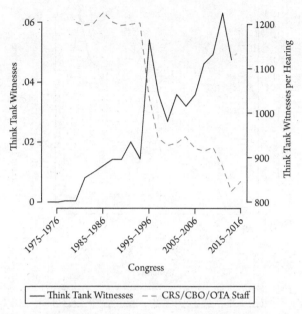

Figure 6.7 Partisan think tank witnesses per hearing and CBO, CRS, and OTA Staff, 1973–2016. Source: Author estimates using ProQuest Congressional, Brookings Vital Statistics on Congress (2019).

lowering internal congressional capacity to process information. Figure 6.7 shows the number of staff working at the Congressional Budget Office, Congressional Research Service, and Office of Technology Assessment. These agencies provide expert and unbiased policy analysis to Congress on a broad range of issues (Baumgartner and Jones 2015; Fagan and McGee 2020; Kosar 2016). For example, the CRS creates "reports, memoranda, customized briefings, seminars, videotaped presentations, information obtained from automated data bases, and consultations in person and by telephone" (Brudnick 2008, iv). Between 1997 and 2017, CRS published 13,536 reports on a broad range of domestic and foreign policy issues (Fagan and McGee 2020). Collectively, they lost about 25% of their staff in 1995, and another 12% due to the Budget Control Act of 2011.

The cuts to congressional staff were even more severe. Figure 6.8 shows the trends in committee staff and partisan think tanks per hearing during the same period. Members of Congress have two types of staff: personal staff and committee staff. Most personal staff focus primarily on constituency services and communication, while committee staff tend to be more focused on substantive policy concerns (Baumgartner and Jones 2015). Much of the specialized knowledge in Congress lies with professional committee staff, who develop long-term relationships with stakeholders, bureaucrats, and experts (Krehbiel 2006). Formal caucuses also lost nearly all their professional staff. These organizations provided considerable

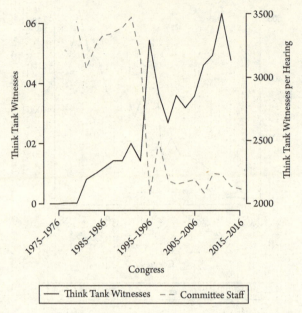

Figure 6.8 Partisan witnesses per hearing and committee staff, 1973–2016. Source: Author estimates using ProQuest Congressional, Brookings Vital Statistics on Congress (2019).

information to members of Congress, often addressing local concerns that cut across party lines (Ainsworth and Akins 1997; Ringe, Victor, and Gross 2013; Victor and Ringe 2009).

Congress lost about one-third of these staff to the 1995 cuts, forcing individual members to rely on other information sources. One of these was increased staff in party leadership offices, who sought to centralize control over policy and legislative information (Curry 2015; Lewallen, Theriault, and Jones 2016). Members of Congress were also forced to rely upon more external information sources, either in the executive branch (Mills and Selin 2017) or outside of government entirely (Baumgartner et al. 2009; Rich 2005). The result was a decline in Congress's ability to search for and define problems, identify solutions, and ultimately take action to pass laws (Glastris and Edwards 2014; Jones, Theriault, and Whyman 2019; Lewallen, Theriault, and Jones 2016).

Conservative Republicans saw the decline of congressional capacity as a feature, rather than a bug or mere side effect, of reducing costs. A legislature with a reduced ability to search for policy problems will pass less legislation to solve those problems, reducing the size of the government's policy agenda (Baumgartner and Jones 2015). While the Republican rhetoric in the Contract with America focused on overspending in Congress, earlier work made it clear that their goal was to reduce congressional capacity to process information. In an influential 1989 book, two Heritage Foundation authors argued that an "Imperial Congress" had stymied public mandates given to Republican presidents Nixon and Reagan to reduce the size and scope of government,[9] and it needed to be hobbled to maintain the separation of powers (Jones and Marini 1988). Gingrich, then the Republican minority whip, wrote the book's foreword. These ideas were eventually incorporated into a promise to cut staffing laid out in the Contract with America (Gayner 1995).

Thus, the reduction of congressional capacity represents an important confounding variable in our analysis. Congress may have sought out not more partisan information, but rather more information from outside of government to compensate for losses in staff. A reduction in capacity for rank-and-file members of Congress (as opposed to leadership) may increase polarization, as they become forced to rely on the judgment of party leaders (Curry 2015). We can test for this potential confounding variable by examining trends in testimony from external nonpartisan information sources. While the data structure does not allow us to search for all sources of nonpartisan information, we can collect data on individual organizations. I selected four organizations to measure demand for external nonpartisan policy analysis. The first three, Harvard, Stanford, and Yale, were leading research universities during the entire period. The fourth, the Brookings Institution, is the leading nonpartisan think tank in the United States (McGann 2019). Figure 6.9 compares frequency of testimony per congressional hearing of these organizations with testimony from the four partisan think tanks. During this same period, all three universities saw significant declines in testimony. As a group, they declined

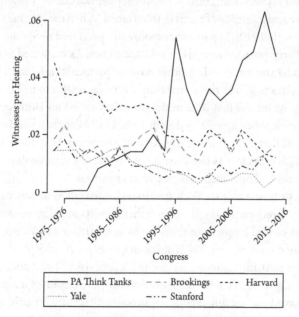

Figure 6.9 Partisan think tank witnesses per hearing and selected nonpartisan witnesses per hearing. Source: Author estimates using ProQuest Congressional.

from 0.07 witnesses per hearing to 0.03. Ultimately, all three universities declined by at least 50%. Brookings Institution testimony was stable, ranging between 0.01 and 0.02 witnesses per hearing. These data suggest that congressional demand for external nonpartisan information decreased during this period. Therefore, demand for external information in general is unlikely to be a confounding variable causing both demand for partisan think tank information and polarization. Indeed, if Congress consumes more partisan think tank information and less nonpartisan information, the impact of partisan think tank information should be greater than if nonpartisan information was stable as the balance of the overall information environment becomes even more partisan.

We can conclude from these results that conservative Republicans chose not only to cut congressional capacity to process information but to also replace it with partisan information. Indeed, the same process has played out in U.S. states. States with lower legislative professionalism are more likely to pass laws supported by the American Legislative Exchange Council, a conservative corporate-funding interest group; Americans for Prosperity, a conservative organization funded by the Koch brothers; and the State Policy Network, a group of state-based conservative think tanks (Hertel-Fernandez 2019).

Summary

There is a very close relationship between polarization in Congress and the increasing size and influence of partisan think tanks. When the Heritage Foundation arrived in the early 1970s, in part as a response to a perceived moderate streak in the Republican Party, polarization was near historic lows. As it entered politics and its advocacy model was emulated by other nascent partisan think tanks, polarization began to accelerate. When the Republican Party regained control of both chambers of Congress for the first time in decades, they called on Heritage and AEI to inform their new policy agenda. A decade later, CAP brought a similar dynamic to the Democratic Party. The statistical relationship between the growth of think tanks and polarization is as close as two time series can be. The relationship between partisan think tanks and polarization is clearly not spurious.

However, to turn a statistical cliché around, correlation in this case is far too close to imply direct causation. If we took these results literally, we would infer polarization was caused by partisan think tanks and partisan think tanks alone. This inference is, of course, wrong. Polarization in Congress is a complex phenomenon. Numerous political, institutional, and feedback processes caused polarization to increase, especially once initial factors kicked off the polarization of the parties. Other factors reinforced and solidified polarization once it increased. Partisan think tanks are likely an important part of a larger story of how elites in both parties, first the Republican Party and later the Democratic Party, began to diverge. Many of those factors likely increased the reach and resources of partisan think tanks at the same time that they impacted elites in other ways, such as the rise of well-organized and politically active billionaires like the Koch brothers, which began in the late 1970s (Hacker and Pierson 2010; Page, Seawright, and Lacombe 2019). To be sure, any inferences are made more tenuous by the nature of polarization in the United States since the 1970s. The line goes up and to the right. If polarization waxed and waned, we might be able to learn more about how partisan think tanks and other factors interact to increase it. If one day polarization decreases, we would expect less partisan think tank activity. However, we have only one modern history. In Chapter 7, we will instead look at the polarization of individual issues, finding a significant though noisier link between the two variables.

7

Partisan Think Tanks and Polarization across Issues

After Democrats regained unified control of the presidency and Congress in 2022, Joe Biden proposed an ambitious legislative agenda, a sweeping package of policy changes titled "Build Back Better" (White House 2021). Those changes could be divided into three broad categories: a large investment in infrastructure, a significant expansion of the American welfare state, and funding for renewable energy projects to address climate change. On infrastructure, Biden and Vice President Kamala Harris promised to repair bridges, build new rail and transit lines, replace aging lead pipes, and expand rural broadband access (Biden-Harris 2020). On social policy and climate policy, they promised to enact universal Pre-K, extend expanded child tax credit monthly payments, increase healthcare subsidies in Medicaid, Medicare, and the Affordable Care Act exchanges, and invest hundreds of billions in renewable energy projects and subsidies, paid for mostly by raising taxes on the richest Americans and corporations.

However, the three sides of Build Back Better saw very different receptions in Congress. The infrastructure package attracted broad bipartisan support. Groups of moderate Republicans and Democrats met for repeated meetings at the White House and hashed out a $1.2 trillion deal. The Infrastructure Investment and Jobs Act passed the Senate 69 to 30, and eventually passed the House on a narrower but bipartisan vote. Biden had originally proposed a much larger infrastructure plan but was willing to settle for a smaller but still historic investment in American infrastructure. The social and climate policy side, however, never gained any support from the Republican Party. Republicans want to contract the social welfare state, not expand it, and strongly opposed raising corporate taxes to pay for social or environmental programs. Both parties preferred the status quo to the other party's positions on these issues. There was never any path for achieving a bipartisan social and climate policy bill.

The Thinkers. E. J. Fagan, Oxford University Press. © Oxford University Press 2024.
DOI: 10.1093/oso/9780197759653.003.0007

This contrast between issues that still see significant bipartisan cooperation and issues where the parties have polarized is on constant display. Yet even as the system has become more polarized, Congress routinely passes laws, including significant laws, with bipartisan support (Mayhew 2005). However, as polarization has increased, the space for bipartisanship has decreased. Fewer issues attract the kind of bipartisan support built for the infrastructure bill, while more receive intense partisan opposition. Many of the core issues in Build Back Better—such as healthcare, environmental policy, and federal aid to support children—have long historical records of bipartisan cooperation. Today there is little space for bipartisan cooperation on any issue.

Partisan think tanks have played an important role in creating this change. As they shift their party's positions on issues, they decrease the potential for bipartisan cooperation. They can short-circuit the consensus-driven problem-solving processes that used to bring lawmakers together. We often think about polarization as a broad process pushing the parties toward the extremes, but reality is more complicated. Throughout the history of partisan think tanks, each individual issue has been its own battle. And battle by battle, partisan think tanks have helped political entrepreneurs convince their allies of steadily more extreme policy preferences.

Polarization of Issues

Political scientists tend to treat polarization the same way economists think about inflation, as a general increase in the level of conflict between the parties. But as a top-line inflation estimate masking interesting variation in prices between industries, overall levels of polarization similarly mask interesting variation among issues. Unfortunately, the literature on issue polarization is thin. Issues related to the redistribution of wealth and conflict between labor and capital were highly polarized even before the increase in polarization started in the 1970s, while others became more polarized in the 1980s and 1990s (Jochim and Jones 2013). These "new" issues mostly became part of the national policy debate during the Great Broadening period of the 1950s–1970s, when the federal government entered scores of new policy areas that had previously been left to states or the market (Jones, Theriault, and Whyman 2019). Issues become more polarized when the president takes a position on a vote, thus raising its profile (Lee 2009). At the state and local level, issues related to socioeconomic problems like healthcare polarized in the 2000s, but not in criminal justice policy and some other areas (Grumbach 2018). It took a few decades for political parties to crystallize their positions on these issues.

We saw these dynamics play out in environmental policy (Karol 2019). In the 1970s, environmental policy was a bipartisan issue. Environmental groups endorsed candidates from both parties or declined to endorse any candidates at all (Karol 2019). The Nixon and Ford administrations oversaw the creation of the Environmental Protection Agency, and bipartisan environmental legislation continued to pass Congress into the early 1990s. Republican support for the environment extended back to the 19th century, when Republican Teddy Roosevelt established the National Parks System and supported a growing conservation movement. At the same time, the Democratic Party was cross-pressured on environmental issues by the policy priorities of labor unions, which often opposed regulations that would impede building and manufacturing. This dynamic is common in many other democracies where environmental policy does not fall cleanly on the liberal-conservative economic policy spectrum (Abou-Chadi 2016). However, the Republican Party moved sharply to the right during the mid-1990s, forcing environmental groups to align with the Democratic Party (Karol 2019). Republicans opposed many different types of environment regulations, culminating in their fierce opposition to laws and policies that address climate change. Democrats became much more united on the issue, which is today one of the most polarizing in Congress (Jochim and Jones 2013).

A similar yet distinct process played out around the issue of women's rights. During the 1960s and early 1970s, there was little partisan conflict on women's rights issues (Wolbrecht 2000). Republicans and Democrats both supported granting women equal protection under the law, universal suffrage, and the Equal Rights Amendment. However, the parties swiftly realigned on women's rights when the debate shifted toward issues like equal pay, women's inclusion in the draft, abortion, and broader gender roles in society (Wolbrecht 2000). The shift was elite-driven; Republican Party elites moved to the right on women's rights issues long before conservative voters did (Wolbrecht 2002). In her study of delegates to the party conventions in the 1970s and 1980s, Wolbrecht finds that Democratic and Republican delegates began to express more liberal and conservative attitudes on women's rights around 1980, driven both by the introduction of abortion as a salient national issue and by the more ideological attitudes of new delegates replacing older, less ideological delegates.

One pattern common to both issue polarization and polarization in general is that elites have polarized before their voters have. The shifts on both women's rights and environmental policy came out of each party's elites and the incorporation of previously unaligned groups into the party's coalition. Voters came along much later, expressing consistent liberal and conservative attitudes across a range of issues only in the late 2000s or 2010s (Dimock et al. 2014).

Issue Polarization and Partisan Think Tanks

Partisan think tanks want their allies to take more conservative or progressive positions on any given issue. If they are successful, we should find a strong relationship between their activities and polarization of issues. As they become more prevalent in an issue area, that issue will become more polarized.

However, we might not expect a short-term relationship between issue attention from partisan think tanks and polarization in Congress. Issues are more complicated than that. There is considerable variation in partisan disagreement over individual policies on the policy agenda on similar issues. For example, the parties may disagree intensely on healthcare plans to help poor people access health insurance, but largely agree on a plan to provide generous federal funding to develop new cancer treatments. On both issues, partisan think tanks might weigh in and try to persuade their allies to adopt more extreme positions when the issue hits the agenda. However, the specifics of the issue will impact how polarized lawmaking is in the short term. Furthermore, many partisan think tank activities take time to move their preferences. Progressive think tanks may want to persuade Democrats that a more expansive public healthcare regime is the best way to provide insurance to Americans, but those arguments likely take place over many years. Thus we should expect polarization to be higher when partisan think tanks prioritize an issue area over the long term, but not in the short term.

I measure four different types of outputs by partisan think tanks. All outputs are assigned to a PAP major topic area. The first two outputs measure the production of information by partisan think tanks. First, I use the same white papers used in the previous chapter. Second, I use bills named by partisan think tanks on lobbying disclosure reports if they have a $501(c)(4)$ companion organization. Taken together, these white papers and lobbying disclosure reports account for issues that think tanks produce and attempt to disseminate to policymakers. Next, I use two data sets to measure the consumption of information by members of Congress. I use citations by name of partisan think tanks referenced by members of Congress in the *Congressional Record*. Here, members use partisan think tank reports to make public policy arguments, indicating both that they have consumed the information and that they choose to drop the think tank's name when referencing the information. Finally, I use the policy content of hearings which received partisan think tank testimony. As with citations, when we observe a partisan think tank researcher called to testify before a hearing, we both understand that at least some members of the committee are seeking to consult with the think tank for policy advice and that they would prefer to be publicly associated with the think tank. All data collected are from 2004–17. A full explanation of how these data were collected and coded is available in the Methodological Appendix.

I measure polarization using a voice-vote adjusted party disagreement score by policy topic. These data capture the average amount of party disagreement on an issue area; 0 indicates that both parties voted for a bill in equal quantities, and 1 indicates a perfectly party-line vote. Bills that pass via voice vote, unanimous consent, or other consensual mechanism are hereafter referred to as "voice votes."

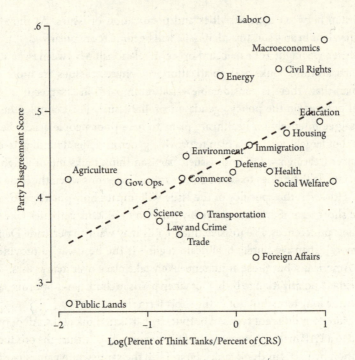

Figure 7.1 Relative white paper policy attention and polarization.

We begin by examining the production of information by partisan think tanks and its relationship with polarization. Issues that receive more attention in partisan think tank white papers are significantly more polarized (p = 0.002, β = 0.06, r^2 = 0.44). The x-axis in Figure 7.1 compares the ratio of partisan think tank reports to CRS reports, while the y-axis shows the average partisan disagreement score. This relationship shows several patterns that are common among many of the upcoming comparisons. A cluster of issues that receive the most attention from partisan think tanks relative to CRS—energy, civil rights, labor, and macroeconomics—are much more polarized than predicted and have, in fact, sharply divided the political parties for most of American history. Labor and macroeconomics contain issues of taxes, budgets, unionization, and other core debates that have defined the liberal-conservative spectrum since the 19th century (Gerring 2001). The umbrella of civil rights is filled with highly contentious issues, ranging from women's rights to racial equality, LGBTQ+ rights, voting rights, and abortion. While these issues receive considerable attention from partisan think tanks, other factors also likely contribute to polarization when they receive roll call votes. Other issues are less polarized than expected. Notably, foreign affairs and trade policy receive considerable attention, but are the second and third least polarized issues. The old saying that "politics stops at the water's edge" appears to still hold some weight, even though partisan think tanks are heavily interested in issues beyond America's borders.

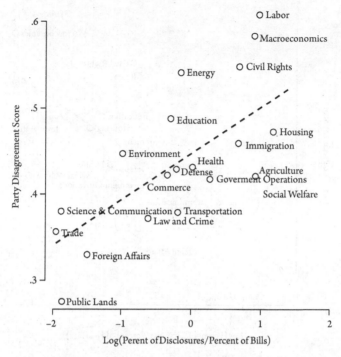

Figure 7.2 Lobbying disclosure reports and polarization.

Next we compare the policy content of bills named in partisan think tank lobbying disclosure reports with measures of polarization (Figure 7.2). Lobbying is a higher-cost activity than releasing a report. Partisan think tanks must devote time and resources to pushing the issue to members of Congress rather than just posting a new report on their website. We should expect this activity to have a stronger impact on polarization. Indeed, there is a stronger relationship between issues emphasized in lobbying disclosure reports and polarization (p = 0.001, β = 0.04). Model fit is also strong, suggesting a closer relationship between bills that think tanks prioritize in their lobbying and polarization in Congress (r^2 = 0.44). These data suggest that a partisan think tank's most important legislative priorities tend to be more polarized.

In Figure 7.3 we turn to measuring consumption of information by members of Congress. Instead of partisan think tanks producing information, these outputs are dependent on members of Congress choosing to both use and highlight the information. However, we see a relationship between partisan think tanks and polarization very similar to the previous two models. Members of Congress are significantly more likely to cite partisan think tanks on the floor of Congress on more polarized issues (p = 0.001, β = 0.04). While the overall amount of error is like the previous two models (r^2 = 0.45), the error is more balanced among the policy areas.

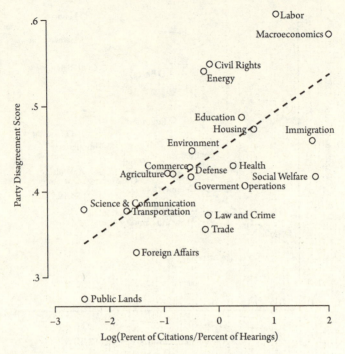

Figure 7.3 Congressional Record citations and polarization across issues.

We turn in Figure 7.4 to partisan think tank testimony before congressional hearings. Inviting a partisan think tank researcher to testify is a higher-cost activity than citing them in the *Congressional Record*. There are a limited number of hearings and witness slots in each hearing, especially for the minority party. Members likely consult with allied witnesses before the hearing. They then choose to use the public forum to highlight the think tank's argument on an issue. As with the previous outputs, there is a positive and significant relationship between partisan think tank testimony and polarization ($p = 0.026$, $\beta = 0.04$), but there is considerably more error than in the other three models ($r^2 = 0.26$). Error in both directions increases as relative partisan think tank testimony increases. Given that there are just 774 witnesses during the observation period, the error could be due to sample size issues. There could also be strong selection effects, where partisan think tank witnesses are called before some types of hearings but not others.

Each of the four operationalizations of relative think tank attention derive from independent measurements of partisan think tank activities. If the distribution of attention to issues is also sufficiently independent, we can average the four independent variables together to produce one measure of partisan think tank policy attention across outputs.[1] The most closely related outputs are the relative attention to issues in *Congressional Record* citations and hearing witnesses, which is expected given that they share a denominator ($\rho = 0.81$). The least closely related data sets

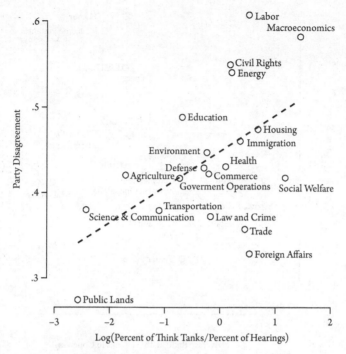

Figure 7.4 Witness testimony and polarization.

are white papers and bills ($\rho = 0.48$). Figure 7.5 shows the relationship between this averaged variable and polarization. Model fit improves slightly over the other models ($r^2 = 0.50$), while the result remains positive and significant ($p = 0.001$, $\beta = 0.06$). We can conclude confidently that issues that are more polarized receive more attention from partisan think tanks relative to Congress. The similarity between these three models is remarkable as each independent variable is measured independently of the other three. While the three data sets are correlated ($\rho = 0.65$; see Table A.1), they are not strongly multicollinear. Each output emphasizes different issues, but all three share a similar relationship with polarization.

While the result is robust across bivariate models, we must also rule out potential confounding omitted variables that are endogenous to both polarization and partisan think tank attention. Partisan think tanks tend to prioritize issues that are owned by their party (Fagan 2021). Issue ownership describes the relationship between the core priorities of a political party and the electorate's trust in the party to handle the issue (Egan 2013). As parties in government prioritize an issue over the long term, the electorate trusts the party to handle that issue in office. If the parties prioritize some issues over others, those issues might polarize. If so, issue ownership presents a potential confounding variable in these models.

Fagan (2021) uses two different specifications of issue ownership across PAP major topics.[2] The first, long-run issue ownership, is a continuous variable derived

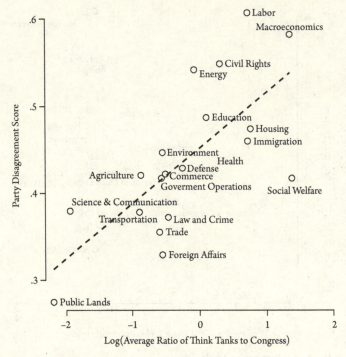

Figure 7.5 Average of partisan think tank outputs and polarization.

from survey data gathered by Egan (2013). A negative score indicates Democratic ownership, while a positive score indicates Republican ownership. The second, a binary measure, assigns each major topic to either Republican, Democrat, or neither. Each has its flaws, as the issue ownership data do not cleanly map onto the PAP major topic areas. The continuous measure has no data on domestic commerce or housing policy and fails to capture both parties' prioritization of different types of macroeconomic policy. The binary measure accurately measures these three issues but fails to capture the degree to which the parties own issues. Because of these limitations, I run models using both measures. Table 7.1 shows the results of a multivariate OLS regression of polarization of issues. We see no evidence that issue ownership is a confounding variable. In Model 1, which contains the continuous issue ownership operationalization, there is no relationship between polarization and issue ownership ($p = 0.788$). In Model 2, which contains the binary ownership variables, there is a negative relationship between issue ownership and polarization. Core party priorities do not drive polarization across issues, and thus are not an endogenous omitted variable.

Next, I test whether issue salience is a potential endogenous omitted variable. Partisan think tanks may produce more information on highly salient issues, either in anticipation of those issues hitting the agenda or because partisan conflict on

Polarization across Issues 95

Table 7.1 **OLS Estimation of Polarization across Issues, Testing for Issue Ownership and Salience as Confounding Variables**

Independent Variables	Model 1	Model 2	Model 3	Model 4
Logged Average Think Tank Attention	0.07**	0.06**	0.06**	0.06**
	(0.02)	(0.02)	(0.02)	(0.02)
Issue Ownership				
Republican Owned	−0.05			
	(0.03)			
Democrat Owned	−0.03			
	(0.04)			
Long-Run Issue Ownership (Squared)		−0.0001		
		(0.001)		
Issue Salience				
Most Important Problem (MIP)			0.06	−0.14
			(0.20)	(0.36)
MIP * Think Tank Attention				0.18
				(0.26)
r^2	0.60	0.50	0.50	0.51
n	19	17	20	20

Note: Standard errors in parenthesis. * p<.05 ** p<.01 *** p<.001. Civil rights policy excluded from both models. Commerce and Housing excluded from Model 2 due to missing issue ownership data.

issues increases issue salience. If these issues are also more polarized, salience would confound estimates of the relationship between partisan think tanks and polarization. Table 7.1 also displays OLS estimates of polarization across issues. There is no evidence that issue salience drives polarization across issues, either on its own (Model 3, p = 0.776) or when interacted with partisan think tank attention (Model 4, p = 0.512). We can rule out issue salience as a potential source of endogeneity.

Panel Models

We can examine the short-term relationship between polarization and partisan think tank attention using time-series cross-sectional methods, where each major topic area represents one panel with multiple observations across congresses. Agenda-setting scholars frequently use error correction or autoregressive distributed lag models to test whether an input can "set the agenda" for an output

(Bevan and Jennings 2014; Bevan and Rasmussen 2017; Fagan 2018; Froio, Bevan, and Jennings 2017; Green-Pedersen and Mortensen 2010; Lovett, Bevan, and Baumgartner 2015; Mortensen et al. 2011), such as whether an executive speech or party platform can push the legislative agenda toward some issues and away from others. Other political scientists use error correction or autoregressive distributed lag models to examine the short-term impact of an independent variable on a dependent variable, such as the impact of changes in public preferences for spending on appropriations (Jennings 2009; Soroka and Wlezien 2010, 2019; Wlezien 1995). In this section, I use similar methods to measure the impact of partisan think tanks on polarization.

Panel methods have several strengths and weaknesses. Most important, they allow models to control for unobserved heterogeneity across panels. They also allow us to separate short-term effects from long-term effects. However, panel models have several important weaknesses when estimating the relationship between polarization and partisan think tank activities. While party disagreement scores require fewer observations than DW-NOMINATE scores to reliable estimate, estimates for many policy topics with fewer votes are much less reliable. While low reliability will not bias estimated beta coefficients, it will increase standard errors. On the independent variable side of the equation, it limits the available data to partisan think tank white papers, as the other three data sets lack enough observations biannually to reliably estimate attention to policy across 20 major topics. Finally, we are limited to just seven Congresses, or six observations per panel with lags. With so few time periods, these models lack the statistical power to perform Granger noncausality tests (Dumitrescu and Hurlin 2012).

I use error correction models to estimate the relationship between polarization and relative attention to policy in partisan tank think white papers.[3] Because polarization in Congress trends upward during the period, but partisan think tank attention always sums to 1 across the 20 issues, I include a trend variable in the equation. I also control for the unobserved heterogeneity in panels,[4] using both fixed effects and panel-corrected standard errors (Beck and Katz 1995). Because both the dependent variable and independent variables are $AR(1)$, I also include an $AR(1)$ disturbance term. Equation 7.1 shows the basic model (Model 2 in Table 7.2).

Equation 7.1: Error Correction Model of Polarization across Issues and Time

$$\Delta Polarization_{it} = Polarizationit-1 + \Delta Think\ Tanksit + Think\ Tanksit-1 + Trendt+e$$

There is a strong long-term relationship between partisan think tank reports and polarization, but only a weak short-term relationship (Table 7.2). In a given Congress, polarization increases when there is an increase in partisan think tank reports in an issue area, but the relationship is barely statistically significant in a one-tailed test ($p<0.1$). However, there is a strong and significant association between these

Table 7.2 **Time-Series Cross-Sectional Estimates of Δ Party Disagreement (t)**

Independent Variable	Model 1	Model 2
Party Disagreement $_{it-1}$	−0.65***	−0.82***
	(0.18)	(0.18)
Δ Relative Think Tank Attention $_{it}$	0.01	0.02+
	(0.01)	(0.01)
Relative Think Tank Attention $_{it-1}$	0.03**	0.04***
	(0.01)	(0.01)
Trend $_t$	No	Yes***
r^2	0.29	0.38
n	120	120

Note: Standard errors in parenthesis. + p<.1 * p<.05 ** p<.01 *** p<.001. All panels contain panel-corrected standard errors and first-order panel autocorrelation to correct for heteroscedasticity.

variables in the long run (p<0.001), even when accounting for the trend of increased polarization (Model 2). These results strongly suggest that partisan think tanks increase polarization by playing a long game: slowly planting seeds of progressive and conservative policy positions over time and slowly cultivating them through close interaction with lawmakers before finally seeing their efforts bear fruit.

Summary

When legislators search for policy analysis on a given issue, the information they find can vary considerably by issue. On some issues, their searches will return a variety of nonpartisan information from sources like the federal bureaucracy, CRS, and other credible experts. On other issues, the nonpartisan sources will face intense competition from partisan information producers such as partisan think tanks. These differences in the balance of the information environment have substantive implications for legislative behavior on issues. When the information environment is largely nonpartisan, issues tend to have lower levels of polarization. When partisans compete for the information environment, polarization increases dramatically.

These differences hugely impact our understanding of the policy process. On the issues where nonpartisan information is still dominant, our understanding of agenda setting centered around problem-solving persists. These issues tend to be more localized, such as transportation, agriculture, public lands, science, and communication. On these issues, the government's agenda will be set by emerging problems and an impetus to offer effective solutions to those problems. The parties will find it easier to come to a consensus around problem-solving. If they disagree over who will bear the trade-offs of those policies, the parties can bargain over the policy response. On the other hand, areas of traditional ideological conflict over domestic redistributive economic policy attract the most attention from partisan think tanks. These issue areas include social welfare, labor, macroeconomics, and housing policy. When one of these issues is on the congressional agenda, the partisan disagreement is unlikely to be limited to a simple ideological dispute over the proper role of government. Rather, legislators of opposite parties are likely to believe that enacting certain policy outputs will lead to vastly different outcomes. They will struggle to come to a bipartisan consensus on these issues, because even as they may agree that the problem requires a policy solution, they disagree about whether the solution will solve the problem or its secondary consequences. These disagreements will break down the problem-solving process, driving agenda setting. Problems will continue to become more severe until one party is able to act narrowly on its own to enact some sort of policy solution or until things become bad enough to force a consensus.

8

Polarized Policy Analysis

After losing the 2012 presidential election, the Republican National Committee wrote a report diagnosing the party's loss in the election and examining its long-term electoral prospects. The report concluded that the Republican Party needed to embrace immigration reform to be successful in the long term:

> If Hispanic Americans perceive that a GOP nominee or candidate does not want them in the United States (i.e. self-deportation), they will not pay attention to our next sentence. It does not matter what we say about education, jobs or the economy; if Hispanics think we do not want them here, they will close their ears to our policies. In the last election, Governor Romney received just 27 percent of the Hispanic vote. Other minority communities, including Asian and Pacific Islander Americans, also view the Party as unwelcoming. President Bush got 44 percent of the Asian vote in 2004; our presidential nominee received only 26 percent in 2012....
>
> We are not a policy committee, but among the steps Republicans take in the Hispanic community and beyond, we must embrace and champion comprehensive immigration reform. (RNC 2013, 8)

The Border Security, Economic Opportunity and Immigration Modernization Act of 2013 was an attempt to enact the policy changes recommended by the RNC report. The immigration bill was structured as a compromise between the pro- and anti-immigration sides of the debate. For pro-immigration proponents, it would have allowed most undocumented immigrants in the United States who came to the country before 2012 to pay a $500 penalty and become permanent residents and eventually citizens. It also provided an easier path to citizenship for undocumented immigrants who were brought to the United States as children. For the anti-immigration side, it would have provided large increases in funding for border security, with the goal of intercepting 90% of crossings on the Southern border. It would have also implemented a national E-Verify system to prevent undocumented

The Thinkers. E. J. Fagan, Oxford University Press. © Oxford University Press 2024.
DOI: 10.1093/oso/9780197759653.003.0008

immigrants from legally working. Many of the policy changes affecting undocumented immigrants would not go into place until after the Southern border targets were met. Finally, the bill also made several important changes to the legal immigration system with support from both sides, including replacing country-based quotas with a Canadian-style merit system and increasing employment-based visas for high-skilled immigrants.

The immigration bill was bipartisan. It was introduced to the Senate by a "Gang of Eight," including prominent Republicans John McCain, Lindsey Graham, Marco Rubio, and Jeff Flake, in April 2013. It was supported by several key interest groups, most notably the conservative U.S. Chamber of Commerce and liberal labor unions. It quickly moved through the Judiciary Committee and passed the full Senate on a 68–32 vote in late June. All Democrats and 14 Republicans voted in favor of it. However, the bill received intense opposition from ideological conservatives. Rush Limbaugh, an influential conservative talk radio host, argued against it relentlessly on grounds that it would hurt Republicans at the ballot box:

> But regardless, whenever they get the vote, if it's 10 years, if it's two hours, if it's five years, if there are 11, 12 million people here currently unable to vote, and they are Hispanic, and if they fit the profile that polling data gives us, a full 70% of them are gonna vote Democrats. So the numbers work out this way. If you got 11 or 12 million people here that can't vote right now, not legally, but someday will be able to, and 70% of those people are gonna vote Democrat, how in the world does the Republican Party stay—I hate using this word 'cause it's used incorrectly, but viable, how does the Republican Party stay viable, when they get 30% of whatever that number of millions of new people is? (*The Rush Limbaugh Show* 2013b)

Two related policy analysis debates emerged from contentious parts of the bill. First, analysts asked what impact legitimizing tens of millions of undocumented immigrants and eventually granting them citizenship would have on economic growth. Relatedly, analysts also asked what impact the bill would have on the deficit. The impacts of changes to legal immigration and increased enforcement were not the subject of partisan debate.

The Congressional Budget Office produced two reports on the bill. The first examined its cost (Congressional Budget Office and Joint Committee on Taxation 2013), estimating that the overall bill would decrease the federal deficit by $197 billion over 10 years, while the second examined its economic impact (Congressional Budget Office 2013). On the revenue side, CBO anticipated that the bill would increase federal revenue by $459 billion, about $451 billion of which would come from increased income and payroll tax revenue from newly legitimized residents and increased legal immigration. The bill would increase the population of prime-age taxpayers by allowing more immigrants into the country, all of whom would be employed and many of whom would be highly skilled and earning high wages. On the other hand, it would increase spending by $262 billion.[1] Of the new spending, $238 billion would come in the form of refundable earned income tax credits, child tax credits, and federal healthcare spending. The first report noted that most new adult immigrants would not be eligible for most federal means-tested benefits. While CBO did not break down spending estimates between the two groups, it acknowledged that most of the costs would likely be concentrated in the lower-skilled, poorer group of formerly undocumented immigrants.

In the second report, on the impact of the bill on economic growth, CBO estimated that real GDP in 2023 would be 3.3% higher if the bill was passed than if it was not passed.[2] While it did not break down the impact of the expansion of legal immigration and legitimization of undocumented immigrants, the report specified that the majority of increased economic growth would come from increasing the size of the U.S. population through increased legal immigration and increases to total factor productivity caused by a more skilled workforce. The legitimization of undocumented immigrants would have a smaller effect through increased productivity given that those workers were already in the labor force.

Both major Democratic-aligned think tanks produced reports on the impact of immigration reforms on the economy and deficit. The Center for American Progress produced a primary analysis of the impact of the legalization portion of the immigration bill, while the Center on Budget and Policy Priorities produced only a secondary analysis. The CAP report, which was co-authored by a CAP research associate and an economist at Washington College, produced three different scenarios of the impact on revenue and economic growth of legalizing 11 million undocumented immigrants. This analysis varied the time when citizenship was granted in each scenario (Lynch and Oakford 2013). Based on research on the 1980s amnesty, the report concluded that granting undocumented immigrants citizenship increases their economic productivity. Under its most optimistic scenario, where undocumented immigrants are granted citizenship shortly after being granted legal status, the authors projected GDP in 2023 to be 3.20% larger than under the counterfactual of current law. They did not include in their estimates the changes to legal immigration proposed by the bill. CBPP published one detailed secondary analysis, authored by two CBPP researchers, on the impact of the immigration bill on the economy and deficit. The report was a detailed summary and explanation of the CBO cost estimate and made little effort to reframe the issue (Stone and Parrot 2013).

Heritage strongly opposed the immigration bill. The think tank had worked to defeat the Bush administration's previous attempt at a compromise immigration reform bill during the 110th Congress (2007–8), publishing over 60 reports opposing it.[3] Written by longtime Heritage Foundation researcher Robert Rector and Jason Richwine, a newer Heritage staffer who earned his Ph.D. from Harvard in 2009 and briefly worked at the American Enterprise Institute, the Heritage report was controversial. It estimated the cost of legitimizing 11 million undocumented immigrants over 50 years to be $7.3 trillion. If legitimized, Rector and Richwine estimated, these immigrants would receive federal, state, and local services and transfers totaling $9.4 trillion, while paying $3.1 trillion in taxes. Under current law, their net cost during the same time period would be just $1 trillion. Services included everything from means-tested benefits to the use of roads, public schools, and the criminal justice system.[4] Beyond Heritage, AEI scholars did produce commentary supporting the bill, but the think tank did not publish any policy analysis to predict its impacts.[5]

There was a quick and decisive backlash to the Heritage report. Two days after it was released, *Washington Post* blogger Dylan Matthews (2013a) pointed out significant methodological errors made by Rector and Richwine, including (1) assuming no macroeconomic feedback effect from legalizing 11 million undocumented immigrants despite considerable evidence that previous amnesties had increased productivity and human capital; (2) assuming that all current undocumented immigrants would return to their home countries when they hit retirement age; and (3) selectively counting tax expenditures and spending. Two days later, Matthews (2013b) published a second blog post on Richwine's 2009 dissertation, "IQ and Immigration Policy," and its argument against Latino immigration based in a belief that Latinos are genetically inferior to whites: "Richwine's dissertation asserts that there are deep-set differentials in intelligence between races. While it's clear he thinks it is partly due to genetics—'the totality of the evidence suggests a genetic component to group differences in IQ'—he argues the most important thing is that the differences in group IQs are persistent, for whatever reason. He writes, 'No one knows whether Hispanics will ever reach IQ parity with whites, but the prediction that new Hispanic immigrants will have low-IQ children and grandchildren is difficult to argue against.'" Following an intense media backlash, the Heritage Foundation noted that it had not published the dissertation (Palmer and Vogel 2013). Richwine resigned from Heritage two days later (Blake 2013).

Biased Policy Analysis

Chapter 2 discussed how information about public policy—policy analysis—might change the preferences of a policymaker looking to solve some policy problem, or even just looking to impact some policy output in the world. Policymaking is instrumental to affecting some policy output in an intended way, such as increasing wages, decreasing infant mortality, avoiding a financial crisis, or controlling crime. Policymakers may care about these goals in and of themselves, or because they expect constituents to care about them in the next election, or from some other motivation. The instrumental nature of policy depends on the policymaker's belief about its cause-and-effect relationship with the outcome. That belief is ultimately derived from policy analysis, either specific studies or evaluations of a policy or long-term ideas about how classes of policy interventions in general influence outcomes.

If a policy analyst wants to convince a policymaker to change their preferences for policy outputs by persuading them that the output has some different relationship to outcomes than they currently believe, the analysis must itself reach a different conclusion than the policymaker's beliefs. For example, a policymaker might prefer that her constituents drink clean water, both because she expects to pay an electoral cost if her constituents' water quality decreases and because she values clean water as an important goal for public policy. Normally, she is advised by scientists and government agencies that a nearby mining project she might otherwise support will significantly increase the chances of a pollutant affecting her district's water supply; she thus opposes the policy choice. However, if a rival information source, perhaps one that supports the new project, can convince her that the scientists are incorrect and the mine poses only a mild risk to the water supply, she might change her preferences and support the policy change.

If partisan think tanks want to pursue this strategy, they must produce biased policy analysis. I define biased policy analysis as *policy analysis that materially differs from the scientific or nonpartisan consensus in the policy author's preferred direction*. In the above example, the policy analysis published by the mine's supporters is biased because it materially disagrees with the nonpartisan consensus in ways that substantiate the mine supporter's preferred direction. While it is unlikely that the author would publish such information, the policy analysis would not be biased if it erred in the opposite direction, for example, with conclusions that suggested the mine would be more harmful to public health than suggested by the consensus of nonpartisan experts. Partisan think tanks, with their ideological missions and patrons, have a clear preference for policy to the left or right of center. Thus, if a Democratic-aligned think tank published a piece of research with estimates supporting a more progressive conclusion than nonpartisan experts have reached, that information would be biased. However, if they published a piece of research that accepted the conclusions of nonpartisans but emphasized the aspects of the issue which appealed to progressive values, it would not be considered biased by this definition.

Several studies have found that partisan think tanks tend to produce biased information. Most of these studies examine information about climate change. Carbon taxes and emissions trading policies were first developed as a market-based alternative to command-and-control policy designs. Meant to address the issue of acid rain, these solutions were designed by bureaucrats in the Environmental Protection Agency under the George H. W. Bush administration (Voß 2007). However, wealthy ideological conservatives such as the Koch brothers, who also happen to own a major oil and gas company, opposed any emissions trading program that targeted greenhouse gases. These elites funded think tanks who published research opposing such programs (Brulle 2014). As a result, Republican-aligned think tanks became the primary source of information questioning climate science. Since the 1970s, over 90% of books promoting skepticism about climate change were published by conservative authors based at conservative think tanks (Dunlap and Jacques 2013; Jacques, Dunlap, and Freeman 2008). Nearly all conservative think tanks either produced numerous white papers, op-eds, and other material supporting climate change skepticism in various forms, or declined to publish research on climate change entirely (Boussalis and Coan 2016). They successfully exploited strong journalistic norms toward balance in political debates by casting disagreements over the facts of climate change as political rather than scientific issues (Bolsen and Shapiro 2018; Boykoff and Boykoff 2004; McCright 2016; McCright and Dunlap 2003). They also spread their biased information throughout the extended party network (Albert 2019). Heterodox scientific researchers would likely have been less successful at promoting climate change skepticism than conservative think tanks, as they had no access to adversarial norms and would have been expressing opinions outside of their field's consensus. Because the literature is so well developed, I explore partisan think tank activities on climate change in depth in Chapter 9.

Although there is less research in other areas, Republican-aligned think tanks have successfully introduced biased information into several policy topics. On tax and budget policy, Republican-aligned think tanks have argued extensively that tax cuts reduce long-run deficits, both by growing the economy and through a "starve the beast" mechanism whereby governments cut spending in response to high deficits, despite a strong consensus from economists to the contrary on both premises (Jones and Williams 2008; Prasad 2018). More generally, Republican-aligned think tanks have elevated heterodox macroeconomic research such as the works of Austrian School economist Friedrich Hayek, a prominent critic of Keynesian economics and supporter of libertarian economic policies (Backhouse 2005). Using Austrian arguments about fiscal and monetary policy during recessions, Republican-aligned think tanks argued that any increased government spending during the 2008–9 financial crisis would have no impact on GDP (Watkins and Tyrrell 2009), despite strong predictions from most economists that increased government spending could make up for decreased aggregate demand (for example, see International Monetary Fund 2012).

On welfare policy, Republican-aligned think tanks subsidized studies finding that racial differences in economic inequality was caused by hereditary differences in intelligence rather than public policy, discrimination, or other environmental factors (Medvetz 2014). The most notable of these were authored by Charles Murray, a prominent conservative political scientist who wrote *Losing Ground* and *The Bell Curve* while working at the Manhattan Institute and AEI. *Losing Ground* argued that social welfare programs ultimately hurt the poor. *The Bell Curve* claimed that racial differences in income and education achievement were caused by hereditary differences in general intelligence, rather than environmental factors. Murray's work formed the intellectual foundation of the conservative campaign to cut U.S. welfare spending in the 1990s (Medvetz 2014; O'Connor 2001). However, the core claims of the work were quickly rejected by social scientists and psychologists (Devlin 1997; Heckman 1995). If Murray were a practicing social scientist engaging with his colleagues in a scientific debate, his work would have lost its relevance long before gaining any public traction. The scientific consensus formed by neutral experts concluded that his theories did not accurately describe reality (Devlin 1997). However, Republican-aligned think tanks continue to support his work and promote it to policymakers. Murray currently holds the Hayek Emeritus Chair at AEI and in January 2020 published a new book, *Human Diversity: The Biology of Gender, Race and Class.*

There is little research assessing the nature of policy analysis produced by Democratic-aligned think tanks. Grossmann and Hopkins (2016) find that reports from progressive think tanks tend to include more citations and be authored by better-educated researchers and are more likely to analyze original data when compared to conservative think tanks. They argue that the difference in research quality is caused by differences in Republican and Democratic values, but they do not trace this argument to the level of individual reports or claims. Given their technocratic traditions, we should expect Democratic-aligned think tanks to generally produce information that is more in line with the scientific consensus, although they may also be tempted to release biased conclusions.

Bob Corker's Dilemma

One anecdote from the 2017 debate over the Tax Cuts and Jobs Act (TCJA) of 2017 illustrates the potential impact of biased policy analysis. While considering whether to vote for TCJA, Senator Bob Corker faced a dilemma. Corker, a conservative Republican, supported lowering taxes on the rich and corporations. However, he was also an avowed deficit hawk and opposed legislation that would significantly add to the national debt. As a result of his concerns over the latter, Corker voted against TCJA when its initial version reached the Senate floor on December 2, 2017. He justified his vote by pointing to a report from the CBO estimating that the bill would increase the deficit by over $1 trillion over the next 10 years. Other Republicans, many of whom had spent the 2010s voicing concerns about rising deficits, disagreed, as the *New York Times* reported: "Republicans said Mr. Corker had angered colleagues and overplayed his hand in the wake of that analysis. Mr. Corker was alarmed by the projections. *But many of his colleagues greeted them with distrust, both because they expected tax cuts to generate more robust economic growth than the forecasters projected* and because they felt burned by *unflattering analyses of their health care proposals issued this year by the Congressional Budget Office*" (Tankersley, Kaplan, and Rappeport 2017, emphasis added).

Strong belief in the efficacy of regressive tax cuts in increasing economic growth was not new for Republicans. Since the 1970s, Republicans repeatedly argued that large tax cuts would reduce deficits over the long run despite a strong consensus from economists that the opposite would happen (Jones and Williams 2008; Prasad 2018). Republican-supported tax cuts in the early 1980s and 2000s failed to spur significant economic growth, and as a result exploded the deficit (Jones and Williams 2008). A 2005 report from the CBO found that increased economic growth from a significant reduction in federal taxes would generate a feedback effect to offset only between 1% and 22% of the revenue lost. However, these estimates did not stop conservative economists, subsidized by Republican-aligned think tanks, from producing far rosier estimates. In keeping with the narrative that tax cuts supercharge economic growth, Republicans frequently heard from their think tanks that supply-side cuts do not decrease the deficit in the long run (Jones and Williams 2008).

Before they would approve the law, conservative House Republicans insisted on writing even more tax cuts into the bill to earn their votes on final passage. They convinced Senate negotiators to decrease the top marginal income tax rate from 39.6% to 38.5%, accelerate corporate tax cuts, and make key provisions permanent rather than allow them to expire (Horsley 2017). On December 20, the Senate voted on a new version of the bill before the CBO had time to score it. Corker switched his vote to aye. The bill passed the Senate on a narrow party-line vote. Two days later, Donald Trump signed the TCJA of 2017 into law.

Why did Corker change his vote? While many Republicans would face political pressure to vote for the bill even if they believed it might significantly increase the deficit, Corker did not. He had already announced his retirement from politics earlier that year. He also did not need to protect his relationships with Republicans in preparation for a career as a revolving-door lobbyist earning seven figures (LaPira and Thomas 2017) after retirement, like many of his colleagues. As one of the richest members of the Senate, with a net worth of $70 million (OpenSecrets 2015), Corker didn't need a lobbying paycheck after retirement. Thus he was free to vote his conscience. When he announced the switch, he released an explanation on Twitter. The statement made it clear that, despite disagreement from the consensus of nonpartisan economists, Corker was persuaded that the TCJA would have a sufficiently large impact on the economy:

> But after great thought and consideration, I believe that this once-in-a-generation opportunity to make U.S. businesses domestically more productive and internationally more competitive is one we should not miss. *While many project that it is very possible over the next ten years we could be at least $500 billion short on a $43 trillion policy baseline,* I believe this bill accompanied by significant regulatory changes that are underway, and hopefully, future pro-growth oriented policies relative to trade and immigration, could have significant positive impact on the well-being of Americans and help drive additional foreign direct investment in Tennessee.[6]

A clue to his change of heart may be hidden in the italicized section of the statement. That week the Tax Foundation, a small Republican-aligned think tank that specializes in tax policy, released a report projecting a very large macroeconomic feedback effect on the new bill, anticipating that it would only increase the deficit by $448 billion (Tax Foundation 2018). While the CBO did not have time to perform a full estimate of the revised bill, their preliminary report estimated that it would increase the deficit by $1.46 trillion. CBO's estimate was on the conservative side of nonpartisan estimates of the bill's cost; others estimated it would add more than $2 trillion to the deficit. Corker, a conservative Republican who likely believed that a package of tax cuts for the wealthy would have a strong effect on the economy, appeared to trust the conservative estimate. A few months later, CBO released its full report on the final bill, projecting that it would increase the deficit by $1.9 trillion. In a committee hearing where the report was unveiled, a contrite Corker commented on the estimate, "If it ends up costing what has been laid out here, it could well be one of the worst votes I've made" (Elis 2018). Two years later, a report from the CBO (2019) concluded that revenues would drop by considerably more than even the $1.9 trillionestimate.

Corker could have received policy advice from many sources. Congress employs a robust staff of nonpartisan expert policy analysts at the CBO, the Joint Committee on Taxation, and CRS. Further from Capitol Hill, there are many more economists and tax policy experts who populate nonpartisan Washington think tanks like the RAND Corporation, Brookings Institution, and Urban Institute. Further still, the United States enjoys the best and largest system of research universities in the world, each with a large department of economists who would have been eager to take his call. Instead, he chose to take the advice of the Tax Foundation, a small right-leaning nonprofit think tank that advocates for lower taxes by publishing policy analyses. If we take Corker at his word, he cared deeply about the country's exploding deficit. However, thanks to suspect policy analysis from a source with a policy agenda, he was the deciding vote in favor of one of the largest debt increases in American history.

Comparing Policy Analysis

"Bias" is a difficult concept to approach when considering the quality of policy analysis. When political parties disagree, journalists often default to "both sides" norms, aiming to give each opinion equal weight (Boykoff and Boykoff 2004). Similarly, one way that social scientists have measured media bias is by listing the ideological affiliations of experts interviewed by journalists and comparing them to experts cited by politicians (Groseclose and Milyo 2005). This kind of equity makes less sense when discussing policy analysis. The goal of a policy analyst is to accurately answer the question asked given their expertise and the information available to them. The predictions developed by analysts always come with uncertainty, but unlike many of the normative issues debated by politicians, their analyses are ultimately organized around facts. Policy analysts aim to predict the future as closely as possible to reality. There may be good-faith disagreements among experts about a given prediction, but there should be no credible "progressive" or "conservative" viewpoint on a particular policy question, just as there are no credible progressive or conservative answers to other scientific questions. If progressives and conservatives are coming to wildly different answers from those arrived at by neutral experts, then we should consider those estimates to be biased.[7]

For the purposes of this chapter, I assume that predictions by well-respected nonpartisan sources represent the best possible scientific estimate given the information available at the time. Estimates are biased when they are both more conservative or liberal than the conclusions of nonpartisan sources and the discrepancy is in the preferred direction of the publishing organization. I collected information produced by partisan think tanks and nonpartisan information sources across a range of issues to compare their claims. I hypothesize that Democrats and Republicans will tend to produce information biased to the left or right of the nonpartisan sources. However, Republican bias will be farther to the right than Democratic bias is to the left due to stronger Republican rejection of the technocratic knowledge regime (see Chapter 3).

One problem that arises with this research design is comparability. Researchers often make conflicting claims about policy, but they can also ask slightly different questions. One report may ask about the efficacy of a specific plan to affect some outcome, while another may ask about the general efficacy of a policy option but not focus on specific aspects. It can be difficult to perform apples-to-apples comparisons between reports that are not predicting very similar outcomes. In a deep qualitative design, a researcher with subject-matter expertise could thoroughly document the claims made by both partisan think tanks and nonpartisan experts and assess whether the partisan think tank information is biased to the left or right of nonpartisans. However, such deep qualitative work is beyond the scope of this project. Rather, I solve this problem using the quantitative predictions of impact analyses. An impact analysis is an estimation by the information producer of an outcome, such as the effect of a policy on GDP, the deficit, unemployment, or some other output. If multiple information sources estimate the effect of the policy on the same output, we can make valid comparisons among the estimates. If information is biased, it will produce a more favorable result for its supporter's party. If it is unbiased, it will be similar to the results produced by nonpartisan information sources.

It is rare that a range of think tanks and nonpartisan sources will produce apples-to-apples impact analyses of a policy output. Typically, nonpartisan information providers such as CBO evaluate specific bills after they have emerged from committee. Outside information sources such as think tanks tend to produce policy analysis at the early stages of the policy process, before policy proposals are precisely defined (Mooney 1991). Often, partisan think tanks will produce a report on the impact of some proposed policy, but the proposal never advances far enough to garner attention from nonpartisan providers. At other times, the proposal does advance, but details change from the time the early report was issued and when the estimates were produced by other sources. Because these factors rarely line up sufficiently to allow for comparison, this research design limits generalizability to information produced on policy that attracts the attention of multiple information producers over a short period.

I selected three cases where there was sufficient alignment between partisan think tank and nonpartisan impact analyses. Not coincidentally, each of these cases was a signature policy goal at the beginning of the Obama, Trump, and Biden administrations. The first case looks at analyses of the cost of Obama's Patient Protection and Affordable Care Act. All four partisan think tanks as well as two nonpartisan organizations produced impact estimates. The second case examines analyses of the cost and impact on economic growth of Trump's TCJA. All partisan think tanks other than CAP produced policy analyses, along with one nonpartisan think tank, one academic center, the CBO, and the Joint Committee on Taxation. The final case covers analyses of the Biden-Harris tax proposal during the 2020 presidential election. There were fewer reports on the Biden-Harris tax plan, with no Democratic-aligned think tanks weighing in against the Republican-aligned think tanks, CBO, and an academic center. I extracted data on the common impact predictions offered by each set of reports.

Two broad types of analyses emerged from these cases: primary and secondary analyses. Think tanks often perform their own primary analysis to predict the impact of a policy on some outcome. These analyses often require complex models and considerable expertise to set parameters and perform a credible estimate. Some think tanks retain this expertise in house, as with the Heritage Foundation's Center for Data Analysis, which produced several of the reports analyzed below. Others contracted with outside firms or academics to produce a report to be released under the think tank's brand, such as CAP's report on the impact of the ACA on the deficit. However, many think tank reports on the impact of a policy are themselves re-analyses of primary research. These secondary reports often accept the finding of the independent analysis they reference, but also examine different aspects of the policy, such as how its impact differs across income distributions or geography. In other cases, secondary reports modify the assumptions of the independent report they are referencing, creating a different estimate than the original source. For each case, I noted whether the report was a primary or secondary impact analysis.

Patient Protection and Affordable Care Act of 2010

The ACA was the signature legislative achievement of the Obama administration. It was the culmination of decades of advocacy by progressives to bring near-universal healthcare coverage to Americans (Hacker 2010). It resulted in between 24 million and 26 million Americans receiving health insurance; 15 million received health insurance through an expansion of Medicaid above the poverty line, and 10 million through subsidies that allowed working-class families to purchase health insurance on publicly run individual exchanges (Congressional Budget Office 2016). The bill also created numerous consumer protections for Americans buying health insurance. Most notably, it prohibited insurance companies from denying coverage to Americans with preexisting conditions, allowed them to vary premiums only by age and location, banned lifetime caps on health insurance coverage, and required insurers to spend a certain percentage of premiums on coverage (Meltzer 2011).

Furthermore, the bill sought to "bend the cost curve" of American health insurance through a number of regulatory measures. These included a mandate that all individuals carry health insurance, changes to how the federal government pays providers, and incentives to increase preventative care and vaccinations. It paid for these changes largely by increasing Medicare payroll taxes by 0.9% and taxing 3.8% on investment income for wealthy households, as well as through cuts to federal Medicare spending (Congressional Budget Office 2010). The final reconciliation bill also included a significant change to federal student loan financing under the Higher Education Act of 1965, a provision that was unrelated to healthcare. The analyses consider only the healthcare portion of the ACA.

The biggest policy analysis debate surrounding the ACA was its cost. Debate centered around the amount of new government spending on healthcare that the bill would authorize, rather than the relatively uncontroversial impact of the taxes used to pay for the new spending. All but one of the reports agreed that the ACA would raise $420 billion in new tax revenue and cut $511 billion in federal spending, primarily to Medicare. Analysts disagreed on both the impact of new regulations on overall healthcare costs and how much the complex regime of subsidies and Medicaid expansion would cost. Two nonpartisan sources modeled the impact of the ACA on the deficit. The CBO estimated that the ACA would increase government spending by $730 billion. It would spend $358 billion on subsidies to the individual marketplaces and $434 billion from the Medicaid expansion. Thus the bill would decrease the deficit by $124 billion over the 10-year budget window (Congressional Budget Office 2010). RAND (2010) released its own independent estimate, using its in-house COMPARE simulation model. RAND estimated that government spending on healthcare would increase by $899 billion. Their model assumed that plans on the individual market would cost considerably more than CBO's estimate, thus increasing the cost of federal subsidies and slightly increasing taxes paid by noncompliant individuals. It also estimated slightly different spending costs. RAND estimated that subsidies would cost the federal government $499 billion. However, it also estimated a slightly lower cost of the federal Medicaid expansion, at $400 billion. Thus, while RAND did not estimate the revenue side of the the law its estimates on federal spending imply that the bill would decrease the deficit by $32 billion.

Both Republican-aligned think tanks produced reports estimating the impact of the ACA on the deficit. The AEI report was written by Scott Harrington (2010), a respected professor of insurance and risk management with an endowed chair at the Wharton School who also held an affiliation with AEI. His report summarized and deferred to the CBO on estimates of the bill's impact on healthcare spending and the deficit. Harrington argued that the cuts to Medicare would likely need to be revisited or reversed by a future Congress, and that the same problems could have been solved with free-market policy alternatives contained in the 2008 Republican Party platform. The Heritage Foundation, on the other hand, created its own primary estimate by modifying the assumptions used by the CBO to determine the bill's "real" cost (Capretta 2010). The Heritage report argued that the CBO's estimate double-counted many of the spending cuts contained in the bill and expected Congress to continue to raise Medicare and Medicaid payments to providers (known as the "Doc Fix"). It concluded that the true cost of the spending provisions in the House version of the bill would be $1.495 trillion,[8] implying that it would increase the deficit by $564 billion.

Both Democratic-aligned think tanks also issued reports. CBPP published three secondary analyses on the impact of the ACA on the deficit, all of which referred to the CBO estimate (Lueck et al. 2010; Van De Water 2010; Van De Water and Horney 2010). The reports framed the ACA as a victory for working- and middle-class families who struggle with healthcare costs, but also one that would bend the cost curve on healthcare and improve the federal government's long-term budget outlook. CAP, on the other hand, performed its own primary analysis of the impact of the ACA on the deficit, which it co-published with the Commonwealth Fund (Cutler, Davis, and Stremikis 2010). The primary author, David Cutler, is an endowed chair in economics at Harvard University who had advised numerous Democratic presidents and presidential campaigns on healthcare issues. The report argued that the ACA would decrease the deficit by $505 billion from its healthcare provisions,[9] largely due to the bill's payments, modernization, and regulatory reforms. Specifically, it estimated that the federal savings from Medicare payment cuts would be $171 billion greater than CBO's $511 billion estimate, that the reforms would decrease the growth of Medicare costs by $124 billion, and that lowered private healthcare costs would result in employers shifting compensation from tax-free health insurance to taxed wages, resulting in an additional $86 billion federal revenue. The CAP report argued that the inefficiencies in healthcare systems, when compared with our private-sector industries, create sufficient slack for the federal reforms to target and reduce costs.

These predictions are summarized in Table 8.1. The nonpartisan sources predicted that the ACA would decrease the federal deficit by between $32 billion and $124 billion over 10 years. The CBO and RAND both forecast that almost all of the savings in the bill would come from relatively straightforward tax increases and direct cuts to federal spending. The two centrist-leaning partisan think tanks,

Table 8.1 **Analyses of the Impact of the Affordable Care Act on the Deficit**

	Organization	Deficit	Type
Democratic			
	CAP	$-505 billion	Primary
	CBPP[1]	$-124 billion	Secondary
Nonpartisan			
	CBO	$-124 billion	Primary
	RAND Corporation[2]	$-32 billion	Primary
Republican			
	Heritage Foundation	$400 billion	Primary
	AEI[3]	$-124 billion	Secondary

[1] The CBPP report references the CBO report.

[2] RAND Corporation report estimates only the cost of the ACA's spending. I calculated the impact on the deficit using the CBO's tax revenue estimates.

[3] The AEI report references the CBO report.

AEI and CBPP, both accepted this assessment with the barest reframing. However, CAP and Heritage each issued reports that were biased in their preferred directions at similar magnitudes. CAP predicted that the payment and regulatory reforms in the ACA would decrease the bill's cost, saving an additional $381 billion. Heritage predicted that many of the cuts would fail to materialize in actual spending due to "double-counting" and anticipated payment policy changes, and it would cost $524 billion more than the CBO estimated.

Tax Cuts and Jobs Act of 2017

TCJA was the signature legislative achievement of the 115th Congress. The CBO now estimates that it reduced federal revenues by $2.6 trillion over 10 years (Congressional Budget Office 2019). Its largest reductions were focused on corporations and the very rich. TCJA reduced the corporate income tax rate from 35% to 21%, allowed pass-through corporations to claim income at the lower corporate rate rather than as income, and moved U.S. corporate taxes from a worldwide to a territorial system. TCJA also raised the threshold on the estate tax from $7.6 million to $11.2 million and tweaked the structure of income tax brackets to decrease taxes on the rich and slightly increase taxes on the poor. It also raised the standard deduction and changed the way that some tax deductions are claimed. TCJA narrowly passed both the House of Representatives and the Senate with no Democratic votes in December 2017.

Polarized Policy Analysis

Much of the debate over TCJA centered around macroeconomic feedback effects. While all analysts estimated that the law would cause a small macroeconomic boost and large increase in the deficit in the short term, they disagreed about the long-term impact of the law on economic growth and therefore the deficit. Republicans argued that the corporate tax cuts in TCJA were designed to encourage investment into the economy, and thus greatly increase economic growth while only marginally impacting the deficit over the long run. Democrats argued that the cuts were pro-cyclical giveaways to the rich that would explode the deficit. These arguments mirror the same debates that the two parties had over the two tax cuts under George W. Bush as well as many of the Reagan-era tax cuts (Jones and Williams 2008; Prasad 2018). In both of those cases, the tax cuts failed to spur economic growth enough to beat their deficit projections (Jones and Williams 2008).

Four nonpartisan information sources published primary estimates of the impact of TCJA on real GDP in 2027, at the end of the 10-year budget window required by the Senate's budget reconciliation procedure. The CBO published estimates for each version of the bill as it passed the House and Senate and eventually emerged from conference committee. However, a rushed legislative process meant that the CBO did not have time to conduct its most thorough estimate of the version of the bill that eventually emerged. The preliminary CBO cost estimate released on December 15, 2017, forecast that the final bill would increase real 2027 GDP by 0.7%, therefore increasing the deficit by $1.5 trillion (Congressional Budget Office 2017).[10] The Joint Committee on Taxation produced a similar estimate of 0.8% GDP and $1.5 trillion over 10 years. Two outside groups also provided detailed primary estimates of TCJA's macroeconomic impact. The first was published by an academic research group at the Wharton School of the University of Pennsylvania led by economist Kent Smetters, who estimated the macroeconomic impact of the bill using a model known as the Penn Wharton Budget Model (2017). This group published two predictions. First, when assuming that the bill increases productivity with a high return to capital investments into the economy, the model estimated that 2027 GDP would increase by 1.1% while the deficit would increase by $1.94 trillion. Second, when assuming a lower return to capital investments, the model estimated that GDP would increase by 0.6% and the deficit by $2.23 trillion.[11] Finally, the Tax Policy Center (TPC), a joint program of the Brookings Institution and Urban Institute, produced their own estimate led by Benjamin Page, a former CBO analyst (Page et al. 2017). They predicted that TCJA would have a much smaller impact on the economy, increasing 2027 GDP by just 0.4%. Both the Penn Wharton Budget Model and TPC also estimated the long-run impact of TCJA on GDP, coming to much different conclusions. The Penn Wharton Budget Model predicted that the bill would increase 2040 GDP by between 0.7% and 1.6%. TPC predicted that it would have no long-run impact on GDP by 2037.

No Democratic-aligned think tank produced its own impact analysis of the TCJA. CAP published numerous reports criticizing the bill but focused on how it would raise middle-class taxes while lowering taxes for the rich, rather than its impact on the deficit or economy (for example, see Rowell and Schwartz 2017). CBPP published two detailed secondary analyses on the macroeconomic impact of the bill. The first compared the impact estimates of the four nonpartisan sources, averaging their predictions together (Friedman and Stone 2017). The second argued that many of the bill's most popular tax cuts were set to expire in the middle of the 10-year budget window in order to keep the headline cost of the bill down, that even a Democratic-controlled Congress would likely feel pressure to maintain these tax cuts, and that therefore the true headline cost of the bill would likely be $200 billion over the official estimates. In both cases, the Democratic-aligned think tanks engaged in framing, rather than in the strategy of elite persuasion.

Both the Heritage Foundation and AEI published primary estimates of the impact of TCJA on economic growth. Both reports estimated the impact of TCJA on economic growth but did not estimate its impact on the deficit. Each used in-house models to estimate the impact of tax changes on the economy but came to different conclusions. The AEI report, written by two resident AEI researchers, estimated the macroeconomic impact of both the House and Senate versions of the bill, but not the conference report, which resolved the differences between the bills passed by each chamber. The AEI researchers predicted that the Senate version of the bill would increase 2027 GDP by 0.92% and long-run GDP by 2.2%. Two Heritage researchers used their own model to estimate the macroeconomic impact of TCJA. They released a more detailed report on the House and Senate bills in November 2017 (Sheppard and Burton 2017b) and a brief updated estimate using the same model on the conference report in December of that year (Sheppard and Burton 2017a). They predicted that the TCJA would dramatically increase capital stock and working hours, resulting in a 2.2% increase in long-run GDP. While they did not estimate the bill's impact on 2027 GDP, they noted that "most of the increase in GDP would likely occur within the 10-year budget window" (Sheppard and Burton 2017a, 1). Neither the AEI nor the Heritage report estimated the impact of the TCJA on the deficit, although we can assume that it would be smaller than estimates predicting a weaker feedback effect on economic growth.[12] The Tax Foundation, the relatively small conservative think tank that persuaded Bob Corker to support the bill, published an estimate of TCJA's impact on the deficit, suggesting that it would decrease revenues by just $448 billion.

Table 8.2 shows these estimates. The four nonpartisans predicted that the TCJA would increase 2027 GDP by between 0.4% and 0.85% and increase the deficit by between $1.1 trillion and $2.05 trillion. In the long run, they predicted that GDP would increase by between 0 and 1.1%. Democratic-aligned think tanks accepted these conclusions and focused their efforts on reframing the issue as one of "rich versus poor." Republican-aligned think tanks, on the other hand, chose to engage in elite persuasion by publishing biased research that found a much larger impact of the tax cuts on the economy. This bias showed up most strongly in their long-term analysis. Both predicted a much larger long-run impact on economic growth than the nonpartisan sources that attempted to estimate long-run growth. In the short term, AEI's prediction was in line with the high end of nonpartisan expectations. While Heritage did not offer a specific short-term prediction, the report stated that most of their long-run 2.2% prediction would come in the first 10 years, which would far exceed nonpartisan predictions for the bill's short-term impact. Finally, while the Republican-aligned think tanks did not formally estimate TCJA's impact on the deficit, their predictions suggested a much lower cost than the nonpartisan estimates.

To summarize, the nonpartisan reports from both inside and outside of government predicted that the TCJA of 2017 would have a relatively modest positive impact on economic growth at a very high cost to the deficit. The Republican-aligned think tanks published reports predicting a much larger impact on economic growth and therefore much lower cost to the deficit. CAP and CBPP did not issue their own reports, CBPP opting to average the four nonpartisan reports together to reach a conclusion.

Biden-Harris Tax Plan

During the 2020 presidential race, the Biden-Harris campaign released a detailed plan on how to raise revenue for its ambitious domestic policy agenda. The plan sought to raise considerable revenue without increasing taxes on Americans making under $400,000 a year. The strategy was about evenly divided between provisions to raise revenue from corporate taxes and from individual and payroll taxes for households making over $400,000. On corporate taxes, the Biden-Harris campaign proposed to raise most of the needed revenue by increasing the corporate tax rate from 20% to 28% and closing loopholes that allowed U.S. companies to avoid taxes by shifting profits to offshore tax havens. On individual taxes, the proposal was to raise revenue through taxing capital gains over $1 million as normal income, exposing income over $400,000 to the Social Security payroll tax, limiting itemized deductions on adjusted gross income over $400,000, and increasing the estate tax.

Five organizations weighed in on the amount of revenue that the Biden-Harris tax plan would raise and its anticipated impact on economic growth (Table 8.3). Unlike the TCJA of 2017, the Biden-Harris plan was not a proposed law, so the CBO did not produce its own cost estimate. As they did for the TCJA, the Penn Wharton Budget Model and TPC published nonpartisan estimates of the proposal's overall impact on the deficit and GDP over 10 years, as well as individual estimates for the impact of its largest provisions. Three Republican-aligned think tanks provided estimates. The Tax Foundation, a Republican-aligned think tank that specializes in tax policy, provided a full score of the proposal's impact on both outputs. Heritage produced an estimate of just the impact of the proposal's corporate tax provisions

Table 8.2 **Analyses of the Impact of the Tax Cuts and Jobs Act on Real GDP in 2027**

	Organization	GDP -2027	GDP (Long Run)	Deficit -2027	Type
Democratic					
	CAP[1]	n/a	n/a	n/a	n/a
	CBPP[2]	0.66%	n/a	$1.6 trillion	Secondary
Nonpartisan					
	CBO	0.70%	n/a	$1.46 trillion	Primary
	Joint Committee on Taxation	0.80%	n/a	$1.1 trillion	Primary
	Penn Wharton Budget Model[3]	0.85%	1.15%	$2.05 trillion	Primary
	TPC	0.40%	0.00%	$1.8 trillion	Primary
Republican					
	Tax Foundation	n/a	1.70%	$448 billion	
	Heritage Foundation	n/a[4]	2.20%	n/a	Primary
	AEI[5]	0.92%	2.05%	n/a	Primary

[1] CAP did not issue a report on the impact of TCJA on the economy.

[2] The CBPP report averaged together the four nonpartisan sources.

[3] The Penn Wharton Budget Model estimated both a high and a low scenario for the impact of TCJA on economic growth. The average of the two scenarios is 0.85%.

[4] The Heritage Foundation report did not estimate the impact of TCJA on 2027 GDP but noted that "most of the increase in GDP would likely occur within the 10-year budget window." (Sheppard and Burton 2017a, 1)

[5] The AEI report estimated the impact of the House and Senate versions of the bill, but not the conference report. Estimates here are for the Senate version.

on GDP. AEI published a report predicting the full plan's impact on both the deficit and GDP, but only projected the corporate tax provision's impact on GDP.

All four nonpartisan sources estimated that the proposal would raise a similar amount of revenue for the federal government. The Penn Wharton Budget Model was the high estimate at $3.34 trillion, while the TPC was the low estimate at $2.1 trillion. AEI and the Tax Foundation estimated that the proposal would raise a higher amount of revenue than the TPC, at $2.8 trillion. There was much more disagreement on the plan's impact on economic growth. The Penn Wharton Budget Model projected that the full plan would only modestly decrease GDP in 2031 by 0.20%, while the TPC projected no significant decrease in economic growth. Both

Polarized Policy Analysis 117

Table 8.3 **Analyses of the Biden-Harris Campaign Tax Plan**

| | Organization | Full Campaign Plan | | Corporate Tax | | Type |
		Deficit	GDP	Deficit	GDP	
Democratic						
	CAP	n/a	n/a	n/a	n/a	n/a
	CBPP	n/a	n/a	n/a	n/a	n/a
Nonpartisan						
	Penn Wharton Budget Model[1]	$3.34tn	−0.20%	$1.03tn	−0.05%	Primary
	TPC	$2.1tn	0.00%	$730 bn	0.00%	Primary
Republican						
	Tax Foundation	$2.8tn	−1.62%	$1.05 tn	−0.97%	Primary
	Heritage Foundation	n/a	n/a	n/a	−0.96%	Primary
	AEI [2]	$2.8tn	−0.16%	$1.02 tn	n/a	Primary

[1] The Penn Wharton Budget Model estimates immigration and tax plan effects together at + 0.8% GDP. Estimates subtract out immigration plan (+1%).

[2] Both the Penn Wharton Budget Model and the AEI report examined the impact of all of the Biden corporate tax proposals collectively on GDP, rather than each individually.

agreed that the corporate tax provisions would have almost no impact on economic growth. AEI broadly agreed with these estimates, projecting that the full plan would lower 2031 GDP by 0.16%. The Tax Foundation and Heritage projected a much more severe impact on the economy. The Tax Foundation projected that the full plan would decrease 2031 GDP by 1.62%, while the corporate tax provisions alone would damage the economy by −0.97%. Heritage did not provide a GDP estimate for the full plan but estimated that the corporate tax provisions would have a similar −0.96% impact.

No Democratic-aligned think tank wrote a report on the impact of the Biden-Harris tax plan on GDP or on the deficit.

Summary

When CAP and Heritage put out an estimate of the impact of a policy, they are likelier to provide more liberal or conservative predictions than the consensus of nonpartisan experts in government, academia, and nonpartisan think tanks. When the CBPP does the same, they produce estimates that are either broadly in line with nonpartisan experts or that simply reference and reframe nonpartisan findings. AEI is somewhere in between. These results conform with each think tank's reputation. CAP and Heritage are broadly understood as friendly partisan organizations that are willing to publish analyses that support partisan and ideological goals. We can draw the conclusion that when policymakers search for expert information on a problem they are considering, they should expect biased policy analysis from their largest and most important partisan think tanks.

However, we should be careful to avoid generalizing too many conclusions from these cases. They are limited in several key ways: these cases relate to policy analyses where a bill is in its final stages, where the parameters to estimate are relatively constrained, and where trusted nonpartisans are producing estimates to compare against highly salient issues. At earlier stages, with fewer constraints and less nonpartisan competition, a variety of information sources, including more or less partisan think tanks, may credibly make more extreme claims about public policy. Furthermore, including the comprehensive immigration reform analyses presented in the chapter's introduction, we have only two examples of CAP case studies. While both were biased to the left of the nonpartisan estimates, only one diverged as far as the estimates released by Heritage. Other research suggests that CAP work is more rigorous than Heritage work (Grossmann and Hopkins 2016). We need more research to judge whether CAP and similar smaller Democratic-leaning think tanks are producing work as far to the left as Heritage and its peers are producing to the right.

9

Green Jobs and Climate Change Denial

The late 2000s and early 2010s saw a remarkable and rapid polarization of party positions on climate change policy. In 2008 all major Republican Party leaders in legislative and executive branches endorsed a significant policy change to address climate change. By 2012 all major Republican Party leaders not only opposed all policy changes, but openly denied the science behind climate change. At the same time, the Democratic Party doubled down on the issue, supporting huge new spending programs on renewable energy and weaker federal mandates to create what they called "green jobs." Why did party positions on climate change policy polarize so rapidly, and what role did partisan think tanks play in the change?

The Republican Party's reversal on climate change is remarkable given the party's past leadership on environmental policy and air pollution (Karol 2019). Richard Nixon signed the Clean Air Act amendments of 1970 into law, significantly expanding federal authority to reduce emissions from automobiles and smokestacks. Nixon was one of California's senators during the height of its smog emergencies, when deadly particulate matter regularly cast a thick fog over Los Angeles, killing thousands (Nussbaum 1998). In many U.S. cities, drivers had to use their headlights as late as 11:00 in the morning. The amendments vastly expanded federal authority to regulate pollution from automobiles and smokestacks. It called for a 90% reduction in particulate emissions from automobiles. To implement the new regulations, Nixon proposed an executive branch reorganization to create the Environmental Protection Agency (EPA) and appointed William Ruckelshaus, who supported strong environmental protections, to lead it. After Ruckelshaus left, Nixon appointed Russell Train, the founder of the World Wildlife Fund, to the position. Under Nixon and later Gerald Ford, Train required all new vehicles to be equipped with catalytic converters, dramatically decreasing the amount of smog-inducing particulate matter and lead emitted from cars and trucks. Nixon and Ford did not stop at air pollution, signing the Endangered Species Act, the Clean Water Act, and the Toxic Substances Control Act into law and banning DDT, among other

The Thinkers. E. J. Fagan, Oxford University Press. © Oxford University Press 2024.
DOI: 10.1093/oso/9780197759653.003.0009

regulations. The programs were wildly successful; U.S. air pollution from all sources has been steadily falling since the 1970s (Aldy et al. 2022).

These positions conflicted with the laissez-faire approaches to policymaking supported by ideological conservatives. In 1977, Heritage published two reports criticizing the incoming Carter administration's environmental policies (Copulous 1977a, 1977b). The first sounded the alarm about the growing power and resources of leading environmental organizations, listing their donors and noting when their "liberal activists" were hired by the Carter administration. The other report addressed the Clean Air Act specifically, arguing that the aggressive regulations passed by Ruckelshaus and especially Train overstepped the statutory authority given to the EPA under the Clean Air Act. It criticized the policies as being too damaging to the economy: "The most important factor in the ongoing debate over environmental controls may wind up being a philosophical one rather than a technological one. If reason and rationality are used, along with a certain amount of common sense, it may be possible to work out solutions to the problems. If, however, environmentalists insist on the most stringent standards without consideration to their economic and social consequences, the eventual result may be significant deterioration of the country's standard of living" (Copulos 1977a).

Heritage continued to oppose the EPA into the Reagan administration.[1] In its first *Mandate for Leadership*, Heritage's Louis J. Cordia called for significantly curtailing the EPA's authority to regulate, returning the power to the states (Cordia 1980). Reagan struggled to exert control over the EPA's bureaucracy, which had developed a strong institutional culture during its first decade (Wood 1988). He appointed Cordia as the agency's Office of Federal Activities. Cordia first showed up at the EPA with a "hit list," handwritten on Heritage stationary, of career agency officials to be fired, hired, or promoted (Russakoff and Kurtz 1983). Under Cordia, 24 of the office's 47 career employees left, "many scientists and Ph.Ds. in the office reassigned to clerical jobs such as the cutting and pasting of organization charts and hole-punching documents that needed to be bound" (Russakoff and Kurtz 1983). He resigned two years later, after the EPA's inspector general found that he had tampered with agency records and ordered the destruction of data. Under pressure from the Cordia episode and other scandals relating to failures to control the EPA, Reagan reappointed Ruckelshaus to lead it in 1983.

As late as the George H. W. Bush administration, Republicans were often leaders in the federal regulation of air pollution (Karol 2019). Facing increased acid rain caused by sulfur dioxide emissions from coal smokestacks, Bush signed into law the Clean Air Act amendments of 1990, giving the EPA authority to address acid rain as well as additional authority to regulate ozone, carbon monoxide, and home appliances (Aldy et al. 2022). Unlike the Nixon and Ford administrations, Bush opposed "command and control" style regulations, either by setting emission rates on classes of emitters or by specifying the type of equipment emitters must install (Schmalensee and Stavins 2013). Environmental Defense Fund president Fred

Krupp convinced Bush that he could address acid rain with market forces rather than command-and-control regulations, by using an emissions trading system known as cap-and-trade (Horn and Krupp 2009). Bush liked the idea and proposed that Congress create a mechanism to allow the EPA to create a cap-and-trade system to address acid rain. Heritage supported the plan, publishing a report titled "Two Cheers for Bush's Clean Air Plan" (Kent 1989).The report called the plan innovative and efficient, a model that should be applied to other types of air pollution.

Over the next decade, the Republican Party steadily grew more conservative on environmental policy (Karol 2019). However, Republican leaders remained committed to reducing air pollution using market-based mechanisms. The George W. Bush administration proposed the Clear Skies Initiative during each of the 107th, 108th, and 109th Congresses, which would have established broader cap-and-trade systems to restrict sulfur dioxide, nitrogen dioxide, and mercury emissions from power plants. The Bush White House (2002) cited the success of the acid rain program as justification for a broader cap-and-trade regime to regulate air pollution. Democrats opposed the plan, calling it a looser regulation of emissions than current law (U.S. House of Representatives 2003). Through the mid-2000s, cap-and-trade was an idea that belonged to conservative Republicans, who were eager to use it as an instrument to decrease air pollution.

The Democratic Party's positions on environmental policy amount to a simpler story. Democrats have long been considered the "owners" of environmental policy in American politics, having incorporated pro-environment interest groups into their coalition by the early 1990s (Egan 2013). This relationship is common in most democracies, where the public tends to trust left-leaning parties to handle environmental issues more than any other issues (Seeberg 2017). Like many left-of-center parties, Democrats are eager to address environmental problems. When in government, they prioritize environmental problems over others (Egan 2013). By the 1990s, most major environmental groups in the United States supported the Democratic Party, often as well-funded insiders (Karol 2019). When the agenda moves toward an environmental problem, Democrats do not need much convincing.

The Reluctant Climate Consensus of the Mid-2000s

Democratic and Republican elites began to reach a reluctant consensus on climate change policy in the mid-2000s. Democrats were more eager than Republicans to address the problem, but the emerging scientific consensus and normal agenda-setting mechanisms dragged Republicans toward supporting action by the middle of the decade.

In 2001, the International Panel on Climate Change (IPCC) released its third assessment report on the scientific literature on climate change (Houghton et al. 2001). The IPCC had released two previous reports in 1990 and 1995, both finding considerable evidence for anthropogenic climate change but expressing some uncertainty and need for more research. The third IPCC report concluded that climate scientists had refined their models over the decade and could be much more confident in the impact of greenhouse gas emissions on the environment. It also sounded the alarm: absent policy interventions, the average global temperature would increase by between 1.4° C and 5.8° C over the next century, up from the 1.0° C to 3.5° C estimate from the initial assessment. Increased temperature would mean longer droughts, more extreme weather, and rising sea levels.

With the 2001 IPCC report, climate change burst onto the global policy agenda. Figure 9.1 shows the frequency of the words "climate change" or "global warming" in books archived by Google Books. The topic saw a huge jump in prevalence in the mid-2000s. In 2004, the climate change–themed disaster movie *The Day after Tomorrow* made $552 million worldwide. In 2006, former vice president Al Gore released *An Inconvenient Truth*, a documentary about climate change. It won the Academy Award for Best Documentary, grossed $50 million worldwide, and further elevated the issue. In 2007, the IPCC issued its fourth assessment, finding even more consensus among scientists about the impacts of climate change and offering even more dire warnings, including a potential temperature increase of 6.4° C by 2100. Neutral experts were telling policymakers worldwide that they had to reduce greenhouse gas emissions, fast.

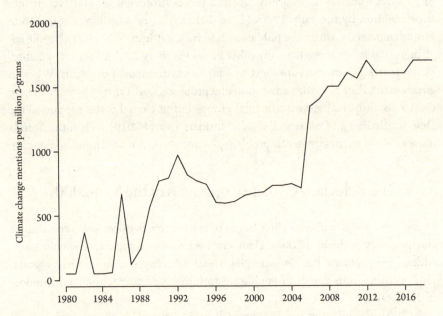

Figure 9.1 Frequency of climate change words in books. Frequency of "climate change" or "global warming" found in published books. Source: Google Books Ngram Viewer; Michel et al. (2011).

Now that the problem was on the agenda, policymakers in both parties came together around solutions. States controlled by both parties had enacted renewable or clean energy mandates and subsidies for wind and solar electricity generation throughout the late 1990s and 2000s, although utility companies were often successful in blunting their implementation (Stokes 2020). In Congress, senators coalesced around the Lieberman-Warner Climate Security Act of 2008, which would have established a cap-and-trade system for coal and natural gas electricity generation. The senate invoked cloture on the bill by a 74–14 vote (12 absent), with 32 Republicans voting in favor. However, the bill died as crude oil prices spiked during the summer of 2008 and the election approached. The George W. Bush administration threatened to veto the bill if passed, citing it as too stringent.

However, both the Republican and Democratic parties remained committed to enacting a climate change solution. Later that summer, both party platforms contained climate change planks. The Democratic platform mentioned climate change in several sections, including this plank calling attention to the severity of the problem: "We will lead to defeat the epochal, man-made threat to the planet: climate change. Without dramatic changes, rising sea levels will flood coastal regions around the world. Warmer temperatures and declining rainfall will reduce crop yields, increasing conflict, famine, disease, and poverty. By 2050, famine could displace more than 250 million people worldwide. That means increased instability in some of the most volatile parts of the world" (Democratic Party Platform 2008).

The Republican Party platform did not discuss climate change as an emergency, but was more specific about what solutions they endorsed. John McCain, the Republican presidential nominee in 2008, gave a campaign speech at a wind power company where he came out against Bush's veto threat and promised to support a cap-and-trade policy. With Democratic moderate Joe Lieberman, McCain had previously introduced carbon cap-and-trade bills in each of the previous three Congresses. A few months later, the platform reiterated his position:

> The same human economic activity that has brought freedom and opportunity to billions has also increased the amount of carbon in the atmosphere. While the scope and long-term consequences of this are the subject of ongoing scientific research, common sense dictates that the United States should take measured and reasonable steps today to reduce any impact on the environment. Those steps, if consistent with our global competitiveness will also be good for our national security, our energy independence, and our economy. Any policies should be global in nature, based on sound science and technology, and should not harm the economy.

The Solution: Technology and the Market
As part of a global climate change strategy, Republicans support technology-driven, market-based solutions that will decrease emissions,

reduce excess greenhouse gasses in the atmosphere, increase energy efficiency, mitigate the impact of climate change where it occurs, and maximize any ancillary benefits climate change might offer for the economy.

To reduce emissions in the short run, we will rely upon the power of new technologies, as discussed above, especially zero-emission energy sources such as nuclear and other alternate power sources. But innovation must not be hamstrung by Washington bickering, regulatory briar patches, or obstructionist lawsuits. Empowering Washington will only lead to unintended consequences and unimagined economic and environmental pain; instead, we must unleash the power of scientific know-how and competitive markets. (Republican Party Platform 2008)

Even the George W. Bush administration, well-known for its ties to the oil and gas industries, got in on the act. Bush, like many Republicans, was skeptical of policy interventions to regulate greenhouse gas emissions. He maintained close relationships with fossil fuel industries and in the earlier part of the decade often flirted with climate change denial and the suppression of federal scientific research on climate change (Harris 2003). However, he still professed a desire to address the problem during his presidency by subsidizing biofuels and hydrogen electricity. While governor of Texas, he signed an ambitious bill that successfully made Texas a leader in wind energy throughout the 2000s (Stokes 2020). In the summer of 2008, the White House released documents claiming credit for the administration's policy to address climate change: "President Bush has taken a reasoned, balanced approach to the serious challenges of energy security and climate change. The President supports a climate change policy that takes advantage of new clean energy technologies; increases our use of alternative fuels; works towards an international agreement that will slow, stop, and eventually reverse the growth of greenhouse gases; and includes binding commitments from all major economies" (White House 2008).

The bottom line of the story of climate change in the 2000s is that the nonpartisan, expert-driven problem-solving process detailed in Chapter 2 was working. The problem of climate change was prioritized externally to the political parties. Both political parties offered solutions to it. The political system organized around a broad, bipartisan climate plan that was based on past successful policies. Democrats were more enthusiastic about addressing climate change, while Republicans had to be dragged kicking and screaming toward it, but they both reached a similar destination.

However, ideological conservatives opposed cap-and-trade to address climate change. They saw it as a massive expansion in both federal taxation and regulatory interventions into the domestic economy. A cap-and-trade system to limit greenhouse gas emissions was a much larger and more intrusive policy than previous cap-and-trade systems to address particulate emissions. They were inherently skeptical of any claims coming from scientists, academics, and bureaucrats about climate change, and convinced that the economic costs would be tremendous. While some Republicans joined them in their skepticism, ideological conservatives saw most of their fellow Republicans endorsing a cap-and-trade policy for greenhouse gas emission.

Partisan Think Tanks Expand Climate Change Denial

Climate change denial began long before the moment that climate change hit the policy agenda in the late 2000s. Fossil fuel industries understood that the regulation of greenhouse gases presented an existential threat to their businesses in a way that previous environmental regulations did not. They promoted climate change skepticism in the 1980s and 1990s by claiming that the scientific literature was more uncertain than it was in reality (Supran and Oreskes 2021). They used public relations tactics and consultants similar to those the tobacco industry had used to fight claims of the negative health effects of smoking cigarettes (Michaels 2008). However, as with that campaign, they were ultimately fighting a losing battle. By the early 2000s, most Americans reported concern about climate change; Republicans were less concerned than Democrats, but public opinion was not highly polarized (Guber 2013).

As with polarization trends generally, elites polarized around the issue of climate change before the mass public followed suit. In 2001, 49% of Republicans and 60% of Democrats said they believe that climate change was occurring (McCright and Dunlap 2011). Democrats began to believe that climate change was more serious by 2008, when 70% believed that climate change was occurring against 46% of Republicans (McCright and Dunlap 2011). However, the bottom fell out after Republican elites began to endorse climate change denial. By 2010, only 29% of Republicans believed that climate change was occurring (McCright and Dunlap 2011).

Partisan think tanks were a vital part of the push for climate change skepticism from the beginning. In the mid-1990s, congressional Republicans tended to prefer experts who disagreed with the scientific consensus across a range of environmental issues, often finding them at conservative think tanks (McCright and Dunlap 2003). Partisan think tanks were able to elevate to prominence a relatively small number of scientists who disagreed with the consensus (Oreskes and Conway 2011). The overwhelming majority of books that promoted climate change denial and skepticism were published or authored by researchers at Republican-aligned think tanks (Dunlap and Jacques 2013; McCright and Dunlap 2003). They were able to exploit "both-sides" norms in the media, where journalists created the appearance of a scientific debate over climate change by giving both the vast majority of mainstream scientists who were affirming the risks of climate change and the tiny minority of scientist dissenters similar credibility (Boykoff and Boykoff 2004). Republican elites regularly denied climate change science. As early as 2003, the Republican chair of the Environment and Public Works Committee Jim Inhofe loudly opposed climate change science, saying in a floor speech, "With all of the hysteria, all of the fear, all of the phony science, could it be that man-made global warming is the greatest hoax ever perpetrated on the American people? It sure sounds like it" (Revkin 2003).

However, this strategy remained marginal until the late 2000s, when something changed. As climate change rocketed up the policy agenda, Heritage snapped into action. They published a huge number of reports opposing climate change, more than quintupling their previous pace of publishing on the issue (Figure 9.2). None of the other three think tanks studied here had a similar countermobilization, although many smaller think tanks joined Heritage on the right in surging attention to climate change policy (Dunlap and Jacques 2013).

In one study of the diffusion of ideas throughout political networks, Heritage and AEI were found to be the most central actors. Albert (2019) studied the use of bigrams, or sets of two words, associated with cap-and-trade policy in statements, reports, and other online publications issued by interest groups and e-newsletters sent by members of Congress. He found that phrases disproportionately used by Republican interest groups and members of Congress were most influenced by reports from Heritage and AEI. Both think tanks were the original developers of much of the language on climate change that was later adopted by Republican members of Congress. On cap-and-trade, Albert found that they were most

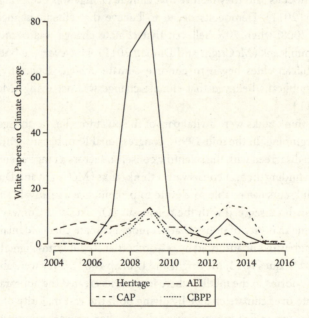

Figure 9.2 Partisan think tank white papers on climate change. Source: Author's counts of white papers published on each think tank's website.

influential on spreading language about the costs of the policy rather than language questioning the underlying science of climate change.

Exaggerated Costs of Climate Solutions

But did they exaggerate the costs of cap-and-trade? We can answer the question by repeating the comparative policy analysis design from Chapter 8. After Democrats took control of the presidency and gained seats in both chambers in the 2008 elections, they introduced the American Clean Energy and Security Act (ACES), which was similar to the Lieberman-Warner bill that had nearly passed a year earlier. It would have capped U.S. emissions at 97% relative to 2005 levels beginning in 2012, slowly decreasing to 17% by 2050. ACES would have directed revenue from permit sales into subsidies for clean energy, carbon sequestration, and other technology. ACES passed the House of Representatives 219 to 212, with just 8 Republicans supporting it, but it did not receive a vote in the Senate.

One of the key policy debates for analysts on ACES was the impact of its cap-and-trade system on the economy. A cap-and-trade system sets hard limits on the amount of greenhouse gases that can be emitted each year and relies on market forces to either reduce energy use or find alternative clean energy sources. If the economy develops cheap and available substitutes for carbon-burning energy, the cap should have a relatively small impact on the economy. If it does not, high energy prices could decrease economic activity. Thus several analysts estimated the impact of the ACES cap-and-trade system on long-run real GDP.

Seven sources produced analyses of the impact of the ACES Act on GDP in 2030, five of which were independent analyses and three of which were secondary (see Table 9.1). Four of these sources were nonpartisan.[2] The first, published by a group of scientists at the MIT Joint Program on the Science and Policy of Global Change led by Sergey Paltsev (Paltsev et al. 2009), used the center's Emissions Predictions and Policy Analysis model to estimate the impact of a number of climate policy alternatives on the economy, including ACES. Paltsev and his coauthors expected ACES to have a relatively small impact on the economy, with 2030 GDP being only 0.37% smaller than the counterfactual of no policy change. Two government agencies also produced detailed reports. The first was published by the Energy Information Administration (2009; EIA), the Department of Energy's policy analysis organization. The second was published by the Environmental Protection Agency (2009). The agencies were split as to the bill's impact; EIA estimated that GDP would be 0.30% lower, like the Paltsev estimate, while the EPA estimated it would be 0.90% lower.

Both the Center for American Progress and the Center on Budget and Policy Priorities produced secondary reports analyzing the impact of cap and trade. The CAP report summarized seven estimates made by nonpartisan organizations of

Table 9.1 **Analyses of the Effect of the American Clean Energy and Security Act on GDP in 2030**

	Organization	GDP (2030)
Democratic		
	CAP[1]	−0.70%
	CBPP[2]	−0.90%
Nonpartisan		
	Paltsev et al. (2009)	−0.40%
	EIA	−0.30%
	EPA	−0.90%
Republican		
	Heritage Foundation	−2.30%
	AEI[3]	−1.00%

1. The Center for American Progress report uses both the EPA and Palstev et al. estimates

2. The Center on Budget and Policy Priorities report references the EPA estimates.

3. The American Enterprise Institute report references predictions from a report by Charles Rivers Associates, an energy consulting firm.

the impact of both the ACES cap-and-trade system and estimates of a similar bill proposed during the previous Congress (Pollin, Heintz, and Garrett-Peltier 2009). CAP noted that the EPA report represented the worst-case scenario when compared with the Paltsev report and, even then, decreased annualized economic growth by just 0.05% annually. They also emphasized benefits of spending on renewable energy, arguing that any cap-and-trade system paired with large increases in public spending on renewable energy would have a net positive impact on growth. CBPP's report also accepted the EPA's analysis as credible and accurate but emphasized that the estimate did include the economic benefits of decreasing the risk of climate-related catastrophic environmental and economic effects (Stone 2009). Thus, both Democratic-aligned think tanks declined to produce biased estimates and instead focused on a progressive framing of the policy analysis.

The two Republican-aligned think tanks published very different information on the impact of ACES. The Heritage Foundation commissioned a primary analysis from IHS Global Insight, an economics consulting firm (Beach et al. 2009). They projected that additional renewable energy capacity would not increase versus the counterfactual despite the price on carbon. Instead, electricity and transportation prices would rise in response to the cap on carbon emissions by as much as 90%. This increased price would decrease economic activity. They projected that

2030 GDP would be 2.31% lower than the counterfactual where no policy changed. Conversely, AEI did not produce a primary analysis, or even a substantial report specifically dedicated to the bill. However, AEI did produce commentary on ACES from Lee Lane, head of the organization's geoengineering program. While much of his commentary focused on the challenges of a cap-and-trade strategy in reducing greenhouse gas emissions given international collective action problems, Lane (2009) commented on economic growth in one article titled "What Will the Climate Bill Cost?," in which he criticized nonpartisan reports for being too optimistic about costs. Lane referred to a study by Charles Rivers Associates, an energy consulting firm, which projected 2030 GDP to decrease by 1%. In short, the Heritage report created a primary estimate biased far to the right of nonpartisans, while the AEI commentary produced a secondary report slightly to the right of the nonpartisans.

These predictions are summarized in Table 9.1. The nonpartisan sources predicted that the cap-and-trade program proposed under ACES would decrease GDP in 2030 by between 0.3% and 0.9%. Neither Democratic-aligned think tank produced their own primary estimate of the impact of cap-and-trade and accepted the EPA's estimate, which was considerably more negative than even the other nonpartisan sources, as the authoritative word on the bill's impact. However, both think tanks also engaged in some mild reframing of the cost-benefit calculus offered by the EPA report. On the other side, both Republican-aligned think tanks offered their own estimates on the impact of the bill. The Heritage Foundation's secondary report was strongly biased to the right, estimating that GDP in 2030 would be 2.3% lower than the counterfactual. AEI provided only secondary analysis, referring to a third-party report by an energy consulting firm that estimated only a slightly larger impact on GDP than the EPA report, although AEI's framing de-emphasized the environmental benefit of decreasing greenhouse gas emissions and strongly emphasized its economic impact.

After ACES failed to pass and Republicans took control of the House of Representatives in the 2010 elections, Democrats turned to a federal clean energy portfolio standard as a compromise policy to address climate change. Clean or renewable portfolio standards (RPS) require utility companies to produce a portion of their electricity from non-fossil-fuel sources. Beginning in the late 1990s, 29 states adopted RPS, including Texas and several Republican-controlled states (Barbose 2018). Republican senators such as Lindsey Graham and Sam Brownback signaled support for an RPS during the 112th Congress (Howell 2010).

The most advanced RPS proposal in the Senate was the Clean Energy Standard Act of 2012 (CES), which was introduced by Democratic senator Jeff Bingaman. CES would require electric utilities to generate 24% of their electricity from clean sources beginning in 2015, slowly increasing to 54% by 2025 and 84% by 2037. It would have set up a credit-trading scheme allowing states with less access to cheap solar or wind power to pay states with better access to overproduce clean electricity and make up for their shortfall (Ye 2012). Carbon emissions from electricity generation in 2035 would drop to 60% of 2010 levels. A similar bill was bipartisan during the 111th Congress, but no Republicans joined Democrats in cosponsoring CES in the 112th. It never received a vote.

Like the debate over cap-and-trade, the policy analysis debate over the portfolio standards contained in CES centered around the ability of utility companies to adjust to a post-coal paradigm. If utilities could generate clean electricity cheaply, there would be a relatively small impact on electricity prices. If they could not, prices would increase under constrained electricity supply. These prices would be paid by retail consumers and businesses, resulting in loss of household income and potentially lower economic growth. Unlike the cap-and-trade estimates, analysts could use data from the 29 states that adopted RPS to estimate the impact of a federal standard on prices. Because the law phased in electricity prices over time, analysts predicted the impact of the policy change at different time intervals.

The Energy Information Administration (2012) performed a detailed analysis of the impact of CES. EIA estimated that the 54% requirement in 2025 would increase average retail electricity prices from $0.0929/kWh to $0.0965/kWh, a 4% increase. In 2035, the impact would be stronger, shifting prices from $0.0954/kWh to $0.1129/kWh, an 18% increase. The Congressional Budget Office (2011) also published an extensive report on various RPS in 2011, but only estimated the impact of a more modest 25% clean energy standard.

On the Democratic side, only CAP published a report estimating the impact of CES on electricity prices (Caperton 2012). Borrowing a method from Hickey and Carlson (2010), the CAP report examined the difference in electricity prices before and after states implemented a renewable energy standard. It found that, on average, state electricity prices did not increase following the introduction of a portfolio standard. Therefore, the report concluded, consumers should not expect any net increase in electricity prices from CES or similar laws in the decade following the introduction of a federal standard. The report's conclusions differed from the EIA report because it ignored the size of the standards, which were much less ambitious than the federal standard proposed by CES. CBPP did not produce a report on RPS.

Both the Heritage Foundation and AEI produced reports skeptical of RPS standards, but for different reasons. During the 111th Congress, Heritage published a report on RPS in response to the requirements included in the ACES bill (Kreutzer et al. 2010). The Heritage report assumed that utilities would have to substitute coal electricity generation for wind and solar at current costs to comply with any portfolio standard, rather than costs coming down with technological change or scale. Coal cost $78/mWh and natural gas cost $140/mWh, while onshore wind cost $149/mWh and photovoltaic solar electricity cost $396/mWh.[3] The report calculated that shifting from coal and natural gas to renewable energy would increase electricity prices by 22.5% in 2025 and 36% in 2035, dramatically increasing household costs by $189 per month in 2037. AEI, on the other hand, accepted the EIA data (Zycher 2012). Rather than dispute these data, Zycher, author of the AEI report, argued that recent changes in natural gas extraction technology would make renewables less competitive, especially as they attempted to scale up. He also emphasized the long-term negative impact that higher energy prices would have on the economy, and de-emphasized the potential risks associated with climate change.

Table 9.2 summarizes these predictions. EIA predicted that real retail electricity prices would increase under a renewable energy portfolio standard by 4% in 2025 and 18% in 2035, as utility companies adapted to the changing environment by switching from lower-cost coal to higher-cost renewable energy sources. AEI published a secondary analysis which largely accepted this finding with some reframing, while the CBPP did not issue a report on the topic. CAP published a report which argued that there should be no short-term increases in electricity prices under a renewable portfolio standard, although it did not predict the impact of one on long-term prices. This short-term prediction is slightly to the left of the EIA's prediction of a 4% increase. However, we might also consider the report's omission of a longer-term prediction to be biased in and of itself, since EIA predicted a significant 18% price increase in 2035, as the RPS became more constraining on utility companies, while CAP ignored the more stringent standards of the federal bill relative to state standards. The Heritage Foundation, on the other hand, aggressively

Table 9.2 **Analyses of the Impact of Proposed Renewable Energy Portfolio Standards on Electricity Prices**

Organization	Prices (2025)	Prices (2035)
Democratic		
CAP	0	n/a
CBPP[2]	n/a	n/a
Nonpartisan[1]		
EIA	4.00%	19.00%
Republican		
Heritage Foundation	22.5%[3]	36%
AEI[4]	4.00%	18%

1. The Congressional Budget Office released an extensive report on the impact of renewable energy standards, but their analysis was based on the EIA analysis.

2. The Center on Budget and Policy Priorities did not issue an impact analysis of renewable energy standards.

3. The Heritage Foundation's report released estimates for 2012 and 2035, as well as cumulative impacts in between. The 22.5% figure is interpolated.

4. AEI based its analysis off the Energy Information Agency report.

predicted that prices would rise by 22.5% in 2025, nearly four times as much as the nonpartisan sources, and 36% in 2037. The short-term prediction is biased much farther to the right than CAP's is to the left. However, the long-term prediction is arguably equally biased if we interpret CAP's silence on long-term prices as a prediction of zero change.

To summarize, Heritage's surge in reports was more complicated than just an intensification of questioning the underlying science of climate change. Their reports greatly exaggerated the costs of climate solutions. A Republican policymaker who trusted Heritage would plausibly walk away with the belief that cap-and-trade or federal RPS, solutions they had previously supported, would be prohibitively costly to implement, and might thus change their position.

Climate Change as an Economic Program

As the pushes for regulation of greenhouse gas emissions began to fail, Democratic-aligned think tanks increasingly adopted a policy entrepreneurship strategy to address climate change. This strategy involved using subsidies for renewable energy or "green jobs" as economic stimulus. The Great Recession created both short-term need for a Keynesian economic stimulus and long-term investment in struggling manufacturing and construction industries. By pairing the problems, recession and long-term decline in certain industries, with climate solutions, progressive Democrats hoped to use a window of opportunity to further their policy goals.

After the cap-and-trade bill failed during the summer of 2008, the U.S. economy began to drift toward a recession. Understanding that Congress would have to enact some policy to address the short-term decline in economic output, CAP published their "Green Recovery" report that advocated for renewable energy subsidies, loan guarantees, and energy efficiency (see Chapter 2). They released a companion report claiming that the $100 million investment would also create 2 million good-paying green jobs. Many of their recommendations were incorporated into the American Recovery and Reinvestment Act and contributed to the growth of U.S. renewable energy and electric cars over the next decade but had little direct impact on employment or wages.

When the COVID-19 pandemic hit in 2020, CAP brought out the green jobs argument again. COVID-19 lockdowns caused a historic drop in economic activity, and CAP knew that Congress would need to inject money into a sputtering economy. CAP dusted off some policy proposals that they had discussed in reports in 2018 and 2019, arguing that they would be effective means of addressing both climate change and the economic downturn. In a report titled "Electric Vehicles Should Be a Win for American Workers" (Walter et al. 2020). CAP laid out a plan to subsidize the production of electric vehicles, arguing that increased electric vehicle sales would be a boon for American manufacturing. They argued for job training and apprenticeship programs for electric vehicle manufacturing and maintenance, federal investment in electric car charters, requiring electric vehicle companies that take federal subsidies to use unionized labor, providing generous tax credits for consumers who purchase electric vehicles, and funding transit agency purchases of electric buses.

However, most of CAP's activity on climate change in the 2020s has been to produce traditional policy subsidies for a new Democratic executive branch rather than legislative entrepreneurship. In several reports, they argued that financial regulators should take climate change into account when assessing risk of lending to or investing in companies. For example, the report "The SEC's Time to Act" (Thorn and Green 2021) called for the Security and Exchange Commission to create a mandatory set of environmental social and corporate governance standards and disclosures, improving on the status quo's patchwork of private certifications. They also published reports encouraging auditors to consider climate change risk, for the Federal Reserve to demand increased capital requirements for banks with high climate change risk, and for municipal bonds to disclose climate change risk. These were all modest programs targeted at a small number of executive branch officials with the power to enact such changes without congressional approval. Shortly after the 2020 election, one Biden appointee— Federal Reserve Vice Chair Lael Brainard, in charge of financial regulation—even keynoted a CAP event on financial risk, regulation, and climate change (Center for American Progress 2020).[4]

Summary

The involvement of partisan think tanks on the issue of climate change in the 2000s and 2010s broadly follows patterns to similar those of partisan think tanks and American politics more generally. The political parties took different positions on climate change policy in the early 2000s. In keeping with their basic ideology, Republicans were skeptical of climate science and command-and-control environmental regulation but were initially open to solutions that emphasized clean energy, clean energy mandates, and market-based carbon pricing. Democrats were much more enthusiastic about regulating policy change and tended to regard climate change as an emergency that deserved prioritization. In the mid-2000s, the nonpartisan knowledge regime sounded the alarm about climate change. Impartial experts pushed Republican leaders to attend to the problem despite conservative ideological opposition to another large government intervention into the economy. Leaders in Congress and the White House began to form a bipartisan consensus around a solution, using well-established policy designs that both parties had traditionally supported. The normal mechanisms of problem-solving were working to produce solutions to a pressing problem.

Republican-aligned think tanks then moved aggressively to interrupt the problem-solving process. For years, Heritage and other partisan think tanks had been the leading promoters of climate change denial in American politics. Their Republican allies were sympathetic, often questioning the science of climate change or suppressing nonpartisan scientific information produced by federal bureaucrats. But when the issue hit the agenda more broadly in the mid-2000s, Republicans felt pressure to do something about it. Heritage and their allies snapped into action with a huge surge in reports addressing climate change. They were successful at persuading Republican elites not only to oppose the specific solutions being considered before Congress, but to deny the underlying science of climate change more broadly.

Why were Republican-aligned think tanks more successful in the late 2000s than they had been previously? Heritage, AEI, and others had a long history of climate change skepticism before the late 2000s, but they briefly lost the argument in the Republican Party when the climate change issue hit the agenda. It required a massive surge in attention from Heritage to pull the Republican Party back from addressing the problem when it became salient and cement lasting opposition to any regulation of greenhouse gas emissions in the Republican Party. It may be that partisan think tanks needed a concrete policy alternative to argue against. For their part, Democrats avoided specifying a broad climate solution prior to the late 2000s, even while sounding the alarm about the seriousness of the problem in their platforms. Concrete policy alternatives allowed partisan think tanks to argue against both the abstract concept of climate science or regulation of greenhouse gases and also the costs and benefits of significant policy changes.

Seeing the newly energized Republican Party opposition to doing anything to regulate greenhouse gas emissions, Democratic-aligned think tanks pivoted to a policy entrepreneurship strategy. They linked the economic struggles of the Great Recession to potential "green jobs" created by renewable energy subsidies. They were initially successful, managing to get a large package of renewable energy subsidies into the 2009 stimulus bill, but made few gains afterward. By 2020, they were engaging in far smaller scale policy subsidy strategies, focusing on where they could support allied appointees to use bits of delegated power to make incremental changes to federal policy on climate change.

10

Democracy and the Information Wars

In 2015 a small group of former Cato Institute staffers founded a new think tank called the Niskanen Center. Cato, a large libertarian think tank originally founded by Charles Koch, has at times played a role similar to that of AEI and Heritage, but its importance in the Republican policymaking apparatus waxes and wanes as the importance of libertarianism within the party shifts (Medvetz 2014). At the height of the conservative backlash to the scientific consensus on climate change, the Cato Institute published more books promoting climate change denial than did any other organization (Dunlap and Jacques 2013). Over time, some of Cato's researchers, led by energy scholar Jerry Taylor (2018),[1] became convinced that their skeptical view of climate change was wrong, but they found little interest in engaging with the scientific consensus within Cato. In an essay titled "The Alternative to Ideology," Taylor (2018) argued that ideology, defined as a priori beliefs about the proper role of government in society, has limited utility in policy debates. Motivated reasoning caused normative beliefs to bleed into positivist beliefs about the impacts of public policy. Taylor wrote, "Over and over again, libertarian friends and colleagues were engaged in fierce, uncompromising debate about empirical matters that had nothing to do with libertarian principles or commitments. Is the Keynesian multiplier consequential? Is Thomas Piketty correct that returns to capital are greater than the rate of growth? Do tax cuts pay for themselves? A libertarian could take either side of those disputes without having to recant any of their principles or fundamental beliefs. But to cross the party line on these or an ocean of similar empirical matters was to risk unemployment." This kind of motivated reasoning leads think tanks to produce what Taylor calls "lazy, decoder-ring policy analysis" in support of ideological conclusions. His criticism extends beyond Cato to ideologically motivated think tanks more generally. Taylor argues that if you approach a problem with an ideological conclusion in mind, you will inevitably find evidence to support that conclusion. Thus ideological organizations like partisan think tanks lead to not just more extreme public policy but also incorrect predictions.

Niskanen's solution to the problem is a strong commitment to problem-solving based on the scientific consensus. In an essay titled "The Center Can Hold," Brinks

Lindsey and coauthors (2018) argue for a moderate vision for public policy. Critically, their definition of "moderate" argues that government should solve problems facing the American people without preconceptions about the size or proper role of government:

> Success in this effort will require not just new policies, but a whole new way of thinking about policy. The center can hold, but first it must be fortified with new convictions. There are, to be sure, many reasons why our political system has failed to address the mounting problems and dissatisfactions of the 21st century. But one crucially important and widely neglected factor is that the two prevailing ideological lenses, on the left and right, have gaping blind spots that render the most promising path forward invisible.
>
> To translate these broad principles into programs and policies, we believe there is no substitute for ongoing empirical investigation and critical scrutiny. In the United States and other advanced democracies, we are poised at the frontier of scientific, technological, economic, social, and cultural change. As a result, for many issues facing us the best path forward is far from obvious; we have no choice but to improvise and explore. (3)

Niskanen offers a stark contrast to Heritage, CAP, and the other partisan think tanks discussed in this book. They want to fill a similar partisan think tank role for a reformed Republican party, but without the ideological bias. Wilkinson and other Niskanen co-founders argue that the center-right needs a think tank grounded to help like-minded reformers in the party rebuild it after the Trump and Heritage eras (Klein 2019). They have had some high-profile successes, such as designing Mitt Romney's Family Security Act in 2021 and 2022, which would replace current cash welfare benefits with a monthly tax credit similar to the one temporarily introduced by Democrats in the American Rescue Plan in 2021. In a report titled "The Conservative Case for a Child Allowance" (Hammond and Orr 2021), two Niskanen researchers argued that a monthly child allowance would help reduce child poverty and family instability and increase birth rates. More important, they argued it should appeal to philosophical conservatives who care about supporting families and good childrearing. After Democrats failed to find the votes for a more expansive child tax credit, a group of CBPP researchers released a report supporting the new tax credit's structure but criticizing some of the funding mechanisms, specifically conveying an opposition to cutting too much funding from the childless poor (Marr et al. 2022). These types of dialogues play out among partisan think tanks operating at their best to grapple with the same basic understanding of facts while seeking a consensus to solve a problem.

Unfortunately, Niskanen has neither enjoyed the rapid success of nor influenced emulators in the way that the Heritage did previously. To accomplish that sort of reach it may require its own "Ronald Reagan moment," an opportunity to form an alliance with a powerful and charismatic figure who represents a different vision for the Republican Party. For now, more ideological partisan think tanks continue to dominate the political space.

Niskanen's emergence and relative prominence is a product of growing dissatisfaction with the think tank ecosystem that had matured by the 2010s. Heritage had always been a far-right organization, but became even more ideological when the original generation of Heritage leaders retired or were pushed out. In 2013, when founder Ed Feulner retired, South Carolina senator Jim DeMint abruptly resigned his seat to become Heritage's president, earning a seven-figure salary (Heritage Foundation 2014). DeMint reoriented the think tank away from conservative policy analysis, toward a more confrontational, overtly political role (Ball 2013). He pushed out several longtime Heritage researchers, most notably the think tank's top domestic policy scholar, Stuart Butler, who DeMint thought had spent too much time trying to work out compromises with Democrats.[2] Four years later, Heritage's board, led by Feulner, fired DeMint for pushing the organization too far away from conservative intellectualism and toward electoral politics (Johnson and Cook 2017).

I find it revealing that when Senator Mike Lee introduced a resolution honoring Heritage on its 50th anniversary, all the policy accomplishments it listed were from the mid-1990s or earlier. The accomplishments he listed in the 2010s had nothing to do with policy, including starting its own media organization, creating a 501(c)(4) lobbying organization, and creating research centers named after large donors (Senate Resolution 164 2023).

AEI has largely resisted the Republican Party's turn toward partisan warfare and Trumpism. AEI did not invite Trump or senior Trump allies to its annual private retreat, but did invite leading Republican critics of Trump's plan to overturn the 2020 election, including Arizona governor Doug Ducey, Maryland governor Larry Hogan, and even Biden's director of the National Economic Council Brian Deese (Costa 2022). In 2022, AEI even hired prominent CAP political scientist Ruy Teixeira, who famously authored *The Emerging Democratic Majority* in 2002. Teixeira faulted the organization and broader progressive movement for focusing too much on issues related to identity rather than class (Schaffer 2022).

Similarly, CAP became a more explicitly political organization during the Trump Era. After allegations emerged about connections between the 2016 Trump campaign, Trump associates, and Russia, CAP created a program called the Moscow Project, aimed at explaining and highlighting issues raised during the investigation. They produced a podcast titled *The Asset*, alluding to a belief that Trump was a Russian intelligence asset. They tried to extend the association between Trump and Russia to the broader Republican Party, repeatedly calling Senate Majority Leader Mitch McConnell "Moscow Mitch" for defending Trump.

Other think tanks looking to chart a different course from the big partisan think tanks formed alongside Niskanen, particularly on the right. Five former staffers at the Heartland Institute, a right-wing think tank focused on promoting climate denial, founded the R Street Institute in 2012. The staffers were working on insurance policy when Heartland sponsored a billboard that featured a mugshot of Ted Kaczynski and the message "I still believe in Global Warming. Do you?" They resigned in disgust and sought to create a conservative think tank devoted to high-quality policy analysis under the motto "Free Markets. Real Solutions" (Lehrer 2023). R Street's president Eli Lehrer worked at both Heritage and AEI before Heartland. In contrast to higher-profile think tanks like Heritage, Lehrer's strategy has been to "focus on low salience, highly complex issues. That's another way of saying boring." R Street grew quickly, from a modest $2 million budget in 2013 to more than $10 million in their latest tax filing (R Street Institute 2022).

Oren Cass, a former Romney staffer, founded the think tank American Compass to attempt to steer the Republican Party away from laissez-faire economics and toward a conservative economic policy centered on families (Olson 2020). In an essay published by American Compass, former Heritage staffer James M. Roberts (2022) criticized a "conservatism on autopilot" promoted inside Heritage and other large conservative think tanks for reflexively supporting free-market policy, even if evidence suggests that these policies might be ineffective. Roberts, noting that most conservative policy goals have not changed since the end of the Cold War, argues that the problem is a lack of innovation from conservative think tanks:

> Like Hollywood studios, conservative think tanks have become addicted to making sequels of the blockbusters that clicked in the past. As a result, it's clear that too much of the talent has forgotten how to do original, inspiring work. The audience, meanwhile, becomes comfortable with a particular formula, and stops paying to see anything else.
>
> That narrative will prevent conservatives from ever wielding power effectively. Of course, we need entrepreneurs. But we also need public policy. Young conservatives need to gain experience and knowledge by working in government. Facing a federal bureaucracy that tilts heavily to the left, they will have to compete for career federal jobs and also run for office at every government level. The antiquated, "holier than thou" message tells them instead that government service is bad and they too should become hedge fund managers.

However, the big four partisan think tanks remain strong. AEI, CAP, CBPP, and Heritage reported a combined $236 million in 501(c)(3) expenditures in 2021, each employing hundreds of researchers and support staff (see Chapter 3). The start-ups that seek to challenge their position are still nascent, and a story for another day. The remainder of this chapter summarizes the conclusions that can be drawn from my study of the four major partisan think tanks, as well as the implications of those conclusions for American democracy, and provides suggestions for future researchers.

The Critical Juncture of 1973

The creation of the Heritage Foundation in 1973 was a critical turning point in the development of American party politics. The political entrepreneurs who founded Heritage invented a new organizational structure for think tanks, opening the door to potent new advocacy strategies. This structure allowed think tanks to form closer bonds with policymakers and use policy analysis and control of a party's policy workforce as tools to accomplish their policy goals. Heritage's success spawned imitators: the think tank landscape is now dominated by advocacy-style think tanks.

The Heritage model was particularly well-suited for think tanks that worked closely with political parties, allowing them to carve out a role as privately controlled formal party organizations. Heritage and its imitators became close policy advisors to political parties. Naturally office-seeking organizations, political parties make policy decisions to help them win more seats in future elections. They have a complex relationship with allied interest groups, which seek to win elections to achieve public policy goals. Formal party organizations usually stand firmly on the office-seeking side of the relationship because they are directly controlled by the party and its elected officials. In most democracies, party think tanks function like any other formal party organization. They serve the office-seeking interests of political parties, which in most cases means providing accurate information focused on earning the support of the median voter and effectively solving those problems that emerge on the policy agenda. When forced to rely on privately controlled organizations to perform these same functions, political parties risk being captured by policy-seeking interest groups.

Why did Heritage surface and become so influential so quickly? To some extent, the think tank was pushing on an open door. The scope of the American federal government's policy agenda expanded tremendously during the "Great Broadening" of the 1950s–1970s (Jones, Theriault, and Whyman 2019). National political parties had to make salient policy decisions at the federal level around issues that had previously been left to state and local governments or were not on the agenda at all, such as education, civil rights, energy, and environmental policy. Modern conservatism as a coherent intellectual ideology emerged in the 1950s (Noel 2014) but took decades to produce significant changes in the party's policy positions. Works like *The Road to Serfdom* (Hayek 1944), *God and Man at Yale* (Buckley 1951), the *National Review* (established by Buckley in 1955), and *Capitalism and Freedom* (Friedman 1962) captured the imagination of ideological conservatives. However, they failed to convince the Eisenhower, Nixon, and Ford administrations and their counterparts in congressional leadership to adopt the conservative policy agenda framed in their pages. Indeed, Republicans participated in the expansion of the federal government's policy agenda as much as Democrats did during the period (Jones, Theriault, and Whyman 2019). Republican Party politicians were open to these ideas, but they lacked a vector for transmitting theory into policy. Instead, they sought policy advice from nonpartisans in the federal bureaucracy, nonpartisan think tanks, and academia. Partisan think tanks did not need to invent new ideas; they just had to package those ideas for a receptive audience of conservative Republican politicians. Their early alliance with Ronald Reagan paid off, allowing an organization that did not exist at the beginning of the 1970s access into the party's innermost circle by the 1980s. Conservative donors, professional legal organizations, and grassroots activists emerged concurrently as political forces. Heritage showed up at the right time in the right place to become the most influential partisan think tank in the United States, and it went on to play a key part in the transformation of the Republican Party.

After Heritage and other partisan think tanks emerged as powerful players in American party politics, factual understanding of public policy became much more contested than it had been previously. Interest groups, bureaucrats, and others had always competed to serve as the dominant source of analysis in any policy debate, but Heritage added a powerful partisan dimension. Experts may disagree on the answer to questions related to public policy, but those disagreements were not previously weaponized in policy debates in the ways they were after 1973. Today policymakers seeking answers within most salient policy debates will find multiple competing partisan claims to truth, allowing them to pick the one that confirms their biases or fits their preexisting goals. The environment is still competitive—neutral expertise can be found throughout the policy process—but the competition for "truth" is fiercer than it used to be. Groups like the Niskanen Center are trying to provide the same aggressive advocacy think tank strategies to centrists, but so far have not found similar success and influence. Political parties are great at spreading conflict around a system and bringing in nonparticipants to policy fights (Fagan, McGee, and Thomas 2019). Nonaligned think tanks lack access to similar conflict-expanding mechanisms, limiting their reach when compared with their partisan counterparts.

Partisan Think Tanks as an Instrument for Polarization

Partisan think tanks have clearly played a role in the polarization of American political parties. Their increasing size and influence are strongly correlated with increasing polarization in Congress. When Heritage was created in 1973, the American political system was in many ways at a high point for interparty cooperation on policymaking. The previous two decades saw the two parties work together to reshape the American federal government, with successes including the Civil Rights Act and Voting Rights Act, the building of the Interstate Highway System, the creation of Medicare and Medicaid, and the establishment of the Environmental Protection Agency. A key factor in this cooperation was consensus in accepting neutral expertise as an authoritative source of policy analysis. Heritage's creation was in large part a reaction to that consensus, and their mission was to undermine it to create a more conservative Republican Party.

They succeeded. The policymaking consensus between political parties broke down. Their preferences for public policy, once bound together by problem-solving and a mutual understanding of the costs, impacts, and trade-offs of policy alternatives, diverged. Today political parties integrate partisan think tanks into their policymaking apparatus. On individual issues, partisan think tank reports, lobbying, citations, and hearing testimony are all strongly correlated with polarization.

It would be too simple to conclude that partisan think tanks cause something as complex as polarization. Partisan think tanks were both a manifestation of and a complementary piece to bigger forces pushes the parties apart. Indeed, American political parties have been highly polarized for most of the country's history, while partisan think tanks have been a feature in its party system for less than 50 years. Even if they occupy a role akin to a formal party organization, American political parties are relatively weak compared to political parties in most advanced democracies, and the information environment is competitive. If the Heritage Foundation and its imitators were never established, American politics would likely still be more polarized today than in 1973.

Rather, we should characterize partisan think tanks as instrumental to increasing and accelerating the polarization of American political parties. After ideological conservatives and progressives developed strong and distinct worldviews, they needed assistance to actualize their ideas into public policy. A publication like the *National Review* or a popular academic work like *The Road to Serfdom* produce neither actionable policy proposals nor the entrepreneurship necessary to market them as solutions to problems that hit the agenda. Grassroots organizations, ideological donors, ambitious politicians, and partisan media organizations need policy proposals to get behind if their activities are going to ultimately affect American public policy. Partisan think tanks were the instrument through which these polarizing actors and organizations actualized their broad goals into concrete policy. Under the counterfactual where they never emerged, these actors would likely have had more trouble seeing their extreme ideas reflected in actual public policy. They may have found other avenues for influence, but the nonpartisan knowledge regime may have curbed their positions, moderating the kinds of extreme stances political parties are more able to take today.

The counterfactual, where national American political parties are not reliant on highly ideological and privately controlled think tanks to form the core of their policy advisory systems, is difficult to test. However, researchers might be able to examine variation in partisan think tanks across U.S. states or across democratic countries to better understand their role in shaping how political parties process information. Republican-controlled states that had strong conservative think tanks were more likely to reject the proposed Medicaid expansion despite strong problem-solving reasons to accept large amounts of federal spending and strong support for Medicaid from business associations (Hertel-Fernandez, Skocpol, and Lynch 2016). The same state-based partisan think tanks are associated with opposition to climate policy (Skocpol and Hertel-Fernandez 2016). U.S. state legislatures are often much less professional than the U.S. Congress and have many fewer internal expert resources. They may be especially likely to accept information from partisan think tanks.

There are also opportunities to explore the impact of privately controlled partisan think tanks on political parties outside of the United States. While most democracies give political parties control over partisan think tanks, some do not (Campbell and Pedersen 2014). Israel has recently seen an explosion of think tanks associated with right-wing parties (Weinglass 2019); most prominently, conservative American donors helped fund the creation of the Kohelet Policy Forum in 2012 (Slyomovics 2021). Kohelet carved out a close relationship with Israel's leading center-right Likud Party. The organization saw itself as a counterweight to the Israel Democracy Institute, a nonpartisan centrist think tank like the Brookings Institution. In 2018 its executive director, a former Likud staffer named Meir Rubin, boasted, "We run the Knesset," which was then controlled by a Likud-led coalition (Sadeh 2018). Kohelet has pushed Likud to support more free-market economic policies similar to the policies supported by American conservatives, even though Israeli politics has historically not seen the same kind of support for laissez-faire economics as American politics (Slyomovics 2021; Weinglass 2019). We might expect Kohelet to move Likud and its allies toward the right on issues that it emphasizes, such as opposition to government oversight of daycare and the Israeli healthcare system (Slyomovics 2021).

Asymmetric Polarization of Elite Information

The information polarization enabled by partisan think tanks has pushed both parties toward the extremes but in an asymmetric formation. The Republican Party built its alternative knowledge regime in explicit opposition to the nonpartisan knowledge regime, while the Democratic Party built its regime to supplement and complement the status quo. Both partisan regimes lead to more polarized position-taking by the political parties, but the information they provide varies considerably.

The Republican Party's conservative ideology was created as an explicit critique of the nonpartisan knowledge regime. Buckley's *God and Man at Yale*, which crystallized the intellectual foundation of the modern conservative ideology (Noel

2014), centered around Buckley's opposition to academia and critiques of racial equality, Keynesian economics, and secularism. He characterized these ideas as inherently liberal rather than nonpartisan, and argued that these ideologies required a conservative counterweight. He and other conservative intellectual leaders of the 1950s and 1960s extended this critique to other nonpartisan experts, including the growing bureaucracy, professional classes of policy analysts, and major nonpartisan think tanks. Perceiving these institutions to be liberal rather than impartial, they felt betrayed by fellow Republicans who worked within government to solve problems.

Conservatives grew distrustful of neutral expertise. When Republicans created their knowledge regime in the 1970s, they built it with the express purpose of providing an alternative to the expertise that conservative elites had come to regard as liberal. Today reports by the Heritage Foundation arrive at conclusions that are wildly out of line with the conclusions of neutral experts on a wide variety of issues, but Heritage and others can convince Republicans to adopt these views because they have succeeded in staking a claim to alternative bases of data, fact, and "truth."

The conservative antipathy toward neutral expertise was never clearer than during the Trump administration. Immediately after taking power, the Trump administration eliminated public references to climate change from federal government websites (Davenport 2017). To force out career scientists in federal agencies, it aggressively reassigned civil servants to new locations and responsibilities (Clement 2017). It blocked career federal scientists from traveling to conferences (Friedman 2017) and testifying before Congress (Friedman 2019). It prevented the release of dozens of peer-reviewed studies from the Agricultural Research Service funded by taxpayers (Evich 2019). It retaliated against economists in the Department of Agriculture's Economic Research Service for publishing research finding that farmers were harmed by the administration's trade policies and changes to tax law (Mccrimmon 2019). It created a process of "red team, blue team" exercises to question peer-reviewed research funded by the federal government (Plumer and Davenport 2019). It imposed onerous requirements on scientific research that could be used to inform EPA regulations, such as requiring that public health studies use non-anonymized data (Friedman 2019). It proposed eliminating the Congressional Budget Office's role in estimating the cost of legislation and replacing it with outside estimates, including those from the Heritage Foundation (Klein 2017). Conservatives may have seen these scientists as "liberal," but from the perspectives of the technocrats, they were just doing their jobs in as impartial a manner as possible.

Democrats never had the same antipathic relationship with neutral experts. Modern liberalism rarely came into conflict with the nonpartisan knowledge regime, and thus it was to the advantage of Democrats to regard neutral experts as allies rather than enemies. However, as the party developed a growing progressive movement, it found the nonpartisan regime insufficient to meet its needs. On some issues, like foreign policy, progressives found themselves outside the mainstream consensus and felt the need to elevate analysts who disagreed with the foreign policy experts at nonpartisan think tanks.

However, on most issues they looked for a knowledge regime to fill the same role that party think tanks occupy in other democracies. CAP became a shadow government for the Democratic Party, and in many ways became more explicitly integrated into it than Heritage ever was, with CAP presidents serving in high-level White House roles. CAP and the CBPP did not aggressively change their agendas to match the issues before Congress, instead choosing to play the role of policy entrepreneurs and to subsidize Democratic issue priorities. When their research produced conclusions that conflicted with nonpartisans, their conclusions were less divergent than those of their Republican counterparts. The new partisan think tank knowledge regime helped Democrats support a more progressive policy agenda, but it kept one foot in the technocratic world.

Democracy and the Information Wars

More than many other types of polarization, elite information polarization disrupts American democracy. The many veto points in the U.S. constitutional system usually force both political parties to work together to change public policy. Even as the two political parties came to represent distinct coalitions with fewer cross-cutting issues after the 1970s, they should still be able to find common ground if they have a common understanding of the problems that Americans are concerned about and the causes and effects of public policy. They should be able to find compromise either by finding the middle ground between two opposing viewpoints or by selecting policy solutions that support the parties' orthogonal goals. Problem-solving naturally exerts centripetal forces on a party system, especially when the parties must compromise to overcome veto points. The parties in many advanced democracies strongly disagree with each other yet still manage to build consensus around solutions to major issues.

Yet in the contemporary U.S. context, we see how information polarization can make solving problems impossible. If the two political parties truly believe in a different understanding of how policy works, then they cannot find consensus around problem-solving. They could each try in earnest to solve problems in good faith yet come to opposite conclusions about the impact of a policy alternative. They might strongly disagree about the material costs of a program, making it difficult to calibrate a compromise. The parties may even begin to disagree about whether a problem is a problem, or how severe it is, such as when partisan think tanks helped push Republicans toward climate change denial. Gridlock becomes common when both parties prefer the status quo over policy changes (Binder 1999; Krehbiel 1998). The party system requires more dire problems or dramatic focusing events in order to force the political parties to agree to some policy solution, or else problem-solving becomes limited to more marginal areas where the parties have less disagreement.

Where parties can act alone, they might choose ineffective solutions to solve their problems. Their good intentions might be compromised by partisan think tanks disrupting the problem-solving process with bad policy analysis, or they might hijack the agenda through policy entrepreneurship. These strategies may be less effective when parties are forced to, and able to, find compromise with each other, but not once those avenues are closed off.

The result of information polarization is a less representative democracy. Citizens want their government to do something to solve salient policy problems (Egan 2014). Even if representatives hear this message loud and clear, they may not be able to overcome the blockages created by information polarization to address the real problems facing their constituents. Worse yet, as we've seen with climate change denial, representatives may respond, often in good faith, by telling their voters that the problem they are identifying isn't real or worthy of their attention. Citizens see more and more problems persist, but their concerns get eaten up by a political system unable to do anything about them. They may lose faith that democracy can solve their problems and seek out peronsalitistic or authoritarian leaders.

Problems that go unsolved for longer require more dramatic interventions once they get too bad to ignore. Punctuated equilibrium theory, a political science framework that explains why systems often see long periods of stasis interrupted by short periods of radical policy change, has a concept to explain these kinds of information-processing deficiencies (Jones and Baumgartner 2005). Systems with friction, or institutions and dynamics that impede decision-making, tend to experience this kind of sclerosis. When problems go unsolved for too long, they risk spiraling out of control into a policy disaster (Fagan 2022). The United States is already a high-friction system compared with other democracies due to its fractured and veto-laden constitutional structure (Fagan, Jones, and Wlezien 2017). Punctuated equilibrium scholars understand that institutions that decrease information-processing efficiency will slow down policy change, but they have failed to consider information polarization as a factor impeding decision-making in the context of problem-solving. Privately funded partisan think tanks are one important source of information polarization, but scholars might explore other sources, such as highly ideological political movements like communist or libertarian parties.

Partisan think tanks have an uncertain role in the future of American politics. From the 1970s until the 2010s, American political elites were polarized, but the electorate remained stubbornly centrist (Dimock et al. 2014). Partisan think tanks emerged during this time as an instrument to steer elite opinion away from the median voter and toward the ideological extremes. Sometime around the election of Barack Obama, Americans began to follow elites into coherent and consistent ideological beliefs, stopped splitting their votes between parties, and formed into two distinct political coalitions for the first time in over a century (Sides, Tesler, and

Vavreck 2018). This change radically transformed the ways in which American polarization manifested. Rather than just polarizing over policy, the political parties are now engaged in brutal partisan warfare and constitutional hardball (Drutman 2017; Theriault 2013). The parties still have distinct positions, but those positions matter less today for electoral competition than they did in the 1990s because few voters are open to persuasion. In this environment, partisan think tanks may choose to fade into the background, pushing policy on lower-salience issues while the parties engage in battle. Alternatively, they may enter the fray by producing information attacking the other party or proposing extreme policies that the party can enact.

There has been a generational change in the leadership of the major partisan think tanks. Ed Feulner, who turned 81 in 2023, briefly resumed leading the Heritage Foundation in 2017, but retired for good after handing off the think tank to new leadership. CAP founder John Podesta, 74, returned to government as a senior advisor to the Biden administration on climate issues in 2022 to oversee implementation of renewable energy investments in the Inflation Reduction Act of 2022 (Grandoni and Pager 2022). CBPP founder Robert Greenstein retired from his leadership role in 2021. At his retirement party, Speaker of the House Nancy Pelosi said, "It is my privilege, on behalf of the millions of lives that we know you've saved, to say thank you, thank you for lifting people up, for giving them hope" (Matthews 2022). After being led by philosopher Arthur Brooks for a decade, AEI passed its leadership mantle to Robert Doar, a lower-profile former official in the New York Republican Pataki and Bloomberg mayoral administrations. Unlike their founders, the new generation of leaders inherited a think tank ecosystem at the center of a deeply divided American party politics.

METHODOLOGICAL APPENDIX
TO CHAPTERS 5–7

Data Collection

White Papers

To measure attention to policy in partisan think tank information production, I collected data on their white papers from 2004 to 2016. Writing and disseminating research or policy arguments in the form of reports, books, explainers, and other documents is the heart of any think tank's mission. Each think tank in the sample produced thousands of white papers during this period on a wide range of policy issues. Their subject matters were similarly broad, ranging from a two-page analysis on a pending piece of legislation to comparisons of cost estimates for a range of policy options and full economic analyses that would not be out of place in an academic journal. House styles varied by institution. For example, the Heritage Foundation tended to produce a greater number of shorter white papers focused on making arguments about policy but without much original research, while the American Enterprise Institute tended to produce fewer but longer white papers conducting original research.

I first collected all white papers listed on websites of the American Enterprise Institute, Center on Budget and Policy Priorities, Center for American Progress, and Heritage Foundation from 2001 to 2016. These four think tanks represent the largest partisan think tanks during the period. I collected the title, abstracts or summaries, and any available metadata listed under the website's "Reports" or "Research" section, using filters where available to eliminate blog posts, press releases, or other nonreport outputs (see Figure A.1 for an example). This process yielded 14,255 reports. I then read each title and any available abstract or summary and assigned it to one of 20 Policy Agendas Project major topic codes.[1] If I was unable to assign a code based on these shorter observations, I read the full report to determine which issue the report addressed and assigned it to a major topic area.

Figure A.2 shows the percentage of white papers assigned to each of the 20 major policy topics. We see huge variation in the issues that partisan think tank white

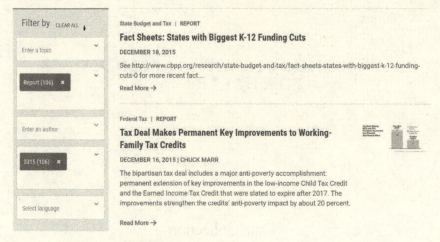

Figure A.1 White paper data collection example.

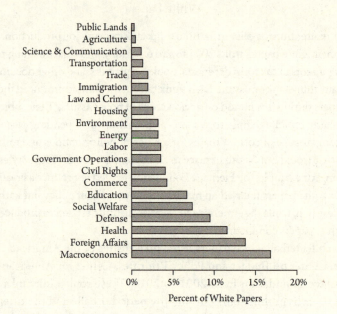

Figure A.2 Distribution of white paper policy attention.

papers address. Macroeconomics, defense, healthcare, and foreign affairs collectively make up about 40% of all white papers. Public lands, agriculture, science and communication, and transportation all receive very small shares of issue attention. However, these raw numbers are difficult to interpret because the government's policy agenda is distributed unevenly across categories. In order to adjust for the baseline demand for white paper–like information by Congress, I compared white paper attention to the policy content of Congressional Research Service reports

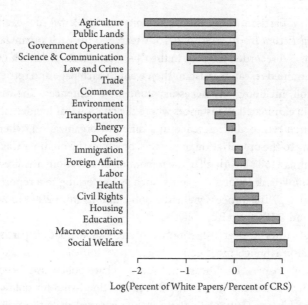

Figure A.3 Distribution of white paper policy attention relative to CRS reports.

(see Fagan and McGee 2022). CRS is Congress's internal think tank. It provides detailed policy reports on a broad range of issues, and thus allows us to compare information produced by outside think tanks to general demand for expert information from a nonpartisan internal congressional information producer. Figure A.3 shows the natural log of the ratio of the percentage of partisan think tank white papers to CRS reports. A positive result indicates that partisan think tanks devote relatively more attention to the issue, while a negative result indicates the opposite. Think tanks tend to focus on social welfare, macroeconomics, healthcare, education, housing, and civil rights when compared to CRS reports.

Congressional Record Citations

To measure the distribution of attention in congressional consumption of partisan think tank information, I used think tank citations by members of Congress in the *Congressional Record*. Members of Congress frequently make arguments about policy either on the floor of Congress or in committee. Their arguments often invoke various forms of policy analysis, including information from partisan think tanks. Citing partisan think tanks indicates that they have both received the information and are using it in policymaking. The information either directly impacted policy decision-making or is being used to support one side in public policy debates. By observing the distribution of policy attention in citations, we can infer the policy topics on which members tend to consume partisan think tank information.

I collected partisan think tank citations using keyword searches of the *Congressional Record* from 2004 to 2016. I searched for each organization's name and acronym and recorded the page in the *Congressional Record* in which the search appeared. A trained research assistant then went to each page and retrieved the text of the citation, including any necessary contextual sentences. The assistant then identified and eliminated all instances where the citation was incidental,[2] where the keyword search returned a reference to a different organization, where members were referring to the organization negatively, or where the member was referencing the think tank as a foil.[3] Nearly all of the remaining observations are direct references to partisan think tank reports or events, such as "According to a report by [organization name]. . . ." This process yielded 1,868 citations from 2004 to 2016, 763 by Democrats and 1,105 from Republicans.

Figure A.4 shows the overall distribution of attention to policy in partisan citations. The distribution is much more concentrated in its top category, macroeconomics, than were white papers. Healthcare and social welfare policy also receive a considerable number of citations. These are often motivating issues for political parties as they are owned by the Democratic Party as their core redistributive policy goals and important to laissez-faire policy goals of the Republican Party (Fagan 2019). The same five issues with significant local dimensions, science and communication, public lands, transportation, agriculture, and trade, receive few citations. Next, Figure A.5 compares citations relative to Congress's attention using the natural log of the ratio of the percentage of citations to the percentage of congressional hearings. We see a distribution similar to that of white papers, with a few exceptions. Immigration policy, one of the emergent highly contentious issues of the 2004–16 period, is significantly

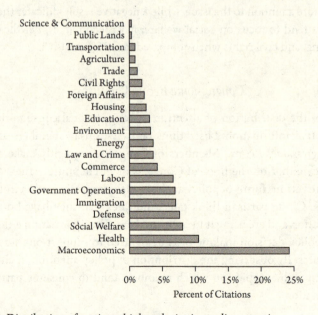

Figure A.4 Distribution of partisan think tank citation policy attention.

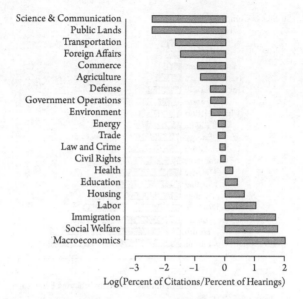

Figure A.5 Distribution of citation policy attention relative to hearings.

overrepresented by partisan think tank citations. Foreign affairs, historically a consensus issue, is significantly underrepresented. Because these citations are drawn from relatively high-profile statements on the floor of Congress, they may represent members using partisan think tank citations in public debates, and thus are more likely to be used on contentious issues than on less contentious issues.

Lobbying Disclosure Reports

While all four partisan think tanks are primarily 501(c)(3) nonprofit corporations that cannot directly lobby, the Heritage Foundation, CAP, and CBPP maintain companion 501(c)(4) lobbying organizations. These organizations employ full-time lobbyists to directly advocate for the organization's policy goals and pay a portion of the 501(c)(3) employees' salaries to allow them to directly advocate for legislation without violating tax law. The 501(c)(4) organizations file quarterly Lobbying Disclosure Act (LDA) reports with the House and Senate to identify all bills that they advocated for. Unlike the other data sets that capture public activity, these lobbying disclosure reports allow us to observe behind-the-scenes lobbying by think tank. The Center for Responsive Politics extracts the bill numbers for each bill named in an LDA report. I collected all 909 bill identifiers named in these reports. I then paired the extracted bills to the Congressional Bills Project data set to identify their policy content.

Figure A.6 shows the overall distribution of bills named in think tank lobbying disclosure reports. Unlike other outputs, government operations is the standout category. This difference is likely due to lobbying on provisions

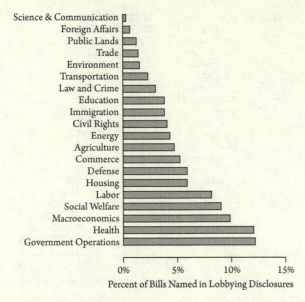

Figure A.6 Distribution of attention to policy in bills named in lobbying disclosures.

in annual omnibus appropriations bills, which are coded under government operations when considered as one package, rather than coded for the policy content of their individual components. Other than government operations, the policy content of lobbying disclosure reports strongly resembles the other outputs, with a heavy focus on domestic redistributive economic policy and less focus on policy with a more localized dimension. However, the picture changes slightly when compared to all Congress bills. In Figure A.7, we see that agriculture policy is the fourth most overrepresented topic in LDA reports. As with government operations, this may be due to the structure of bills and the PAP coding system; large farm bills often include both agriculture policy and means-tested food aid. When means-tested food aid is discussed on its own it would be coded as social welfare policy, which is in line with the partisan think tanks' focus on redistributed domestic economic policy, but the larger bill would be categorized as agriculture policy.

Hearing Witnesses

Finally, I measured partisan think tank testimony before congressional hearings. Members of Congress use hearings to define problems, identify potential solutions, and field public arguments (Bawn 1997; Lewallen, Theriault, and Jones 2016; Workman, Shafran, and Bark 2017). Partisan think tanks frequently testify before these hearings to help members achieve their goals. While a handful of hearings receive substantial media attention each year, many are lower-profile affairs

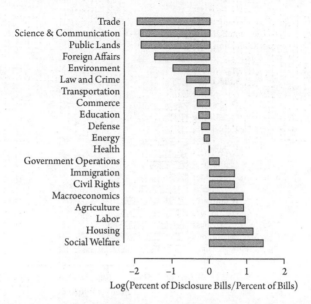

Figure A.7 Attention to policy in bills disclosed in lobbying disclosures relative to bills.

where members of Congress genuinely seek information that may be useful in policymaking (Lewallen, Theriault, and Jones 2016). I identified each instance of testimony recorded in the ProQuest Congressional database using keyword searches, aggregating by Congress. I then paired each identified hearing to one coded by the PAP for policy content. This process yielded 443 witnesses between 2004 and 2016.

Figure A.8 shows the overall distribution of attention to policy in hearings where partisan think tanks testified. The distribution is more mixed than the other three outputs. Think tanks are called to testify frequently in foreign policy, defense, commerce, and energy hearings, as well as the traditional domestic economic policy areas of healthcare and macroeconomics. On the low end, they are rarely called to testify on issues with local dimensions, as well as education. Given that education scholars point to the important role of think tanks in structuring debates over education reform during this period (Haas 2007; McDonald 2014), their decreased presence in hearings is surprising. However, when we compare their testimony to all hearings in Figure A.9 we find that macroeconomics, social welfare, and housing are top issues.

Measuring Polarization across Issues

While numerous scholars have focused on polarization increasing on individual issues or groups of issues (for example, see Karol 2019; Layman and Carsey 2002;

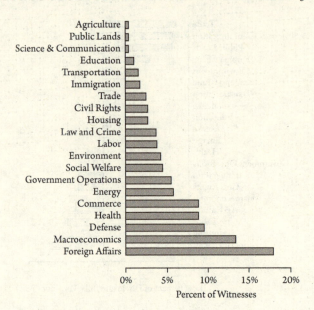

Figure A.8 Distribution of testimony attention to policy.

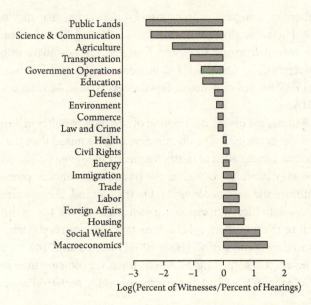

Figure A.9 Distribution of relative testimony policy attention relative to hearings.

Lindaman and Haider-Markel 2002), only a handful of scholars have attempted to measure polarization across the 20 PAP major topics. Jochim and Jones (2013) examined changes in polarization across policy topics and time. They use a scaling procedure similar to NOMINATE to compare the dimensionality of issues. Due to

the large number of roll call votes necessary to use the scaling procedure, they estimate change in dimensionality across two periods of 15 years each. They find that
most of the increased polarization occurred in a handful of major topics: education,
science and communication, public lands, transportation, healthcare, and business,
while the other topics did not change significantly. Thus they attribute increased
polarization to increased disagreement over specific issues, rather than general partisanship. Lee (2009) uses party disagreement scores to measure cross-sectional
polarization across issues and substantive, procedural, or parliamentary votes. She
finds considerable variation in party disagreement by policy topic, although disagreement goes up on all policy topics when votes move from substantive to procedural or parliamentary. Thus Lee attributes the bulk of increased polarization to
general partisanship rather than increased policy differences.

Most modern political science studies use the difference of party means in the
first dimension of DW-NOMINATE to measure polarization in Congress (Lewis,
Poole, and Rosenthal 2019). However, DW-NOMINATE scores are a poor tool
to measure polarization across issues, as it requires a large number of annual
observations to estimate the difference between party means. Modern Congresses
hold between 1,500 and 2,000 roll call votes over each two-year period. When these
votes are broken up into 20 issue categories, some of which are much larger than
others, the bins become very small. For example, the 112th Congress (2011–12)
held the most votes on energy issues in decades, with 176 roll calls, while the previous Congress held just 55. Instead, I follow Lee (2009) and use party disagreement scores, which require many fewer observations to reliably estimate.

Party disagreement scores are calculated using Equation A.1. The party disagreement score of roll call vote i is defined as the absolute value of the proportion of Democrats voting aye minus the proportion of Republicans voting aye. If
all members of one party vote aye and no members of other party do, the score
is 1. If the same proportion of each party votes aye, the score is 0. Abstentions,
missed votes, and third-party or independent members are dropped. A value of 0
indicates that the parties voted aye in equal proportions. As the score increases, it
indicates greater differences between the parties. A score of 1 represents a strictly
party-line vote.

Equation A.1. Party Disagreement Score Formula

$$D_i = \left| \left(\frac{Y_d}{V_d} - \frac{Y_r}{V_r} \right) \right|$$

Next, I improve upon existing measures of party disagreement across issues by
incorporating laws passed without roll call votes. Both traditional party disagreement scores and DW-NOMINATE scores overstate the amount of polarization

in the legislative process because they measure party conflict only in roll call votes. Congress processes some of its legislation through roll call voting, but not all of it. Chambers pass the majority of legislation using voice votes or unanimous consent mechanisms (Clinton and Lapinski 2008).[4] Laws are more likely to pass using these procedures when they are less important, involve particularistic goods, and fall in the second session of each Congress (Clinton and Lapinski 2008). They were most common during the textbook Congress era and have declined since (Shepsle 1989). While they are used more commonly for less important legislation, many laws that are approved by voice vote are substantively meaningful. For example, in late December 2018, the 115th Congress used voice votes to approve reauthorizations of the National Flood Insurance Program, Public Health Services Act, and Museum of Library Services Act, a major reform of sexual harassment policies in congressional offices, an expansion of reporting requirements for electronic service providers in child sexual abuse and child pornography cases, funding for new unmanned marine weather data collection systems, a new program to care for Alzheimer's patients, several bills providing benefits to veterans, $1.5 billion in additional foreign aid to East Asian countries threatened by China and North Korea, and a major reform to juvenile justice systems. While party leaders may use voice votes to prevent their members from having to make a tough vote on the record, neither party objected to any of these laws, and thus there is little meaningful party conflict on them. They are also all absent from analysis of polarization of roll call votes. Their absence will inflate the overall level of polarization. If voice votes are unevenly distributed across issues, they will bias estimates of polarization across issues.

I measured voice votes on final passage by inference, using a procedure similar to Clinton and Lapinski's (2008). I started with the U.S. PAP laws and roll call votes data sets. These contain all laws or roll call votes passed by Congress between 1973 and 2018. During this time, Congress passed 11,068 public laws and held 43,272 roll call votes.[5] In each chamber-Congress pair, I searched for the bill number of each noncommemorative law in the roll call votes data. Where no roll call vote was record, I inferred that the law was passed in the chamber using a voice vote procedure.[6] This process yielded 5,431 laws passed by voice vote in the House and 7,616 in the Senate between 1948 and 2018. Note that this process excludes bills passed by voice vote but not signed into law, bills that passed the chamber but were folded into other public laws before final passage, and nonlegislative voice votes, such as on nominations. Figure A.10 plots these votes over time in the House and Senate. I then calculated an adjusted party disagreement score where each voice vote was assigned a score of zero disagreement. We see that the House and Senate each passed hundreds of laws annually using voice votes but trending downward since the 90th Congress (1967–69). Voice votes decreased in the House faster than the Senate for most of the period. A second large drop-off occurred when Republicans took

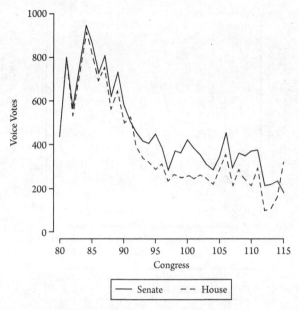

Figure A.10 Laws passed without roll call votes in the House and Senate, 1947–2018.

control of the House of Representatives in the 2010 midterm election, although the House did rebound in the 115th Congress.

Next, I validate voice-vote adjusted party disagreement scores as a valid measurement of polarization in Congress. Party disagreement scores, adjusted for voice votes or not, should be highly correlated with existing methods of measuring polarization like DW-NOMINATE. Figure A.11 compares the average party disagreement score, voice-vote adjusted party disagreement score, and DW-NOMINATE difference of party means for both chambers of Congress from 1973 to 2018. The three series are closely related. All three begin accelerating during the 96th Congress (1979–80), sharply increase around the 104th (1995–96), and increase further after the 112th (2011–12). These results strongly suggest that party disagreement scores, both adjusted for voice votes and unadjusted, are a strong substitute for DW-NOMINATE difference of means as a method for measuring polarization in Congress.

Table A.1 shows the correlations between the three variables for each chamber and the average of both chambers. The unadjusted party disagreement scores and adjusted disagreement scores are almost perfectly correlated (rho = 0.98 for both chambers averaged). Thus, while the inclusion of voice votes changes the y-intercept of party disagreement scores, it does little to change the overall change in polarization over the time series. Excluding laws passed by voice vote increases party disagreement scores by about 0.15. We can examine how voice votes change the

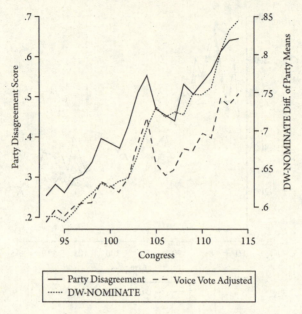

Figure A.11 Comparison between party disagreement scores, voice-vote adjusted scores, and DW-NOMINATE, 1973–2018.

overall distribution of party disagreement scores by plotting each vote or law's score on a histogram. Figure A.12 shows the distribution of party disagreement scores of just roll call votes in the House of Representatives. The distribution is bimodal, with zero or close to zero disagreement being the modal outcome. The second most common outcome is a party-line vote, with about half as many observations as zero disagreement votes. Votes are mostly evenly distributed in between the two polls, with a slight uptick approaching each poll. Figure A.13 shows the distribution once voice votes are added in. Zero disagreement votes now dominate the distribution, at about four times the number of party-line votes. Overall, these results suggest that the level of polarization in Congress is significantly overstated when analyzing just roll call votes, while an analysis of the change in polarization over time using just roll call votes is accurate.

Next, I apply these results to measuring polarization across issue areas. If voice votes are unevenly distributed among issue areas, excluding them from party disagreement scores will change the overall distribution of polarization across issue areas. Unadjusted party disagreement scores will overstate polarization in policy topics that over-index voice votes and understate polarization in policy topics that under-index voice votes. Figure A.14 shows the distribution of voice votes and roll call votes by policy topic during the full 1947–2018 period. Six policy areas—civil rights, macroeconomics, labor, energy, foreign affairs, social welfare, and education—each have a ratio greater than 3:1 roll call votes to voice votes,

METHODOLOGICAL APPENDIX TO CHAPTERS 5-7   159

Table A.1 **Correlations between Party Disagreement Scores, Voice-Vote Adjusted Party Disagreement Scores, and DW-NOMINATE Difference of Means, 1973–2018**

	House		
	Adjusted	Unadjusted	DW-NOMINATE
Adjusted	1		
Unadjusted	0.83	1	
DW-NOMINATE	0.84	0.99	1

	Senate		
	Adjusted	Unadjusted	DW-NOMINATE
Adjusted	1		
Unadjusted	0.96	1	
DW-NOMINATE	0.82	0.76	1

	Congress		
	Adjusted	Unadjusted	DW-NOMINATE
Adjusted	1		
Unadjusted	0.98	1	
DW-NOMINATE	0.94	0.92	1

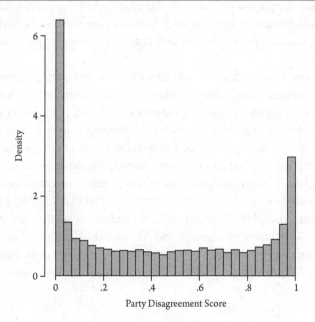

Figure A.12 Histogram without voice votes, House of Representatives.

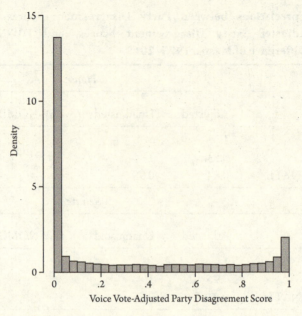

Figure A.13 Histogram, voice vote adjusted, House of Representatives.

with civil rights having a nearly 10:1 ratio. On the other end of the spectrum, law and crime, agriculture, trade, transportation, and public lands each have a ratio of 1.6:1 or fewer roll call votes to voice votes, with public lands as the outlier with 0.38:1 roll call votes to voice votes. Thus, excluding voice votes would make the former group appear less polarized than they are relative to other issues, and vice versa for the latter group. Because voice vote practices changed considerably over time, this cross-sectional variation will also bias change in polarization across time periods.

We can see these results play out across time by comparing the two different party disagreement scores across all 20 policy topics from 1947 to 2018 in Figure A.15. Unlike the aggregate time series compared in Figure A.15, we see that the two series often diverge over time, likely due to changing voice vote practices. Issues like domestic commerce, healthcare, law and crime, agriculture, and environmental policy go through long consensus periods when Congress is passing many laws via voice vote. Adjusted and unadjusted party disagreement scores are only correlated at less than 0.70 on all of these policy topics (see Table A.2). Other issues, such as civil rights, labor, foreign affairs, defense, and social welfare, are correlated at greater than 0.90 during the same period. Thus we should also include voice votes in analyses of change in polarization across issues and time, even though it is not necessary to include them in analyses of overall polarization in Congress.

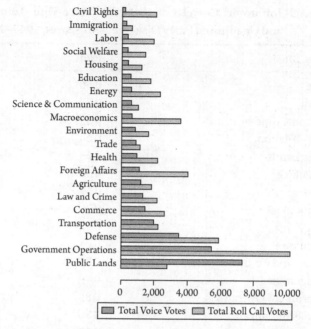

Figure A.14 Total laws passed by voice vote and total roll call votes in Congress, 1947–2018.

We can now explore these data descriptively to understand the variation in polarization across issues. Figure A.16 shows the mean annual voice-vote adjusted party disagreement score across each of the 20 policy topics from 1947 to 2018. We see considerable variation between the policy topics. The most polarized issues tend to be subjects of what Gerring (2001) calls the "Great Debate" between those who favor greater redistribution and government intervention into domestic economic policy and those who favor less. These issues—labor, macroeconomics, social welfare, housing, and education—often define the traditional left-right spectrum in both American politics and other systems. On the other end of the spectrum, issues with local dimensions, such as public lands, transportation, and law and crime, and issues that emerged during the 20th century, such as science, technology and communication, and environmental policy, tend to be far less polarized on average during the full 1947–2018 period.

Table A.2 **Intratopic Correlation between Voice-Vote Adjusted and Unadjusted Party Disagreement Scores, 1947–2018**

Policy Topic	Rho
Trade	0.56
Health	0.57
Law and Crime	0.57
Transportation	0.6
Public Lands	0.63
Commerce	0.65
Housing	0.67
Environment	0.7
Energy	0.72
Agriculture	0.74
Science and Communication	0.75
Immigration	0.79
Government Operations	0.81
Macroeconomics	0.86
Education	0.87
Social Welfare	0.87
Defense	0.91
Foreign Affairs	0.93
Civil Rights	0.94
Labor	0.96

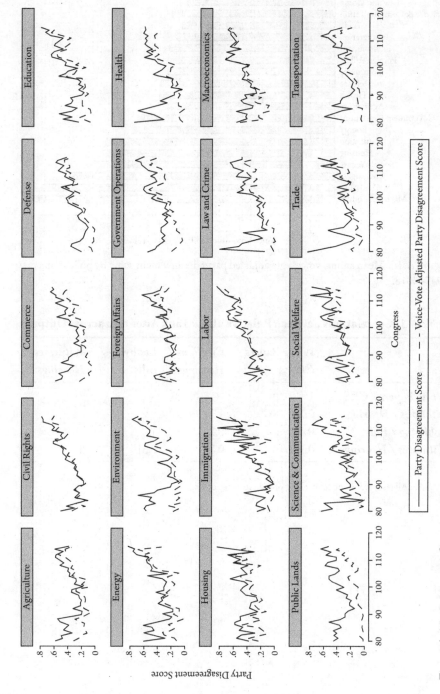

Figure A.15 Comparison between voice-vote adjusted party disagreement scores and unadjusted party disagreement scores, 1947–2018.

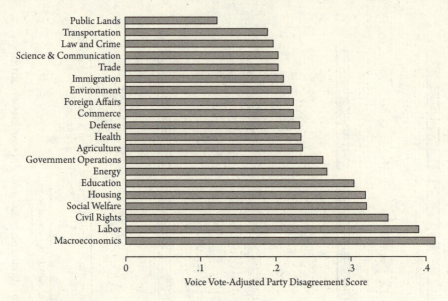

Figure A.16 Mean annual voice-vote adjusted party disagreement score by policy topic, 1947–2018.

Table A.3 **Correlations between Relative Think Tank Attention across Outputs**

	White Papers / CRS	*Citations / Hearings*	*Lobbying / Bills*	*Witnesses / Hearings*
White Papers / CRS	1			
Citations / Hearings	0.72	1		
Lobbying / Bills	0.48	0.75	1	
Witnesses / Hearings	0.78	0.81	0.51	1

Note: All tests are of the natural log of the ratios reported.

Table A.4 **Issue Ownership Values by Comparative Agendas Project Major Policy Topic Area (Fagan 2021)**

Major Topic Area	Egan (2013)[1,2]	Binary Ownership[3]
Agriculture	0	Neither
Civil Rights	n/a	n/a
Defense	14	Republican
Domestic Commerce	n/a	Republican
Education	−10	Democratic
Energy	−3	Neither
Environment	−18	Democratic
Foreign Affairs	6	Republican
Government Operations	0	Neither
Healthcare	−12	Democratic
Housing	n/a	Democratic
Immigration	9	Republican
Labor	−12	Democratic
Law and Crime	7	Republican
Macroeconomics	1	Both
Public Lands	0	Neither
Science and Communication	0	Neither
Social Welfare	−14	Democratic
Trade	5	Republican
Transportation	0	Neither

Note: [1] Values are the coefficient on Egan's (2013) estimate of long-run issue ownership coefficients in public opinion surveys. Negative scores are more Democratic; positive scores are more Republican. Defense is assigned the average of Egan's "Domestic Security" and "Military" category. Macroeconomics is assigned the average of "Inflation," "Taxes," "Economy," "Jobs," and "Inequality" categories. Agriculture, government operations, public lands, science and communication, and transportation policy were coded = 0. No data exist for these areas, all of which tend to have very low levels of party polarization and issue salience (Jochim and Jones 2013).

[2] Civil rights excluded due to conflicting issues contained in the Comparative Agendas Project coding (abortion and civil rights issues), and its failure to meet Egan's consensus issue criteria. Domestic commerce and housing excluded due to a lack of survey data.

[3] Binary values are coded = 1 to the issue area where Egan's data are greater than 5 or less than -5. For housing and commerce, there are no data. I assigned Housing to Democrats as a dimension of social welfare policy and Domestic Commerce to Republicans as a dimension of their advantage on "big government" business or regulatory policy (Petrocik, Benoit, and Hansen 2003).

NOTES

Chapter 1

1. Interview with Stuart Butler, former vice president of domestic and economic policy studies at the Heritage Foundation July 2017.
2. Daschle also worked as a policy advisor for a lobbying firm during the same period.
3. Interview with Robert Greenstein, former president of the Center on Budget and Policy Priorities, June 2023.
4. Interview with James Horney, former Senior Advisor at the Center on Budget and Policy Priorities, June 2023.
5. Horney was an American Political Science Association Congressional Fellow.
6. Interview with Robert Greenstein, June 2023.
7. These data are explained in the Methodological Appendix which follows Chapter 7.

Chapter 2

1. Interview with Robert Greenstein, December 2022.
2. Ibid.
3. Ibid.
4. The child tax credit and EITC provisions were set to expire after 2010 in the original ARRA, but were extended to 2012 by the Tax Relief, Unemployment Insurance Reauthorization and Job Creation Act of 2010.

Chapter 3

1. Interview with a former senior Heritage researcher, July 2017.
2. Like many legends, this story has been repeated many times with slightly different details. Any individual facts may be apocryphal. The version of the story that I recount here is drawn from Edwards (1997), Heritage's internal historian, writing its autobiography to celebrate its 25th anniversary.
3. Interview with a former senior Heritage researcher, July 2017.
4. Interview with a former senior Heritage researcher, July 2017.
5. Interview with a former senior Heritage Foundation researcher, July 2017.
6. Others, such as Rich (2005), propose a similar "marketing" think tank label.
7. Interview with a former Heritage Foundation researcher, July 2019.
8. Interview with Robert Greenstein, December 2022.

9. The CBPP and Economic Policy Institute had budgets of $4 million and $3 million, respectively, in 1996 (Rich 2005). In contrast, the Heritage Foundation, AEI, and Brookings had budgets of $25 million, $13 million, and $17 million, respectively.
10. Author's count of IRS Form 990 filings of partisan think tanks contained in the ProPublica Non-Profit Explorer database.
11. Interview with a former Heritage Foundation researcher, July 2019.
12. The 2020 Democratic platform promised a public option administered by Medicare that will automatically enroll low-income Americans who are not eligible for Medicaid. The CAP plan automatically enrolls children, but not other low-income Americans.
13. Expenditure data drawn from IRS Form 990s contained in ProPublica's Non-Profit Explorer database.
14. A significant portion of CBPP's budget is regranted to state-based organizations that are only loosely affiliated with the Center.
15. Author's count of IRS Form 990 filings of partisan think tanks contained in the ProPublica Non-Profit Explorer database.
16. Interview with a senior Democratic think tank official, July 2017.

Chapter 4

1. Interview with Robert Greenstein, December 2022. Greenstein was frequently invited to speak to Democratic caucus meetings with no other non-think-tank outsiders present to give his opinion on legislation supported by leadership.
2. Interview with Robert Greenstein, June 2022.
3. Accounts often use the phrase "Personnel are policy" and sometimes attribute the quote to Ronald Reagan aid Scott Faulkner. In his autobiography of Heritage, (Edwards 1997) uses "People are policy," attributing the maxim originally to Feulner.
4. Public financing structures vary by country. Some party think tanks are funded through the country's university system (Campbell and Pedersen 2014).

Chapter 5

1. Interview with Robert Greenstein, June 2023.
2. Interview with Robert Greenstein, June 2023.
3. Interview with a senior Democratic-aligned think tank manager, July 2017.
4. A more detailed explanation of how I collected and coded these data is available in the methodological appendix.
5. The international Comparative Agendas Project system uses an additional major topic, cultural policy, that is not used in the U.S. codebook, and thus is not used for this project.

Chapter 6

1. DW-NOMINATE (Lewis, Poole, and Rosenthal 2019) is the most common way that scholars measure polarization of roll call votes in the U.S. Congress. A higher difference in DW-NOMINATE between the average Democrat and Republican indicates that they are less likely to cast the same vote.
2. See Table A.1.
3. Ideally, I would also include *Wall Street Journal* stories, but these data are not available.
4. Unlike revenue and witness testimony, these data suffer from the absence of the total number of political stories produced by these media organizations over the time period. A change in total citations may not be indicative of a change in the total rate of citations.

NOTES

5. I stop the series at 2016 because the Policy Agendas Project hearings data set stops including all hearings in recent years. See the note at the beginning of the 2019 update of the PAP hearings codebook.
6. While the scope of this chapter stops at 2016 due to data availability, polarization continued to increase in the 115th and 116th Congresses. The average difference of party means in the 116th Congress, as of the end of 2019, was 0.91.
7. Each axis contains the residuals of the series when regressed on a trend variable.
8. The relationship remains positive and significant if the 113th Congress, which appears to be an outlier, is excluded (p = 0.012).
9. The book ignores the degree to which the expansions of government under Nixon were by Nixon himself rather than the Democratic-controlled Congress (see Jones, Theriault, and Whyman 2019).

Chapter 7

1. Table A.3 shows the correlations between each of the four outputs.
2. Values for both specifications are found in Table A.4.
3. I use an error correction model instead of an autoregressive distributed lag model. While they produce identical estimates, error correction models offer a simpler interpretation of the short-term impact of an independent variable on a dependent variable.
4. A Hausman test suggests fixed effects are appropriate over random effects (p<.001).

Chapter 8

1. CBO anticipated that Congress would authorize an additional $15 billion in annual spending on border security, but did not include these potential appropriations in the cost estimate.
2. The cost estimate noted that this increased economic growth should lead to macroeconomic feedback effects and thus further increase tax revenues, but did not perform a dynamic analysis of the bill's cost.
3. Author's count based on white papers data set used in previous chapters.
4. While the $7.3 trillion figure seems large, its 50-year period and combination of federal, state, and local analysis exaggerate the bill's impact; the report's estimate comes out to just $106 billion annually. However, the figure was reported as if it were comparable to the CBO's cost estimate of the entire bill (Palmer and Vogel 2013).
5. AEI did produce considerable commentary supporting immigration reform, including using similar political logic as the RNC report. See (Olson 2010; Ponnuru 2013).
6. Tweet from @SenBobCorker, December 15, 2017, https://twitter.com/SenBobCorker/status/941765655497445376, emphasis added.
7. Like any humans, nonpartisan experts bring other types of unconscious biases with them when conducting their analyses. By no means are impartial policy analyses free of these biases, but professions of policy analysts work to minimize unconscious bias where possible. This chapter limits its analysis of bias to policy analysis that tilts toward ideological biases only.
8. The Heritage report was released on January 16, 2010, before the final reconciled version of the bill was available.
9. Because the Cutler report uses the CBO's report on the full bill, including the education provisions, it estimates savings of $524 billion. I subtracted the CBO's $19 billion savings from the education provisions from their estimate.
10. CBO (2018) released a more detailed report on April 19, 2018. It estimated that the deficit impact would be larger, at $1.9 trillion. This chapter uses the December 15 estimate, as it is most comparable to the other impact analyses, which also had little time to perform their final analyses. After gathering data on the TCJA in the field, it further revised the estimate to $2.6 trillion (CBO 2019).

11. The estimates in Table 8.2 average the optimistic and pessimistic scenarios together.
12. One further Republican-aligned think tank report from the Tax Foundation (2017) received considerable attention. It predicted that the TCJA would increase 2027 GDP by 2.68% and the deficit by $448 billion.

Chapter 9

1. AEI's website does not contain all reports it published during the 1970s and 1980s. Of the available reports, none is on environmental policy.
2. Two additional independent nonpartisan estimates of the bill's impact on the economy were produced by the Brookings Institution and CBO. However, neither report specifically predicted the impact on 2030 GDP, so they are not included below.
3. These rates refer to the levelized cost per megawatt hour for new capacity as estimated by U.S. Energy Information Administration, "2016 Levelized Cost of New Generation Resources from the Annual Energy Outlook 2010." Today, the Energy Information Agency (2020) estimates that new capacity for photovoltaic and onshore wind in 2023 at $49/mWh and $43/mWh.
4. The CBPP did not publish any notable reports on climate change in the 2020s.

Chapter 10

1. Taylor was fired from Niskanen in 2021 after domestic violence charges (Ball 2023).
2. Interview with Stuart Butler, July 2017.

Methodological Appendix to Chapters 5–7

1. Two trained graduate students coded a random sample of 500 observations using the procedures of the PAP. They agreed with the major topic codes assigned to 86% of these data.
2. Such as a reference to the think tank on the chamber calendar.
3. Such as a Democrat stating, "Even the ultra-conservative Heritage Foundation supports my plan."
4. There are various processes through which a chamber can approve the final passage of a law without individual members recording their expressed preferences with a roll call vote, such as asking for unanimous consent or for a voice vote. For the sake of simplicity, I refer to all of these processes as "voice votes."
5. Note that some laws receive roll call votes in one chamber but are passed through voice votes in the other chamber.
6. I drew a random sample of 25 of these inferred voice votes and checked them by hand. All 25 were correctly identified as voice votes.

REFERENCES

Abad-Santos, Alex. 2017. "Jimmy Kimmel's Monologue about His Baby's Heart Surgery Is Also a Plea for Affordable Health Care." *Vox*, May 2. https://www.vox.com/2017/5/2/15513404/jimmy-kimmel-monologue-newborn-son-healthcare-surgery.

Abelson, Donald. 2004. "The Business of Ideas: The Think Tank Industry in the USA." In *Think Tank Traditions: Policy Research and the Politics of Ideas*. Manchester: Manchester University Press.

Abou-Chadi, Tarik. 2016. "Niche Party Success and Mainstream Party Policy Shifts—How Green and Radical Right Parties Differ in Their Impact." *British Journal of Political Science* 46 (2): 417–36.

Abramowitz, Alan I., Brad Alexander, and Matthew Gunning. 2006. "Incumbency, Redistricting, and the Decline of Competition in U.S. House Elections." *Journal of Politics* 68 (1): 75–88.

Ainsworth, Scott H., and Frances Akins. 1997. "The Informational Role of Caucuses in the U.S. Congress." *American Politics Quarterly* 25 (4): 407–30.

Albert, Zachary. 2019. "Partisan Policymaking in the Extended Party Network: The Case of Cap-and-Trade Regulations." *Political Research Quarterly* 73 (2): 476–91. 1065912919838326.

Albert, Zachary, and David J. Barney. 2018. "The Party Reacts: The Strategic Nature of Endorsements of Donald Trump." *American Politics Research* 47 (6): 1239–58. 1532673X1880802.

Aldy, Joseph E., et al. 2022. "Looking Back at 50 Years of the Clean Air Act." *Journal of Economic Literature* 60 (1): 179–232.

American Enterprise Institute. N.d. "History of AEI." https://web.archive.org/web/20090708195505/http://www.aei.org/history.

Applebaum, Binyamin. 2020. *Economists Hour: False Prophets, Free Markets, and the Fracture of Society*. New York: Back Bay Books.

Backhouse, Roger. 2005. "The Rise of Free Market Economics: Economists and the Role of the State since 1970." *History of Political Economy* 37 (5): 355–92.

Ball, Molly. 2013. "The Fall of the Heritage Foundation and the Death of Republican Ideas." *The Atlantic*, September. https://www.theatlantic.com/politics/archive/2013/09/the-fall-of-the-heritage-foundation-and-the-death-of-republican-ideas/279955/.

Ball, Molly. 2023. "The Most Interesting Think Tank in American Politics." *Time*, March 7. https://time.com/6258610/niskanen-center-bipartisanship-think-tank-politics/.

Barber, Michael J. 2016. "Ideological Donors, Contribution Limits, and the Polarization of American Legislatures." *Journal of Politics* 78 (1): 296–310.

Barber, Michael, and Nolan McCarty. 2015. "Causes and Consequences of Polarization." In *Political Negotiation: A Handbook*, edited by Jane Mansbridge and Cathie Martin, 39–43. Washington, D.C.: Brookings Institution Press.

Barbose, Galen. 2018. *U.S. Renewables Portfolio Standards: 2018 Annual Status Report*. Berkeley, CA: Lawrence Berkeley National Laboratory.

Baumgartner, Frank R., and Bryan D. Jones. 1993. *Agendas and Instability in American Politics*. Chicago: University of Chicago Press.

Baumgartner, Frank R., and Bryan D. Jones. 2015. *The Politics of Information: Problem Definition and the Course of Public Policy in America*. Chicago: University of Chicago Press.

Baumgartner, Frank R., et al. 2009. *Lobbying and Policy Change: Who Wins, Who Loses, and Why*. Chicago: University of Chicago Press.

Bawn, K. 1997. "Choosing Strategies to Control the Bureaucracy: Statutory Constraints, Oversight, and the Committee System." *Journal of Law, Economics, and Organization* 13 (1): 101–26.

Bawn, Kathleen, Martin Cohen, David Karol, Seth Masket, Hans Noel, and John Zaller. 2012. "A Theory of Political Parties: Groups, Policy Demands and Nominations in American Politics." *Perspectives on Politics* 10 (3): 571–97.

Beach, William W., David Kreutzer, Karen Campbell, and Ben Lieberman. 2009. "Son of Waxman-Markey: More Politics Makes for a More Costly Bill." Heritage Foundation. https://www.heritage.org/government-regulation/report/son-waxman-markey-more-politics-makes-more-costly-bill.

Beck, Nathaniel, and Jonathan N. Katz. 1995. "What to Do (and Not to Do) with Time-Series Cross-Section Data." *American Political Science Review* 89 (3): 634–47.

Berman, Russell. 2016. "The Clinton Transition Team Takes Shape." *The Atlantic*, August. https://www.theatlantic.com/politics/archive/2016/08/the-clinton-transition-team-takes-shape/496034/.

Bertelli, Anthony M., and Jeffrey B. Wenger. 2009. "Demanding Information: Think Tanks and the US Congress." *British Journal of Political Science* 39 (2): 225.

Bevan, Shaun, and Will Jennings. 2014. "Representation, Agendas and Institutions." *European Journal of Political Research* 53 (1): 37–56.

Bevan, Shaun, and Anne Rasmussen. 2017. "When Does Government Listen to the Public? Voluntary Associations and Dynamic Agenda Representation in the United States." *Policy Studies Journal* 00(00): 1–22.

Biden-Harris. 2020. "The Biden Plan to Invest in Middle Class Competitiveness." https://web.archive.org/web/20220630082932/https://joebiden.com/infrastructure-plan/.

Binder, Sarah A. 1999. "The Dynamics of Legislative Gridlock, 1947–96." *American Political Science Review* 93 (3): 519–33.

Binder, Sarah. 2017. "This Is Why the Congressional Budget Office Will Likely Survive Republican Attacks." *Washington Post*, March 15. https://www.washingtonpost.com/news/monkey-cage/wp/2017/03/15/this-is-why-the-congressional-budget-office-will-likely-survive-republican-attacks/?utm_term=.9f7a1471f6d6.

Birkland, Thomas A. 1998. "Focusing Events, Mobilization, and Agenda Setting." *Journal of Public Policy* 18 (1): 53–74.

Birnbaum, Jeffrey H., and Alan S. Murray. 1988. *Showdown at Gucci Gulch: Lawmakers, Lobbyists, and the Unlikely Triumph of Tax Reform*. New York: Vintage Books.

Blake, Aaron. 2013. "Jason Richwine Resigns from Heritage Foundation." *Washington Post*, May 10. https://www.washingtonpost.com/news/post-politics/wp/2013/05/10/jason-richwine-resigns-from-heritage-foundation/.

Bolsen, Toby, and Matthew A. Shapiro. 2018. "The US News Media, Polarization on Climate Change, and Pathways to Effective Communication." *Environmental Communication* 12 (2): 149–63.

Boussalis, Constantine, and Travis G. Coan. 2016. "Text-Mining the Signals of Climate Change Doubt." *Global Environmental Change* 36: 89–100.

Boykoff, Maxwell T., and Jules M. Boykoff. 2004. "Balance as Bias: Global Warming and the US Prestige Press." *Global Environmental Change* 14 (2): 125–36.

Braml, Josef. 2006. "U.S. and German Think Tanks in Comparative Perspective." *German Policy Studies* 3 (3): 222.

REFERENCES

Broaddus, Matt. 2017. "Affordable Care Act's Medicaid Expansion Benefits Hospitals, Particularly in Rural America." Center and Budget on Policy Priorities, June 23. https://www.cbpp.org/resea rch/health/affordable-care-acts-medicaid-expansion-benefits-hospitals-particularly-in-rural.

Brookings Institution. 2019. "Vital Statistics on Congress." https://www.brookings.edu/articles/ vital-statistics-on-congress/.

Brown, Heath. 2011. "Interest Groups and Presidential Transitions." *Congress & the Presidency* 38 (2): 152–70.

Brown, Heath A. 2012. *Lobbying the New President: Interests in Transition.* New York: Routledge.

Brudnick, Ida. 2008. "The Congressional Research Service and the American Legislative Process." Congressional Research Service. https://digitalcommons.ilr.cornell.edu/key_workpl ace/511/.

Bruenig, Matt. 2018. "Thoughts on the Medicare Extra Proposal." *People's Policy Project,* February 26. https://www.peoplespolicyproject.org/2018/02/26/thoughts-on-the-medicare-extra-proposal/.

Brulle, Robert J. 2014. "Institutionalizing Delay: Foundation Funding and the Creation of U.S. Climate Change Counter-Movement Organizations." *Climatic Change* 122 (4): 681–94.

Buckley, William F. 1954. *God and Man at Yale: The Superstitions of "Academic Freedom."* South Bend, IN: ISI Conservative Classics.

Burstein, Paul. 2003. "The Impact of Public Opinion on Public Policy: A Review and an Agenda." *Political Research Quarterly* 56 (1): 29.

Butler, Stuart M. 1989. "Assuring Affordable Health Care for All Americans." Paper presented at the Health Care for the Poor and Underserved, MeHarry Medical College, Nashville, TN. https://web.archive.org/web/20161006185543/http://healthcarereform.procon.org/sour cefiles/1989_assuring_affordable_health_care_for_all_americans.pdf.

Butler, Stuart M., and Edmund F. Haislmaier, eds. 1989. *A National Health System for America.* Washington, D.C.: Heritage Foundation.

Campbell, John L., and Ove K. Pedersen. 2014. *The National Origins of Policy Ideas: Knowledge Regimes in the United States, France, Germany, and Denmark.* Princeton, NJ: Princeton University Press.

Caperton, Richard W. 2012. "Renewable Energy Standards Deliver Affordable, Clean Power." Center for American Progress, April 11. https://www.americanprogress.org/issues/green/ reports/2012/04/11/11397/renewable-energy-standards-deliver-affordable-clean-power/.

CAP Health Policy Team. 2018. *Medicare Extra for All.* Center for American Progress. https://www. americanprogress.org/article/medicare-extra-for-all/.

Capretta, James. 2010. "The Real Budgetary Impact of the House and Senate Health Bills." Heritage Foundation. https://www.heritage.org/health-care-reform/report/the-real-budgetary-imp act-the-house-and-senate-health-bills.

Center for American Progress. 2020. "The Financial System and Climate Change: A Regulatory Imperative." December 18. https://www.americanprogress.org/events/making-money-green/.

Clinton, Joshua D., and John Lapinski. 2008. "Laws and Roll Calls in the U.S. Congress, 1891–1994." *Legislative Studies Quarterly* 33 (4): 511–41.

Clement, Joel. 2017. "I'm a Scientist. I'm Blowing the Whistle on the Trump Administration." *Washington Post.* July 19.

Cohen, Marty, David Karol, Hans Noel, and John Zaller. 2009. *The Party Decides: Presidential Nominations Before and After Reform.* Chicago: University of Chicago Press.

Cohen, Rachel. 2018. "Has the New America Foundation Lost Its Way?" *The Washingtonian,* June 24. https://www.washingtonian.com/2018/06/24/has-new-america-foundation-lost-its-way-anne-marie-slaughter/.

174 REFERENCES

Congressional Budget Office. 2005. "Analyzing the Economic and Budgetary Effects of a 10 Percent Cut in Income Tax Rates." December 1. https://www.cbo.gov/sites/default/files/109th-congress-2005-2006/reports/12-01-10percenttaxcut.pdf.

Congressional Budget Office. 2010. H.R. 4872, Reconciliation Act of 2010 (Final Health Care Legislation). https://www.cbo.gov/publication/21351.

Congressional Budget Office. 2011. "The Effects of Renewable or Clean Electricity Standards." https://www.cbo.gov/sites/default/files/112th-congress-2011-2012/reports/07-26-energy.pdf.

Congressional Budget Office. 2013. "The Economic Impact of S. 744, the Border Security, Economic Opportunity, and Immigration Modernization Act." https://www.cbo.gov/sites/default/files/113th-congress-2013-2014/reports/44346-immigration.pdf.

Congressional Budget Office. 2016. "Federal Subsidies for Health Insurance Coverage for People under Age 65: 2016 to 2026." https://www.cbo.gov/publication/51385.

Congressional Budget Office. 2017. "Cost Estimate for the Conference Agreement on H.R. 1." December 15. https://www.cbo.gov/publication/53415

Congressional Budget Office. 2018. "The Effects of the 2017 Tax Act on CBO's Economic and Budget Projections." April 17. https://www.cbo.gov/sites/default/files/115th-congress-2017-2018/reports/53651-outlook-appendixb.pdf

Congressional Budget Office. 2019. "Additional Information About the Effects of Public Law 115-97." October 28. https://www.cbo.gov/system/files/2019-10/55743-CBO-effects-of-public-law-115-97-on-revenues.pdf.

Congressional Budget Office and Joint Committee on Taxation. 2013. "S. 744: Border Security, Economic Opportunity and Immigration Modernization Act: Cost Estimate." http://www.cbo.gov/sites/default/files/cbofiles/attachments/s744.pdf.

Congressional Research Service. 2019. "The Economic Effects of the 2017 Tax Revision: Preliminary Observations." https://www.everycrsreport.com/reports/R45736.html.

"Conservapedia." *Conservapedia*. https://www.conservapedia.com/Conservapedia

Cooke, Morris L. 1915. "Scientific Management of the Public Business." *American Political Science Review* 9 (3): 488–95.

Copulos, Milton. 1977a. "Clean Air Act Amendments: An Overview." Heritage Foundation. https://www.heritage.org/environment/report/clean-air-act-amendments-overview.

Copulos, Milton. 1977b. "Carter's Energy Program." Heritage Foundation. https://www.heritage.org/environment/report/carters-energy-program.

Cordia, Louis. 1980. "Environmental Protection Agency." In *Mandate for Leadership*. Heritage Foundation.

Costa, Robert. 2022. "Conservative Think Tank's Exclusive Gathering Will Include Biden Official—but Not Trump." CBS News, March 6. https://www.cbsnews.com/news/aei-world-forum-no-trump-biden-official-brian-deese-invited/.

Cox, Gary W., and Matthew D. McCubbins. 1993. *Legislative Leviathan: Party Government in the House*. Berkeley: University of California Press.

Craft, Jonathan, and Michael Howlett. 2012. "Policy Formulation, Governance Shifts and Policy Influence: Location and Content in Policy Advisory Systems." *Journal of Public Policy* 32 (2): 79–98.

Cross-Call, Jesse. 2017. "Affordable Care Act Repeal Puts Veterans' Health Care at Risk." Center on Budget and Policy Priorities, February 10. https://www.cbpp.org/blog/affordable-care-act-repeal-puts-veterans-health-care-at-risk.

Curry, James M. 2015. *Legislating in the Dark: Information and Power in the House of Representatives*. Chicago: University of Chicago Press.

Cutler, David M., Karen Davis, and Kristof Stremikis. 2010. "The Impact of Health Reform on Health System Spending." Center for American Progress, May 21. https://www.americanprogress.org/issues/healthcare/reports/2010/05/21/7731/the-impact-of-health-reform-on-health-system-spending/.

REFERENCES

Daschle, Thomas. 2008. *Critical: What We Can Do about the Health-Care Crisis.* New York: Thomas Dunne Books.

Davenport, Coral. 2017. "With Trump in Charge, Climate Change References Purged From Website." *New York Times.* January 20.

DeLeo, Rob A., Kristin Taylor, Deserai A. Crow, and Thomas A. Birkland. 2021. "During Disaster: Refining the Concept of Focusing Events to Better Explain Long-Duration Crises." *International Review of Public Policy* 3 (1): 5–27. http://journals.openedition.org/irpp/1868.

Democratic Party Platform. 2008. American Presidency Project. https://www.presidency.ucsb.edu/documents/2008-democratic-party-platform.

Desmarais, Bruce A., Raymond J. La Raja, and Michael S. Kowal. 2015. "The Fates of Challengers in U.S. House Elections: The Role of Extended Party Networks in Supporting Candidates and Shaping Electoral Outcomes." *American Journal of Political Science* 59 (1): 194–211.

Devlin, Bernie, ed. 1997. *Intelligence, Genes, and Success: Scientists Respond to The Bell Curve.* New York: Springer.

Dews, Fred. 2016. "What Brookings Did for the 1960 Presidential Transition." Brookings Institution. https://www.brookings.edu/articles/what-brookings-did-for-the-1960-presidential-transition/.

Dimock, Michael, Carol Doherty, Jocelyn Kiley, and Russ Oates. 2014. "Polarization in the American Public." Pew Research Institute, June 12. https://www.pewresearch.org/wp-content/uploads/sites/4/2014/06/6-12-2014-Political-Polarization-Release.pdf.

Downs, Anthony. 1957. "An Economic Theory of Political Action in a Democracy." *Journal of Political Economy* 65 (2): 135–50.

Dreyfuss, Bob. 2004. "An Idea Factory for the Democrats." *The Nation*, February 12. https://www.thenation.com/article/archive/idea-factory-democrats/.

Drutman, Lee. 2017. *The Business of America Is Lobbying: How Corporations Became Politicized and Politics Became More Corporate.* New York: Oxford University Press.

Dumitrescu, Elena-Ivona, and Christophe Hurlin. 2012. "Testing for Granger Non-Causality in Heterogeneous Panels." *Economic Modelling* 29 (4): 1450–60.

Dunlap, Riley E., and Peter J. Jacques. 2013. "Climate Change Denial Books and Conservative Think Tanks: Exploring the Connection." *American Behavioral Scientist* 57 (6): 699–731.

Edwards, Lee. 1997. *The Power of Ideas: The Heritage Foundation at 25 Years.* Ottawa, IL: Jameson Books.

Egan, Patrick J. 2013. *Partisan Priorities: How Issue Ownership Drives and Distorts American Politics.* Cambridge: Cambridge University Press.

Egan, Patrick J. 2014. "'Do Something' Politics and Double-Peaked Policy Preferences." *Journal of Politics* 76 (2): 333–49.

Elis, Niv. 2018. "Corker: Tax Cuts Could Be 'One of the Worst Votes I've Made.'" *The Hill*, April 11.

Energy Information Administration. 2009. "Energy Market and Economic Impacts of H.R. 2454." https://www.eia.gov/analysis/requests/2009/hr2454/pdf/sroiaf(2009)05.pdf.

Energy Information Administration. 2012. "Analysis of the Clean Energy Standards Act of 2012." https://www.eia.gov/analysis/requests/bces12/pdf/cesbing.pdf.

Environmental Protection Agency. 2009. "Economic Impacts of S. 1733: The Clean Energy Jobs and American Power Act of 2009." https://archive.epa.gov/epa/sites/production/files/2016-07/documents/epa_s1733_analysis.pdf.

Erickson, Rosemary J., and Rita J. Simon. 1998. *The Use of Social Science Data in Supreme Court Decisions.* Urbana: University of Illinois Press.

Evich, Helena Bottemiller. 2019. "Agriculture Department Buries Studies Showing Dangers of Climate Change." *POLITICO.* June 23.

Fagan, E. J. 2021. "Issue Ownership and the Priorities of Party Elites in the United States, 2004–2016." *Party Politics*: 27 (2): 149–60.

Fagan, E. J. 2023. "Political Institutions, Punctuated Equilibrium Theory, and Policy Disasters." *Policy Studies Journal* 51 (2): 243–63. https://onlinelibrary.wiley.com/doi/10.1111/psj.12460.

Fagan, E. J., and Alexander C. Furnas. 2024. "Lobbying Responsiveness to Congressional Policy Agendas." *Policy Studies Journal* 52 (1): 11–29.

Fagan, E.J., Bryan D. Jones, and Brooke Shannon. 2023. "Linking Party and Congressional Agendas: New Datasets on Policymaking During the Gilded Age and Progressive Era." *Journal of Historical Political Economy* 3 (3): 305–35.

Fagan, E. J., Bryan D. Jones, and Christopher Wlezien. 2017. "Representative Systems and Policy Punctuations." *Journal of European Public Policy* 24 (6): 809–31.

Fagan, E. J., and Zachary A. McGee. 2022. "Problem Solving and the Demand for Expert Information in Congress." *Legislative Studies Quarterly* 47 (1): 53–77.

Fagan, E. J., Zachary A. McGee, and Herschel F. Thomas. 2021. "The Power of the Party: Conflict Expansion and the Agenda Diversity of Interest Groups." *Political Research Quarterly* 74 (1): 90–102.

Feulner, Edwin. 2000. "The Heritage Foundation." In *Think Tanks and Civil Societies: Catalysts for Ideas and Actions*, edited by James G. McGann and R. Kent Weaver, 67–84. New Brunswick, NJ: Transaction.

Fiorina, Morris P. 2017. *Unstable Majorities: Polarization, Party Sorting, and Political Stalemate*. Stanford, CA: Hoover Institution Press, Stanford University.

Fiorina, Morris P., Samuel J. Abrams, and Jeremy Pope. 2011. *Culture War? The Myth of a Polarized America*. 3rd edition. Boston: Longman.

Fraussen, Bert, and Darren Halpin. 2017. "Think Tanks and Strategic Policy-Making: The Contribution of Think Tanks to Policy Advisory Systems." *Policy Sciences* 50 (1): 105–24.

Friedman, Gerald. 2018. "Center for American Progress' Health Care Plan Does Have Real Merit." *The Hill*, March 4. https://thehill.com/opinion/healthcare/376657-center-for-american-progress-health-care-plan-does-have-real-merit.

Friedman, Joel, and Chad Stone. 2017. "Republican Tax Plans Cost More—and Add Less to Growth—Than Proponents Claim." Center on Budget and Policy Priorities. https://www.cbpp.org/research/federal-tax/republican-tax-plans-cost-more-and-add-less-to-growth-than-proponents-claim.

Friedman, Lisa. 2017. "E.P.A. Cancels Talk on Climate Change by Agency Scientists." *New York Times*. October 22.

Friedman, Lisa. 2019. "White House Tried to Stop Climate Science Testimony, Documents Show." *New York Times*. June 8.

Friedman, Milton. 1962. *Capitalism and Freedom*. Chicago, IL: University of Chicago Press.

Froio, Caterina, Shaun Bevan, and Will Jennings. 2017. "Party Mandates and the Politics of Attention: Party Platforms, Public Priorities and the Policy Agenda in Britain." *Party Politics* 23 (6): 692–703.

Furnas, Alexander C., Timothy M. LaPira, Alexander Hertel-Fernandez, Lee Drutman, and Kevin Kosar. 2023. "More Than Mere Access: An Experiment on Moneyed Interests, Information Provision, and Legislative Action in Congress." *Political Research Quarterly* 76 (1): 348–64.

Furnas, Alexander, Timothy Michael LaPira, and Dashun Wang. 2024. "Partisan Disparities in the Use of Science in Policy." Institute For Policy Research Working Paper. doi:10.31235/osf.io/aep9v.

Furnas, Alexander C., Michael T. Heaney, and Timothy M. LaPira. 2019. "The Partisan Ties of Lobbying Firms." *Research & Politics* 6 (3): 2053168019877039.

Gailmard, Sean, and John W. Patty. 2012. *Learning While Governing: Expertise and Accountability in the Executive Branch*. Chicago: University of Chicago Press.

Gayner, Jeffrey. 1995. "The Contract with America: Implementing New Ideas in the U.S." Heritage Foundation. /political-process/report/the-contract-america-implementing-new-ideas-the-us.

Gerring, John. 2001. *Party Ideologies in America, 1828–1996*. Reprint edition. Cambridge: Cambridge University Press.

REFERENCES

Glastris, Paul, and Haley Sweetland Edwards. 2014. "The Big Lobotomy." *Washington Monthly*, June–August. https://washingtonmonthly.com/magazine/junejulyaug-2014/the-big-lobotomy/.

Grandoni, Dino, and Tyler Pager. 2022. "Biden Reshuffles Top White House Climate Team." *Washington Post*, September 2. https://www.washingtonpost.com/climate-environment/2022/09/02/gina-mccarthy-stepping-down-climate-advisor/.

Gray, Tim. 2016. "Jimmy Kimmel on His First Hollywood Job and How He Got Into TV." *Variety*. September 16. https://variety.com/2016/tv/awards/emmy-host-jimmy-kimmel-120 1859652/.

Green-Pedersen, Christoffer, and Peter B. Mortensen. 2010. "Who Sets the Agenda and Who Responds to It in the Danish Parliament? A New Model of Issue Competition and Agenda-Setting." *European Journal of Political Research* 49 (2): 257–81.

Groseclose, Tim, and Jeffrey Milyo. 2005. "A Measure of Media Bias." *Quarterly Journal of Economics* 120 (4): 1191–237.

Grossmann, Matt. 2014. *Artists of the Possible: Governing Networks and American Policy Change since 1945*. Oxford: Oxford University Press.

Grossmann, Matt, and Casey B. K. Dominguez. 2009. "Party Coalitions and Interest Group Networks." *American Politics Research* 37 (5): 767–800.

Grossmann, Matt, and David A. Hopkins. 2016. *Asymmetric Politics: Ideological Republicans and Group Interest Democrats*. Oxford: Oxford University Press.

Grumbach, Jacob M. 2018. "From Backwaters to Major Policymakers: Policy Polarization in the States, 1970–2014." *Perspectives on Politics* 16 (2): 416–35.

Guber, Deborah Lynn. 2013. "A Cooling Climate for Change? Party Polarization and the Politics of Global Warming." *American Behavioral Scientist* 57 (1): 93–115.

Haas, Eric. 2007. "False Equivalency: Think Tank References on Education in the News Media." *Peabody Journal of Education* 82 (1): 63–102.

Hacker, Jacob S. 2010. "The Road to Somewhere: Why Health Reform Happened: Or Why Political Scientists Who Write about Public Policy Shouldn't Assume They Know How to Shape It." *Perspectives on Politics* 8 (3): 861–76.

Hacker, Jacob S. 2011. "Why Reform Happened." *Journal of Health Politics, Policy and Law* 36 (3): 437–41.

Hacker, Jacob S., and Paul Pierson. 2010. *Winner-Take-All Politics: How Washington Made the Rich Richer—and Turned Its Back on the Middle Class*. New York: Simon & Schuster.

Halberstam, David. 1992. *The Best and the Brightest*. New York: Ballantine Books.

Hall, Richard L., and Alan V. Deardorff. 2006. "Lobbying as Legislative Subsidy." *American Political Science Review* 100 (1): 69–84.

Hammond, Samuel, and Robert Orr. 2021. "The Conservative Case for a Child Allowance." Niskanen Center, February 4. https://www.niskanencenter.org/report-the-conservative-case-for-a-child-allowance/.

Harrington, Scott. 2010. "The Health Insurance Reform Debate." American Enterprise Institute. https://www.aei.org/articles/the-health-insurance-reform-debate/.

Harris, Paul. 2003. "Bush Covers Up Climate Research." *The Guardian*, September 21. https://www.theguardian.com/environment/2003/sep/21/usnews.georgewbush.

Hayek, Fredrich A. 1944. *The Road to Serfdom*. London: Institute Of Economic Affairs.

Heckman, James J. 1995. "Lessons from the Bell Curve." *Journal of Political Economy* 103 (5): 1091–120.

Heritage Foundation. 2015. "IRS Form 990 Filing, Fiscal Year 2015." https://projects.propublica.org/nonprofits/organizations/237327730/201611799349300971/full.

Heritage Foundation. n.d. "Board of Trustees." https://www.heritage.org/board-trustees.

Hertel-Fernandez, Alexander. 2019. *State Capture: How Conservative Activists, Big Businesses, and Wealthy Donors Reshaped the American States, and the Nation*. New York: Oxford University Press.

Hertel-Fernandez, Alexander, Theda Skocpol, and Daniel Lynch. 2016. "Business Associations, Conservative Networks, and the Ongoing Republican War over Medicaid Expansion." *Journal of Health Politics, Policy and Law* 41 (2): 239–86.

Hickey, Emily A., and J. Lon Carlson. 2010. "An Analysis of Trends in Restructuring of Electricity Markets." *Electricity Journal* 23 (5): 47–56.

Hirano, Shigeo, James Snyder, Stephen Ansolabehere, and John Mark Hansen. 2010. "Primary Elections and Partisan Polarization in the U.S. Congress." *Quarterly Journal of Political Science* 5 (2): 169–91.

Holcombe, Randall G. 1980. "An Empirical Test of the Median Voter Model." *Economic Inquiry* 18 (2): 260–74.

Horn, Miriam, and Fred Krupp. 2009. *Earth: The Sequel: The Race to Reinvent Energy and Stop Global Warming*. Illustrated edition. New York: W. W. Norton.

Horsley, Scott. 2017. "9 Sticking Points the House and Senate Have to Work Out in Their Tax Bills." NPR, December 4. https://www.npr.org/2017/12/04/568329807/9-sticking-points-the-house-and-senate-have-to-work-out-in-their-tax-bills.

Houghton, J. T., Y. Ding, D. J. Griggs, M. Noguer, P. J. van der Linden, X. Dai, and K. Maskell. 2001. "TAR Climate Change 2001: The Scientific Basis." International Panel on Climate Change. https://www.ipcc.ch/site/assets/uploads/2018/03/WGI_TAR_full_report.pdf.

Howell, Katie. 2010. "Frustration on Senate's Failure to Act on Energy Policy May Pave Way for 'Clean Energy Standard.'" *New York Times*, December 14. https://archive.nytimes.com/www.nytimes.com/gwire/2010/12/14/14greenwire-frustration-on-senates-failure-to-act-on-energ-90076.html?pagewanted=all.

Howlett, Michael. 2019. "Comparing Policy Advisory Systems beyond the OECD: Models, Dynamics and the Second-Generation Research Agenda." *Policy Studies* 40 (3–4): 241–59.

International Monetary Fund. 2012. "IMF Fiscal Monitor Update: As Downside Risks Rise, Fiscal Policy Has to Walk a Narrow Path, January 2012." Fiscal Monitor. https://www.imf.org/en/Publications/FM/Issues/2016/12/31/As-Downside-Risks-Rise-Fiscal-Policy-Has-To-Walk-a-Narrow-Path.

Jacobson, Gary C. 2015. "It's Nothing Personal: The Decline of the Incumbency Advantage in US House Elections." *Journal of Politics* 77 (3): 861–73.

Jacques, Peter J., Riley E. Dunlap, and Mark Freeman. 2008. "The Organisation of Denial: Conservative Think Tanks and Environmental Scepticism." *Environmental Politics* 17 (3): 349–85.

Jeffreys, Kent. 1989. "Two Cheers for Bush's Clean Air Plan." Heritage Foundation Backgrounder. Heritage later published a report opposing the other provisions of the amendments, but still supporting a cap-and-trade system to reduce acid rain.

Jennings, Will. 2009. "The Public Thermostat, Political Responsiveness and Error-Correction: Border Control and Asylum in Britain, 1994-2007." *British Journal of Political Science* 39 (4): 847–70.

Jochim, Ashley E., and Bryan D. Jones. 2013. "Issue Politics in a Polarized Congress." *Political Research Quarterly* 66 (2): 352–69.

Johnson, Eliana, and Nancy Cook. 2017. "The Real Reason Jim DeMint Got the Boot." *Politico*, May 2. https://www.politico.com/story/2017/05/02/why-jim-demint-was-ousted-from-heritage-237876.

Joint Committee on Taxation. 2017. "Macroeconomic Analysis of the Conference Agreement For H.R. 1, the 'Tax Cuts and Jobs Act.'" December 22. https://www.jct.gov/getattachment/53ad7658-20ac-4c10-b4d0-2759305432aa/x-69-17-5055.pdf.

Jones, Bryan D. 2001. *Politics and the Architecture of Choice: Bounded Rationality and Governance*. Chicago: University of Chicago Press.

Jones, Bryan D., and Frank R. Baumgartner. 2004. "Representation and Agenda Setting." *Policy Studies Journal* 32 (1): 1–24.

Jones, Bryan D., and Frank R. Baumgartner. 2005. *The Politics of Attention: How Government Prioritizes Problems*. Chicago: University of Chicago Press.

Jones, Bryan D., Heather Larsen-Price, and John Wilkerson. 2009. "Representation and American Governing Institutions." *Journal of Politics* 71 (1): 277–90.

Jones, Bryan D., Sean M. Theriault, and Michelle Whyman. 2019. *The Great Broadening: How the Vast Expansion of the Policy-Making Agenda Transformed American Politics*. Chicago: University of Chicago Press.

Jones, Bryan D., and Walter Williams. 2008. *The Politics of Bad Ideas: The Great Tax Cut Delusion and the Decline of Good Government in America*. New York: Pearson Longman.

Jones, Gordon S., and John A. Marini, eds. 1988. *The Imperial Congress: Crisis in the Separation of Powers*. New York: Pharos Books.

Karni, Annie. 2016. "2016 Election: Ken Salazar to Lead Hillary Clinton's Transition Team." *Politico*, August 16. https://www.politico.com/story/2016/08/clinton-transition-team-white-house-salazar-227044.

Karol, David. 2019. *Red, Green, and Blue: The Partisan Divide on Environmental Issues*. Cambridge, UK: Cambridge University Press.

Kim, Seung Min, Jennifer Haberkorn, and Burgess Everett. 2017. "Senate Won't Vote on Last-Ditch Obamacare Repeal Bill." *Politico*, September 26. https://www.politico.com/story/2017/09/26/obamacare-repeal-failure-republican-senate-243148.

Kingdon, John W. 2011. *Agendas, Alternatives, and Public Policies*. Updated 2nd edition. Boston: Longman.

Klein, Ezra. 2012. "Unpopular Mandate." *New Yorker*, June 25. https://www.newyorker.com/magazine/2012/06/25/unpopular-mandate.

Klein, Philip. 2017. "Mick Mulvaney: The Day of the CBO 'Has Probably Come and Gone.'" *Washington Examiner*. May 31.

Klein, Ezra. 2019. "How 'Medicare Extra' Gets to Universal Coverage without Single-Payer." *Vox*, July 23. https://www.vox.com/policy-and-politics/2019/7/23/20699958/medicare-extra-center-american-progress-single-payer-health-reform.

Klein, Ezra. 2019. "An Ex-Libertarian's Quest to Rebuild the Center Right." *The Ezra Klein Show*.

Klein, Ezra. 2021. *Why We're Polarized*. New York: Avid Reader Press.

Kliff, Sarah. 2017. "Jimmy Kimmel Defines the 'Jimmy Kimmel Test' on Health Care." *Vox*, May 9. https://www.vox.com/health-care/2017/5/9/15591764/jimmy-kimmel-test-ahca (June 24, 2023).

Kliff, Sarah. 2018. "Democrats Are Shifting toward Single-Payer. Here's Proof." *Vox*, February 23. https://www.vox.com/policy-and-politics/2018/2/23/17041638/single-payer-medicare-extra-health.

Knobloch-Westerwick, Silvia, Cornelia Mothes, and Nick Polavin. 2020. "Confirmation Bias, Ingroup Bias, and Negativity Bias in Selective Exposure to Political Information." *Communication Research* 47 (1): 104–24.

Koger, Gregory, Seth Masket, and Hans Noel. 2009. "Partisan Webs: Information Exchange and Party Networks." *British Journal of Political Science* 39 (3): 633–53.

Koger, Gregory, Seth Masket, and Hans Noel. 2010. "Cooperative Party Factions in American Politics." *American Politics Research* 38 (1): 33–53.

Konrad Adenauer Stiftung. n.d. "Board of Directors." https://www.kas.de/en/board-of-directors.

Kosar, Kevin. 2016. "Restoring Congress as the First Branch." *R Street Policy Study* 50. https://www.rstreet.org/2016/01/28/restoring-congress-as-the-first-branch/.

Kravitz, Derek, et al. 2018. "Trump Town." *ProPublica*. https://projects.propublica.org/trump-town/.

Krehbiel, Keith. 1998. *Pivotal Politics: A Theory of U.S. Lawmaking*. Chicago: University of Chicago Press.

Krehbiel, Keith. 2006. *Information and Legislative Organization*. Ann Arbor: University of Michigan Press.

Kreutzer, David, Karen Campbell, William Beach, Ben Lieberman, and Nicolas Loris. 2010. "A Renewable Electricity Standard: What It Will Really Cost Americans." Heritage Foundation.

https://www.heritage.org/environment/report/renewable-electricity-standard-what-it-will-really-cost-americans.

Lane, Lee. 2009. "What Will the Climate Bill Cost?" American Enterprise Institute. https://www.aei.org/economics/us-economy/what-will-the-climate-bill-cost/.

LaPira, Timothy M., and Herschel F. Thomas. 2017. *Revolving Door Lobbying: Public Service, Private Influence, and the Unequal Representation of Interests.* Lawrence: University Press of Kansas.

Layman, Geoffrey C., and Thomas M. Carsey. 2002. "Party Polarization and 'Conflict Extension' in the American Electorate." *American Journal of Political Science* 46 (4): 786–802.

Layman, Geoffrey C., Thomas M. Carsey, and Juliana Menasce Horowitz. 2006. "Party Polarization in American Politics: Characteristics, Causes, and Consequences." *Annual Review of Political Science* 9 (1): 83–110.

Lee, Frances E. 2009. *Beyond Ideology: Politics, Principles, and Partisanship in the U.S. Senate.* Chicago: University of Chicago Press.

Lee, Kurtis. 2016. "Bernie Sanders Says Hillary Clinton 'Insulting' California Voters by Not Debating." *Los Angeles Times.* May 23. https://www.latimes.com/nation/politics/trailguide/la-na-trailguide-05232016-htmlstory.html.

Leech, Beth L., Frank R. Baumgartner, Timothy M. La Pira, and Nicholas A. Semanko. 2005. "Drawing Lobbyists to Washington: Government Activity and the Demand for Advocacy." *Political Research Quarterly* 58 (1): 19–30.

Lehrer, Eli. 2023. "An Interview with Eli Lehrer of the R Street Institute: Part I." R Street Institute. https://www.rstreet.org/commentary/an-interview-with-eli-lehrer-of-the-r-street-institute-part-i/.

Levendusky, Matthew S. 2013. "Why Do Partisan Media Polarize Viewers?" *American Journal of Political Science* 57 (3): 611–23.

Lewallen, Jonathan, Sean M. Theriault, and Bryan D. Jones. 2016. "Congressional Dysfunction: An Information Processing Perspective: Congressional Dysfunction and Hearings." *Regulation & Governance* 10 (2): 179–90.

Lewis, Jeffrey B., Keith Poole, and Howard Rosenthal. 2019. "Voteview: Congressional Roll-Call Votes Database." https://www.voteview.com.

Lim, Taekyoung, Tian Tang, and William M. Bowen. 2021. "The Impact of Intergovernmental Grants on Innovation in Clean Energy and Energy Conservation: Evidence from the American Recovery and Reinvestment Act." *Energy Policy* 148: 111923.

Lindaman, Kara, and Donald P. Haider-Markel. 2002. "Issue Evolution, Political Parties, and the Culture Wars." *Political Research Quarterly* 55 (1): 91–110.

Lindsey, Brink, Steven Teles, William Wilkinson, and Samuiel Hammond. 2018. *The Center Can Hold: Public Policy for an Age of Extremes.* Niskanen Center.

Lovett, John, Shaun Bevan, and Frank R. Baumgartner. 2015. "Popular Presidents Can Affect Congressional Attention, for a Little While." *Policy Studies Journal* 43 (1): 22–43.

Lueck, Sarah, January Angeles, Paul N. Van de Water, Edwin Park, and Judith Solomon. 2010. "Health Reform Package Represents Historic Chance to Expand Coverage, Improve Insurance Markets, Slow Cost Growth, and Reduce Deficits." Center on Budget and Policy Priorities. https://www.cbpp.org/research/health-reform-package-represents-historic-chance-to-expand-coverage-improve-insurance.

Lynch, Robert, and Patrick Oakford. 2013. "The Economic Effects of Granting Legal Status and Citizenship to Undocumented Immigrants." Center for American Progress. https://cdn.americanprogress.org/wpcontent/uploads/2013/03/EconomicEffectsCitizenship-1.pdf.

Maher, Thomas V., Charles Seguin, Yongjun Zhang, and Andrew P. Davis. 2020. "Social Scientists' Testimony before Congress in the United States between 1946–2016, Trends from a New Dataset." *PLOS One* 15 (3): e0230104.

Marmor, Theodore. 2014. "Book Review: Critical: What We Can Do about the Health-Care Crisis." *Notre Dame Journal of Law, Ethics & Public Policy* 25 (2): 481.

REFERENCES

Marr, Chuck, Kris Cox, Stephanie Hinggen, Arloc Sherman, Sarah Calame, and Jabari Cook. 2022. "Romney Tax Credit Proposal Is a Step Forward but Falls Short, Targets Low Income Families to Pay for It." Center on Budget and Policy Priorities, July 6. https://www.cbpp.org/sites/defa ult/files/Romney%20CTC%20Proposal%20--%20Paper.pdf.

Masket, Seth E. 2016. *The Inevitable Party: Why Attempts to Kill the Party System Fail and How They Weaken Democracy*. New York: Oxford University Press.

Mason, Lilliana. 2018. *Uncivil Agreement: How Politics Became Our Identity*. Chicago: University of Chicago Press.

Matthews, Dylan. 2013a. "Heritage Says Immigration Reform Will Cost $5.3 Trillion. Here's Why That's Wrong." *Washington Post*, May 6. https://www.washingtonpost.com/news/wonk/ wp/2013/05/06/heritage-says-immigration-reform-will-cost-5-3-trillion-heres-why-thats-wrong/.

Matthews, Dylan. 2013b. "Heritage Study Co-author Opposed Letting in Immigrants with Low IQs." *Washington Post*, May 8. https://www.washingtonpost.com/news/wonk/wp/2013/ 05/08/heritage-study-co-author-opposed-letting-in-immigrants-with-low-iqs/.

Matthews, Dylan. 2022. "How One Man Quietly Stitched the American Safety Net over Four Decades." *Vox*. November 22. https://www.vox.com/the-highlight/23383703/robert-gre enstein-center-budget-policy-priorities.

Mayhew, David R. 1974. *Congress: The Electoral Connection*. New Haven, CT: Yale University Press.

Mayhew, David R. 2005. *Divided We Govern: Party Control, Lawmaking, and Investigations, 1946– 2002*. 2nd edition. New Haven, CT: Yale University Press.

McArdle, John. 2003. "Hillary's Hirings." *Roll Call*, October 17. https://www.rollcall.com/2003/ 10/17/hillarys-hirings/.

McCarty, Nolan, Keith T. Poole, and Howard Rosenthal. 2006. *Polarized America: The Dance of Ideology and Unequal Riches*. Cambridge, MA: MIT Press.

McCarty, Nolan, Keith T. Poole, and Howard Rosenthal. 2009. "Does Gerrymandering Cause Polarization?" *American Journal of Political Science* 53 (3): 666–80.

McConnell, Allan, Anika Gauja, and Linda Courtenay Botterill. 2008. "Policy Fiascos, Blame Management and AWB Limited: The Howard Government's Escape from the Iraq Wheat Scandal." *Australian Journal of Political Science* 43 (4): 599–616.

McCright, Aaron M. 2016. "Anti-Reflexivity and Climate Change Skepticism in the US General Public." *Human Ecology Review* 22 (2): 77–108.

McCright, Aaron M., and Riley E. Dunlap. 2003. "Defeating Kyoto: The Conservative Movement's Impact on U.S. Climate Change Policy." *Social Problems* 50 (3): 348–73.

McCright, Aaron M., and Riley E. Dunlap. 2011. "The Politicization of Climate Change and Polarization in the American Public's Views of Global Warming, 2001–2010." *Sociological Quarterly* 52 (2): 155–94.

McCrimmon, Ryan. 2019. "Economists Flee Agriculture Dept. after Feeling Punished under Trump." *POLITICO*. May 7.

McDonald, Lauren. 2014. "Think Tanks and the Media: How the Conservative Movement Gained Entry into the Education Policy Arena." *Educational Policy* 28 (6): 845–80.

McGann, James. 2016. *The Fifth Estate: Think Tanks, Public Policy, and Governance*. Washington, D.C.: Brookings Institution Press.

McGann, James. 2019. "2018 Global Go To Think Tank Index Report." University of Pennsylvania: Think Tanks and Civil Societies Program. https://repository.upenn.edu/cgi/ viewcontent.cgi?article=1017&context=think_tanks.

McGhee, Eric, Seth Masket, Boris Shor, Steven Rogers, and Nolan McCarty. 2014. "A Primary Cause of Partisanship? Nomination Systems and Legislator Ideology." *American Journal of Political Science* 58 (2): 337–51.

Medvetz, Thomas. 2014. *Think Tanks in America*. Chicago: University of Chicago Press.

Meltzer, C. C. 2011. "Summary of the Affordable Care Act." *American Journal of Neuroradiology* 32 (7): 1165–66.

Michaels, David. 2008. *Doubt Is Their Product: How Industry's Assault on Science Threatens Your Health*. New York: Oxford University Press. http://site.ebrary.com/id/10215788.

Michel, Jean-Baptiste, Yuan Kui Shen, Aviva Presser Aiden, Adrian Veres, Matthew K. Gray. 2011. "Quantitative Analysis of Culture Using Millions of Digitized Books." *Science* 331 (6014): 176–82.

Miller, Chris. 2022. *Chip War: The Fight for the World's Most Critical Technology*. New York: Simon & Schuster.

Miller, Kenneth M. 2017. "Cooperative Media Spending in Senate Campaigns Post–*Citizens United*." *The Forum* 15 (2): 269–89.

Miller, Kenneth M. 2019. "The Divided Labor of Attack Advertising in Congressional Campaigns." *Journal of Politics* 81 (3): 805–19.

Mills, Russell W., and Jennifer L. Selin. 2017. "Don't Sweat the Details! Enhancing Congressional Committee Expertise through the Use of Detailees." *Legislative Studies Quarterly* 42 (4): 611–36.

Mooney, Christopher Z. 1991. "Information Sources in State Legislative Decision Making." *Legislative Studies Quarterly* 16 (3): 445–55.

Mortensen, Peter Bjerre, Christoffer Green-Pedersen, Gerard Breeman, Laura Chaqués-Bonafont, Will Jennings, Peter John, Anna M. Palau, and Arco Timmermans. 2011. "Comparing Government Agendas: Executive Speeches in the Netherlands, United Kingdom, and Denmark." *Comparative Political Studies* 44 (8): 973–1000.

Niskanen Center. 2017. "Conspectus." https://www.niskanencenter.org/wp-content/uploads/2019/09/Niskanen-conspectus-2017-final-1.pdf.

Noel, Hans. 2014. *Political Ideologies and Political Parties in America*. Cambridge: Cambridge University Press.

Nussbaum, Daniel. 1998. "How About a Smog Observance Day in Los Angeles?." *Los Angeles Times*, September 14. https://www.latimes.com/archives/la-xpm-1998-sep-14-me-22627-story.html.

O'Connor, Brendon. 2001. "The Intellectual Origins of 'Welfare Dependency.'" *Australian Journal of Social Issues* 36 (3): 221–36.

Olson, Henry. 2010. "The Way of the Whigs?" American Enterprise Institute. https://www.aei.org/articles/the-way-of-the-whigs/

Olson, Henry. 2020. "Opinion: This New Think Tank Wants to Reform Conservatism. Republicans Ignore It at Their Peril." *Washington Post*, May 5. https://www.washingtonpost.com/opinions/2020/05/05/this-new-think-tank-wants-reform-conservatism-republicans-ignore-it-their-peril/.

Olson, Mancur. 2003. *The Logic of Collective Action: Public Goods and the Theory of Groups*. 21st printing. Cambridge, MA: Harvard University Press.

Open Secrets. 2015. "Bob Corker." https://www.opensecrets.org/personal-finances/net-worth/Bob-Corker?cid=N00027441.

Oreskes, Naomi, and Erik M. Conway. 2011. *Merchants of Doubt: How a Handful of Scientists Obscured the Truth on Issues from Tobacco Smoke to Global Warming*. New York: Bloomsbury Press.

Page, Benjamin I., Jason Seawright, and Matthew J. Lacombe. 2019. *Billionaires and Stealth Politics*. Chicago: University of Chicago Press.

Page, Benjamin R., Joseph Rosenberg, James R. Nunns, Jeffrey Rohaly, and Daniel Berger. 2017. "Macroeconomic Analysis of the Tax Cuts and Jobs Act." Tax Policy Center. https://www.urban.org/sites/default/files/publication/95491/macroeconomic_analysis_of_the_tax_cuts_and_jobs_act_conference_12-20.pdf.

Palmer, Anna, and Kenneth P. Vogel. 2013. "Heritage Does Damage Control." POLITICO. https://www.politico.com/story/2013/05/heritage-foundation-immigration-reform91148.html.

Paltsev, Sergey, John M. Reilly, Henry D. Jacoby, and Jennifer F. Morris. 2009. *The Cost of Climate Policy in the United States*. Report. Cambridge, MA: MIT Joint Program on the Science and Policy of Global Change.

REFERENCES

Pear, Robert. 2008. "Health Care Policy Is in Hands of an Ex-Senator." *New York Times*, December 12. https://www.nytimes.com/2008/12/12/us/politics/12daschle.html.

Penn Wharton Budget Model. 2017. "The Tax Cuts and Jobs Act, as Reported by Conference Committee (12/15/17): Static and Dynamic Effects on the Budget and the Economy." https://budgetmodel.wharton.upenn.edu/issues/2017/12/18/the-tax-cuts-and-jobs-act-reported-by-conference-committee-121517-preliminary-static-and-dynamic-effects-on-the-budget-and-the-economy.

Peterson, Holly L. 2023. "Narrative Policy Images: Intersecting Narrative and Attention in Presidential Stories about the Environment." *Policy Studies Journal* 51 (1): 53–77.

Petrocik, John R., William L. Benoit, and Glenn J. Hansen. 2003. "Issue ownership and presidential campaigning, 1952–2000." *Political Science Quarterly* 118 (4): 599–626.

Plumer, Brad, and Coral Davenport. 2019. "Science Under Attack: How Trump Is Sidelining Researchers and Their Work." *New York Times*. December 28.

Podesta, John. 2008. *Green Recovery*. Center for American Progress. https://www.americanprogress.org/issues/green/reports/2008/09/09/4929/green-recovery/.

Politico Staff. 2012. "Rick Santorum Values Voter Summit: Speech Transcript (Full Text)." *Politico*, September 15. https://www.politico.com/news/stories/0912/81256.html.

Pollin, Robert, James Heintz, and Heidi Garrett-Peltier. 2009. "The Economic Benefits of Investing in Clean Energy." Center for American Progress. https://www.americanprogress.org/issues/green/reports/2009/06/18/6192/the-economic-benefits-of-investing-in-clean-energy/.

Ponnuru, Ramesh. 2013. "New Immigration Bill Has One Terrible Flaw." American Enterprise Institute. https://www.aei.org/articles/new-immigration-bill-has-one-terribleflaw/.

Poole, Keith T., and Howard Rosenthal. 1984. "The Polarization of American Politics." *Journal of Politics* 46 (4): 1061–79.

Popp, David, Francesco Vona, and Joëlle Noailly. 2020. "Green Stimulus, Jobs and the Post-Pandemic Green Recovery." *VoxEU*. July 4. https://voxeu.org/article/green-stimulus-jobs-and-post-pandemic-green-recovery.

Prasad, Monica. 2018. *Starving the Beast: Ronald Reagan and the Tax Cut Revolution*. New York: Russell Sage Foundation.

RAND. 2010. "Analysis of the Patient Protection and Affordable Care Act (HR 3590)." Policy Brief. https://www.rand.org/content/dam/rand/pubs/research_briefs/2010/RAND_RB9514.pdf.

RAND. N.d. a. "A Brief History of RAND." https://www.rand.org/about/history.html.

RAND. N.d. b, "RAND at a Glance." https://www.rand.org/about/glance.html.

Rand, Ayn. 1957. *Atlas Shrugged*. New York: Signet.

Revkin, Andrew C. 2003. "Politics Reasserts Itself in the Debate over Climate Change and Its Hazards." *New York Times*, August 5. https://www.nytimes.com/2003/08/05/science/politics-reasserts-itself-in-the-debate-over-climate-change-and-its-hazards.html.

Republican Party Platform. 2008. American Presidency Project. https://www.presidency.ucsb.edu/documents/2008-republican-party-platform.

Rich, Andrew. 2005. *Think Tanks, Public Policy, and the Politics of Expertise*. Cambridge: Cambridge University Press.

Rich, Andrew, and R. Kent Weaver. 2000. "Think Tanks in the U.S. Media." *Harvard International Journal of Press/Politics* 5 (4): 81–103.

Ringe, Nils, Jennifer Nicoll Victor, and Justin H. Gross. 2013. "Keeping Your Friends Close and Your Enemies Closer? Information Networks in Legislative Politics." *British Journal of Political Science* 43 (3): 601–28.

Roberts, David. 2010. "The Right's Climate Denialism Is Part of Something Much Larger." *Mother Jones*. September 10. https://www.motherjones.com/politics/2010/09/climate-denialism-public-trust.

Roberts, James M. 2022. "Taking the Right Off Autopilot." *American Compass*. April 22.

184   REFERENCES

Rohde, David W. 1991. *Parties and Leaders in the Postreform House*. Chicago: University of Chicago Press.

Rosenfeld, Sam. 2018. *The Polarizers: Postwar Architects of Our Partisan Era*. Chicago: University of Chicago Press.

Rothstein, Samuel. 1990. "The Origins of Legislative Reference Services in the United States." *Legislative Studies Quarterly* 15 (3): 401–11.

Rowell, Alex, and rew Schwartz. 2017. "Millions of Working- and Middle-Class Americans Would See a Tax Increase under the Senate GOP Tax Plan." Center for American Progress. https://www.americanprogress.org/issues/economy/news/2017/11/27/443316/millions-working-middle-class-americans-see-tax-increase-senate-gop-tax-plan/.

R Street Institute. 2002. IRS Form 990 Filing, Fiscal Year 2022. https://projects.propublica.org/nonprofits/organizations/263477125.

The Rush Limbaugh Show. 2013a. "The Four Corners of Deceit." April 29. https://www.rushlimbaugh.com/daily/2013/04/29/the_four_corners_of_deceit_prominent_liberal_social_psychologist_made_it_all_up/.

The Rush Limbaugh Show. 2013b. "We've Been Played on Immigration." June 13. https://www.rushlimbaugh.com/daily/2013/06/13/we_ve_been_played_on_immigration/.

Russakoff, Dale, and Howard Kurtz. 1983. "Compiler of EPA 'Hit Lists' Resigns." *Washington Post*, March 16. https://www.washingtonpost.com/archive/politics/1983/03/16/compiler-of-epa-hit-lists-resigns/a934af45-cdad-4407-927d-a164ca7364ed/.

Sadeh, Shuki. 2018. "The Right-Wing Think Tank That Quietly 'Runs the Knesset.'" *Haaretz*. October 5. https://www.haaretz.com/israel-news/.premium-the-right-wing-think-tank-that-quietly-runs-the-knesset-1.6514722.

Savage, Charlie. 2008. "John Podesta, Shepherd of a Government in Exile." *New York Times*, November 7. https://www.nytimes.com/2008/11/07/us/politics/07podesta.html.

Schaffer, Michael. 2022. "'A Real Chilling Effect': A Lefty Scholar Is Dumping CAP—for AEI." *Politico*, July 15. https://www.politico.com/news/magazine/2022/07/15/capital-city-ruy-teixeira-american-enterprise-institute-00045819.

Scherer, Michael. 2008. "Inside Obama's Idea Factory in Washington." *Time*. November 21. http://content.time.com/time/politics/article/0,8599,1861305,00.html.

Schickler, Eric. 2016. *Racial Realignment: The Transformation of American Liberalism, 1932–1965*. Princeton, NJ: Princeton University Press.

Schmalensee, Richard, and Robert N. Stavins. 2013. "The SO_2 Allowance Trading System: The Ironic History of a Grand Policy Experiment." *Journal of Economic Perspectives* 27 (1): 103–22.

Schwartz, Mildred A. 1990. *The Party Network: The Robust Organization of Illinois Republicans*. Madison: University of Wisconsin Press.

Scott, Dylan. 2017. "Jimmy Kimmel: New Obamacare Repeal Bill Flunks the Jimmy Kimmel Test." *Vox*, September 19. https://www.vox.com/policy-and-politics/2017/9/19/16337466/jimmy-kimmel-test-bill-cassidy-graham.

Seeberg, Henrik Bech. 2017. "How Stable Is Political Parties' Issue Ownership? A Cross-Time, Cross-National Analysis." *Political Studies* 65 (2): 475–92.

Senate Resolution 164. 2023. "A Resolution Honoring the Heritage Foundation on the Occasion of its 50th Anniversary." https://www.congress.gov/bill/118th-congress/senate-resolution/164/.

Shafran, JoBeth S. 2021. "More Than Agents: Federal Bureaucrats as Information Suppliers in Policymaking." *Policy Studies Journal* 50 (4): 921–43. http://onlinelibrary.wiley.com/doi/abs/10.1111/psj.12455.

Shafran, JoBeth Surface. 2015. "Whirlpools of Information: Information Processing in Policy Subsystems 1995–2010." (Thesis, University of Texas). https://repositories.lib.utexas.edu/handle/2152/33349.

REFERENCES

Sheppard, Parker, and David Burton. 2017a. "The Economic Impact of the Tax Cuts and Jobs Act." Heritage Foundation. https://www.heritage.org/taxes/commentary/the-economic-impact-the-tax-cuts-and-jobs-act.

Sheppard, Parker, and David Burton. 2017b. "How the GOP Tax Bill Will Affect the Economy." Issue Brief. Heritage Foundation. https://www.heritage.org/taxes/report/how-the-gop-tax-bill-will-affect-the-economy.

Shepsle, Kenneth W. 1989. "The Changing Textbook Congress." In *Can the Government Govern*, edited by John Chubb and Paul Peterson, 238–66. Washington, D.C.: Brookings Institution Press.

Sides, John, Michael Tesler, and Lynn Vavreck. 2018. *Identity Crisis: The 2016 Presidential Campaign and the Battle for the Meaning of America*. Princeton, NJ: Princeton University Press.

Skocpol, Theda, and Alexander Hertel-Fernandez. 2016. "The Koch Network and Republican Party Extremism." *Perspectives on Politics* 14 (3): 681–99.

Slyomovics, Nettanel. 2021. "The U.S. Billionaires Secretly Funding the Right-Wing Effort to Reshape Israel." *Haaretz*. March 11. https://www.haaretz.com/israel-news/.premium.HIGHLIGHT.MAGAZINE-the-u-s-billionaires-secretly-funding-the-right-wing-effort-to-reshape-israel-1.9611994.

Soroka, Stuart, and Christopher Wlezien. 2010. *Degrees of Democracy: Politics, Public Opinion, and Policy*. Cambridge: Cambridge University Press.

Soroka, Stuart, and Christopher Wlezien. 2019. "Tracking the Coverage of Public Policy in Mass Media." *Policy Studies Journal* 47 (2): 471–91.

Stahl, Jason M. 2016. *Right Moves: The Conservative Think Tank in American Political Culture since 1945*. Chapel Hill: University of North Carolina Press.

Stokes, Leah Cardamore. 2020. *Short Circuiting Policy: Interest Groups and the Battle over Clean Energy and Climate Policy in the American States*. New York: Oxford University Press.

Stone, Chad. 2009. *New EPA and CBO Estimates Refute Claims That House Climate Bill Would Impose Large Costs on Households and the Economy*. Center on Budget and Policy Priorities. https://www.cbpp.org/research/new-epa-and-cbo-estimates-refute-claims-that-house-climate-bill-would-impose-large-costs-on.

Stone, Chad, and Sharon Parrot. 2013. "Examining the Congressional Budget Office Cost Estimate of the Senate Immigration Bill." Center on Budget and Policy Priorities. https://www.cbpp.org/research/examining-the-congressional-budget-office-cost-estimate-of-the-senate-immigration-bill.

Stone, Diane. 1996. *Capturing the Political Imagination: Think Tanks and the Policy Process*. London: Frank Cass.

Supran, Geoffrey, and Naomi Oreskes. 2021. "Rhetoric and Frame Analysis of ExxonMobil's Climate Change Communications." *One Earth* 4 (5): 696–719.

Suskind, Ron. 2004. "Faith, Certainty and the Presidency of George W. Bush." *New York Times*, October 17. https://www.nytimes.com/2004/10/17/magazine/faith-certainty-and-the-presidency-of-george-w-bush.html.

Swan, Jonathan, and Maggie Haberman. 2023. "Heritage Foundation Makes Plans to Staff Next G.O.P. Administration." *New York Times*, April 20. https://www.nytimes.com/2023/04/20/us/politics/republican-president-2024-heritage-foundation.html.

Tankersley, Jim, Thomas Kaplan, and Alan Rappeport. 2017. "Senate Republicans Pass Sweeping Tax Bill." *New York Times*, December 1. https://www.nytimes.com/2017/12/01/us/politics/senate-tax-bill.html.

Tax Foundation. 2017. "Preliminary Details and Analysis of the Tax Cuts and Jobs Act." December 18.

Taylor, Jerry. 2018. "The Alternative to Ideology." Niskanen Center. https://www.niskanencenter.org/the-alternative-to-ideology/.

Teles, Steven Michael. 2008. *The Rise of the Conservative Legal Movement: The Battle for Control of the Law*. Princeton, NJ: Princeton University Press.

Theriault, Sean M. 2003. "The Case of the Vanishing Moderates: Party Polarization in the Modern Congress." https://citeseerx.ist.psu.edu/document?repid=rep1&type=pdf&doi=5ef76d66628028e767fe357c240f04da1fa8e3a9.

Theriault, Sean M. 2006. "Party Polarization in the US Congress: Member Replacement and Member Adaptation." *Party Politics* 12 (4): 483–503.

Theriault, Sean M. 2008. *Party Polarization in Congress.* Cambridge: Cambridge University Press.

Theriault, Sean M. 2013. *The Gingrich Senators.* Oxford: Oxford University Press.

Thiel, Peter. 2009. "The Education of a Libertarian." *Cato Unbound*, April 13. https://www.cato-unbound.org/2009/04/13/peter-thiel/education-libertarian.

Thomsen, Danielle M. 2014. "Ideological Moderates Won't Run: How Party Fit Matters for Partisan Polarization in Congress." *Journal of Politics* 76 (3): 786–97.

Thomsen, Danielle M. 2017. *Opting Out of Congress: Partisan Polarization and the Decline of Moderate Candidates.* Cambridge: Cambridge University Press.

Thorn, Alexandra, and Andy Green. 2021. "The SEC's Time to Act." Center for American Progress, February 19. https://www.americanprogress.org/article/secs-time-act/.

Time Magazine. 1965. "We Are All Keynesians Now," December 31.

U.S. Energy Information Administration. *U.S. Energy Outlook 2010.* 2010. https://www.nrc.gov/docs/ML1111/ML111170385.pdf.

U.S. Energy Information Administration. 2012. "Analysis of the Clean Energy Standard Act of 2012." https://www.eia.gov/analysis/requests/bces12/pdf/cesbing.pdf.

U.S. Energy Information Administration. 2020. *Annual Energy Outlook 2020.* https://www.eia.gov/outlooks/aeo/pdf/AEO2020%20Full%20Report.pdf.

U.S. House of Representatives. 2003. "The Clear Skies Initiative: A Multipollutant Approach to the Clean Air Act." Hearing before the Subcommittee on Energy and Air Quality of the Committee on Energy and Commerce, July 8. https://www.govinfo.gov/content/pkg/CHRG-108hhrg88427/html/CHRG-108hhrg88427.htm.

Van De Water, Paul. 2010. "Health Reform Essential for Reducing Deficit and Slowing Health Care Costs." Center on Budget and Policy Priorities. https://www.cbpp.org/research/health-reform-essential-for-reducing-deficit-and-slowing-health-care-costs.

Van De Water, Paul, and James R. Horney. 2010. "Health Reform Will Reduce the Deficit." Center on Budget and Policy Priorities. https://www.cbpp.org/research/health-reform-will-reduce-the-deficit.

Victor, Jennifer Nicoll, and Nils Ringe. 2009. "The Social Utility of Informal Institutions: Caucuses as Networks in the 110th U.S. House of Representatives." *American Politics Research* 37 (5): 742–66.

Voß, Jan-Peter. 2007. "Innovation Processes in Governance: The Development of 'Emissions Trading' as a New Policy Instrument." *Science and Public Policy* 34 (5): 329–43.

Wadler, Joyce. 2000. "Public Lives: The Wonk, er, Woman behind Mrs. Clinton." *New York Times*, October 4. https://www.nytimes.com/2000/10/04/nyregion/public-lives-the-wonk-er-woman-behind-mrs-clinton.html.

Wall Street Journal. 2008. "Rahm Emanuel on the Opportunities of Crisis." November 19. YouTube. https://www.youtube.com/watch?v=_mzcbXi1Tkk.

Walter, Karla, et al. 2020. "Electric Vehicles Should Be a Win for American Workers." Center for American Progress, September 23. https://www.americanprogress.org/article/electric-vehicles-win-american-workers/.

Watkins, Shanea, and Patrick Tyrrell. 2009. "The Stimulus Bill: $825 Billion in Forgone Family Spending." Heritage Foundation. https://www.heritage.org/budget-and-spending/report/the-stimulus-bill-825-billion-forgone-family-spending.

Weaver, R. Kent. 1986. "The Politics of Blame Avoidance*." *Journal of Public Policy* 6 (4): 371–98.

Weaver, R. Kent. 1989. "The Changing World of Think Tanks." *PS: Political Science and Politics* 22 (3): 563–78.

Weidenbaum, Murray L. 2011. *The Competition of Ideas: The World of the Washington Think Tanks.* New Brunswick, NJ: Transaction.

REFERENCES

Weinglass, Simona. 2019. "Meet the Conservative Activists Who Want to Override the Supreme Court." *Times of Israel*. June 5. https://www.timesofisrael.com/meet-the-conservative-activists-who-want-to-override-the-supreme-court/.

White House. 2021. "The Build Back Better Framework." https://www.whitehouse.gov/build-back-better/.

White House. 2008. "Energy for America's Future: Diversifying Our Energy Supply and Confronting Climate Change." Fact sheet, December 15. https://georgewbush-whitehouse.archives.gov/infocus/energy/.

White House. 2002. "The Clear Skies Initiative." News Release. https://georgewbush-whitehouse.archives.gov/news/releases/2002/02/clearskies.html.

Williams, Walter. 1998. *Honest Numbers and Democracy. Social Policy Analysis in the White House, Congress, and the Federal Agencies*. Washington, DC: Georgetown University Press.

Williamson, Elizabeth, and Kenneth P. Vogel. 2019. "The Rematch: Bernie Sanders vs. a Clinton Loyalist." *New York Times*, April 15. https://www.nytimes.com/2019/04/15/us/politics/tanden-sanders-.html.

Wilsok, V. Seymour. 1973. "The Relationship between Scientific Management and Personnel Policy in North American Administrative Systems." *Public Administration* 51 (2): 193–205.

Wlezien, Christopher. 1995. "The Public as Thermostat: Dynamics of Preferences for Spending." *American Journal of Political Science* 39 (4): 981–1000.

Wlezien, Christopher. 2005. "On the Salience of Political Issues: The Problem with 'Most Important Problem.'" *Electoral Studies* 24 (4): 555–79.

Wolbrecht, Christina. 2000. *The Politics of Women's Rights: Parties, Positions, and Change*. Princeton, NJ: Princeton University Press.

Wolbrecht, Christina. 2002. "Explaining Women's Rights Realignment: Convention Delegates, 1972–1992." *Political Behavior* 24 (3): 237–82.

Wolfe, Michelle. 2012. "Putting on the Brakes or Pressing on the Gas? Media Attention and the Speed of Policymaking." *Policy Studies Journal* 40 (1): 109–26.

Wood, B. Dan. 1988. "Principals, Bureaucrats, and Responsiveness in Clean Air Enforcements." *American Political Science Review* 82 (1): 213–34.

Wood, B. Dan, and Soren Jordan. 2017. *Party Polarization in America: The War over Two Social Contracts*. Cambridge: Cambridge University Press. http://ebooks.cambridge.org/ref/id/CBO9781108164450.

Workman, Samuel. 2015. *The Dynamics of Bureaucracy in the US Government*. Cambridge: Cambridge University Press.

Workman, Samuel, Deven Carlson, Tracey Bark, and Elizabeth Bell. 2021. "Measuring Interest Group Agendas in Regulatory Proposals: A Method and the Case of US Education Policy." *Interest Groups & Advocacy* 11: 26–45. https://doi.org/10.1057/s41309-021-00129-w.

Workman, Samuel, Bryan D. Jones, and Ashley E. Jochim. 2009. "Information Processing and Policy Dynamics." *Policy Studies Journal* 37 (1): 75–92.

Workman, Samuel, JoBeth Shafran, and Tracey Bark. 2017. "Problem Definition and Information Provision by Federal Bureaucrats." *Cognitive Systems Research* 43: 140–52.

Ye, Jason. 2012. "Summary of the Clean Energy Standard Act of 2012 (S.2146)." Center for Climate and Energy Solutions. https://www.c2es.org/document/summary-of-the-clean-energy-standard-act-of-2012-s-2146/.

Zaller, John. 1992. *The Nature and Origins of Mass Opinion*.

Zelizer, Julian E. 2006. *On Capitol Hill: The Struggle to Reform Congress and Its Consequences, 1948–2000*. Cambridge: Cambridge University Press.

Zeller, Shawn. 2007. "Conservapedia: See under 'Right.'" *New York Times*. March 5.

Zhou, Yanmengqian, and Lijiang Shen. 2022. "Confirmation Bias and the Persistence of Misinformation on Climate Change." *Communication Research* 49 (4): 500–523.

Zycher, Benjamin. 2012. "Wind and Solar Power, Part III: Chasing the Green Tail." American Enterprise Institute. https://www.aei.org/research-products/report/wind-and-solar-power-part-iii-chasing-the-green-tail/.

INDEX

For the benefit of digital users, indexed terms that span two pages (e.g., 52–53) may, on occasion, appear on only one of those pages.

Tables and figures are indicated by *t* and *f* following the page number

ACA. *See* Affordable Care Act
advocacy models, 34
AEI. *See* American Enterprise Institute
Affordable Care Act (ACA)
  to CAP, 109, 111
  to CBPP, 54–56, 55*f*
  costs of, 8–9
  to Democratic Party, 1–4
  exchanges, 86
  Medicaid and, 54
  partisanship and, 61*f*, 61
  policy analysis of, 109–12
  politics of, 56–57
  Sebelius for, 45–46
Afghanistan, 10, 61*f*, 61
agenda setting
  comparative agendas, 59–61, 60*t*
  congressional agendas, 66*t*, 67
  dynamic, 63–67
  partisan think tanks and, 54–57, 55*f*, 58–59, 67–68
  scholarship and, 67–68, 95–96
  U.S. Policy Agendas Project, 8, 25–26, 59–61, 60*t*, 89, 93–94, 152–53, 156–57
Albert, Zachary, 52
American Clean Energy and Security Act, 127–32, 128*t*
American Compass, 138
American Enterprise Association, 28, 32
American Enterprise Institute (AEI). *See also* data collection
  CAP and, 5, 39
  CBPP and, 117–18
  climate change to, 126*f*, 126–27, 128–29
  culture of, 32

EPA to, 129
  Harrington for, 111
  Heritage Foundation and, 8, 58, 63, 111–12, 112*t*, 114–15, 130–31, 131*t*
  immigration reform to, 169n.5
  issue attention to, 64*f*, 65–66
  leadership at, 35, 105
  to partisan think tanks, 8
  politics at, 33
  Reagan and, 50
  Republican Party and, 84, 116–17, 117*t*
  scholarship from, 34, 101–2
  Tax Foundation and, 116–17
  Trump to, 137
  white papers at, 59
American Legislative Exchange Council, 84
American Recovery and Reinvestment Act, 10–11, 20, 50
American Rescue Plan (2021), 136
Americans with Disabilities Act, 75–76
analytical bureaucracy formation, 27, 28*f*
Aron-Dine, Aviva, 54
asymmetric polarization, 142–44
Atlas Shrugged (Rand), 31*f*
attention dynamics, 13–14

Backhouse, Roger, 27
Baker, Raymond, 15
Baroody, William, 32, 33
Baroody, William, Jr., 35
The Bell Curve (Murray), 35, 104–5
Bernstein, Jared, 50
bias, scholarship on, 107–9, 169n.7
biased policy analysis, 102–5
Biden, Joe, 45–46, 54, 86, 109, 115–17

INDEX

Bingaman, Jeff, 129–30
Boorstin, Bob, 39
Border Security, Economic Opportunity and Immigration Modernization Act (2013), 99–102
Boskin, Michael, 36
Brainard, Lael, 133
Brookings Institution
  CBO and, 170n.2
  to Kennedy, J. F., 50–51
  reputation of, 107
  scholarship from, 5, 28–29, 32
  testimony, 83–84
  Urban Institute and, 113
Brown, Scott, 3
Brownback, Sam, 129
Buckley, William F., 30–32, 31f, 43, 142–43
Build Back Better, 86
Bush, George H. W., 36, 75–76, 103–4, 120–21
Bush, George W., 121, 124
Butler, Stuart, 2, 137
Buttigieg, Pete, 40

Campbell, John, 25
CAP. *See* Center for American Progress
Capitalism and Freedom (Friedman), 31f, 139–40
CARES Act, 21
Carter, Jimmy, 38, 120
Casey, William, 35
Cass, Oren, 5
Cassidy, Bill, 56–57
CATO Institute, 35, 135
CBO. *See* Congressional Budget Office
CBPP. *See* Center on Budget and Policy Priorities
"The Center Can Hold" (Lindsey), 135–36
Center for American Progress (CAP). *See also* data collection
  ACA to, 109, 111
  AEI and, 5, 39
  American Recovery and Reinvestment Act and, 20
  Boorstin for, 39
  budget of, 40
  CBO and, 101
  CBPP and, 111–12, 112t, 115, 116–17, 117t, 127–28, 143–44
  climate change to, 126–27, 126f, 130, 131t, 132–33
  COVID-19 to, 132–33
  Daschle for, 2–3
  Democratic Party and, 40, 45–46, 84, 118
  health care to, 168n.12
  Heritage Foundation and, 4, 7, 117–18, 131–32
  history of, 43
  issue attention to, 64f, 65–66
  to knowledge regimes, 7

Obama to, 50
Podesta for, 11, 146
policy alternatives from, 10–11
policy analysis from, 109
in policy debates, 40
priorities of, 63
renewable energy to, 12–13
reputation of, 8
TCJA to, 113–14
Trump to, 137
Center for Economic and Policy Research, 5
Center on Budget and Policy Priorities (CBPP). *See also* data collection
  ACA to, 54–56, 55f
  AEI and, 117–18
  budget of, 40, 168n.14
  CAP and, 111–12, 112t, 115, 116–17, 117t, 127–28, 143–44
  CBO and, 8–9, 68
  climate change to, 126–27, 126f, 130, 131t
  earned income tax credit, 11
  foreign policy to, 63
  Greenstein for, 4, 11, 12, 48–49, 146
  Heritage Foundation and, 5, 38–39, 50
  immigration reform to, 101
  issue attention to, 64f, 65–66
  macroeconomics to, 113–14
  to Obama, 4
  policy alternatives from, 10–11
  RAND Corporation and, 111–12, 112t
  reputation of, 4, 8, 39
Chafee, John, 2
Change for America (CAP), 40, 50
Charles Rivers Associates, 128–29
Christian Democratic Party, 51–52
Civil Rights Act, 30, 69, 71, 140–41
Clean Air Act, 119–21
Clean Energy Standard Act, 129–30
Clean Water Act, 119–20
Clear Skies Initiative, 121
climate change
  to AEI, 126–27, 126f, 128–29
  to CAP, 126–27, 126f, 130, 131t, 132–33
  to CBPP, 126–27, 126f, 130, 131t
  to Heritage Foundation, 126–27, 126f, 132
  International Panel on Climate Change, 121–22
  to Republican Party, 119–20
climate change denial
  climate solutions and, 127–32
  economics of, 132–33
  green jobs and, 119–21, 133–34
  in partisan think tanks, 125–27
  scholarship on, 9
  in U.S., 121–25
Clinton, Bill, 1, 38–39, 45, 76
Clinton, Hillary, 40, 45–46, 50

INDEX

Clinton, Joshua, 156–57
Colbert, Stephen, 56–57
Collins, Susan, 56
committee staff, 81–82, 82*f*
comparative agendas, 59–61, 60*t*
confounding variables, 93–95, 97*t*
Congress. *See specific topics*
congressional agendas, 66*t*, 67
Congressional Budget Office (CBO)
    Brookings Institution and, 170n.2
    CBPP and, 8–9, 68
    Congressional Research Office and, 80–81, 81*f*
    data collection from, 169n.10
    immigration reform to, 100–1
    Joint Committee on Taxation and, 109, 113
    legislation costs to, 143
    Office of Technology Assessment and, 29–30
    partisan think tanks to, 108–9
    RAND Corporation and, 110, 111–12
    scholarship and, 111, 130
    TCJA to, 105–6, 107
congressional capacity, cuts to, 80–84
Congressional Record citations, 91, 92*f*, 92–93, 149–51, 164*t*
Congressional Research Office
    CBO and, 80–81, 81*f*
    issues to, 90, 97
    Joint Committee on Taxation and, 107
    reports, 62*f*, 62–63, 64*f*
    scholarship from, 28*f*, 29–30
    think tanks and, 63–66, 65*t*, 66*t*
"The Conservative Case for a Child Allowance" (Hammond and Orr), 136
conservatives. *See* Republican Party
Contract for America, 78*f*, 80–81, 82–83
Coors, Joseph, 32–33, 43, 76–77
Cordia, Louis J., 120
Corker, Bob, 105–7
Corporation Transparency Act, 15
correlations between relative think tank attention across outputs, 164*t*
COVID-19, 21, 132–33
Creative Helpful Incentives to Produce Semiconductors Act, 21
Critical (Daschle), 2–3
Cutler, David, 111, 169n.9

Daschle, Tom, 2–3
data collection
    from CBO, 169n.10
    Congressional Record citations, 149–51
    DW-NOMINATE data, 73–74, 75*f*, 77–79, 77*f*, 78*f*, 80*f*, 96, 155–58, 158*f*, 159*f*
    error correction models in, 169n.3
    hearing witnesses, 152–53
    lobbying disclosure reports, 89, 91, 91*f*, 151–52

    for polarization across issues, 153–61
    voice votes in, 170n.2
    white papers, 147–49
Deese, Brian, 137
DeMint, Jim, 137
democracy
    asymmetric polarization in, 142–44
    Democracy Alliance, 39
    information and, 139–40
    information wars and, 9, 135–39, 140–42, 144–46
    to policymakers, 14
    in U.S., 14
Democratic Party. *See also specific topics*
    ACA to, 1–4
    alliances of, 47–48
    CAP and, 40, 45–46, 84, 118
    compromise to, 21
    Democratic Leadership Council to, 39
    earned income tax credit to, 12
    healthcare to, 168n.12
    Heritage Foundation to, 38
    history of, 87–88, 139–40
    ideology of, 42
    neutral experts to, 143–44
    Nixon and, 76–77, 169n.9
    partisan knowledge regimes to, 38–42
    policy goals of, 12–13, 18
    Republican Party and, 9, 19, 24, 30, 51, 69, 84–85, 111–12, 112*t*, 119, 123
    think tanks to, 35–36, 105, 111
DeMuth, Chris, 35
Department of Agriculture, 143
Department of Education, 18, 75–76
Department of Energy, 127
disclosure reports, 89, 91*f*, 91
distribution of white paper policy attention, 147–49, 148*f*, 149*f*
Doar, Robert, 146
Dole, Bob, 38
Ducey, Doug, 137
Dunn, Anita, 50
DW-NOMINATE data. *See* data collection

earned income tax credit, 11, 12
Edwards, Lee, 33, 50
Egan, Patrick J., 93–94
Eisenhower, Dwight D., 30, 36
Elementary and Secondary Education Act, 30, 69
elites, 71–72, 73–75, 84–85, 88, 142–44
Emanuel, Rahm, 3, 10, 13, 14
The Emerging Democratic Majority (Teixeira), 137
Endangered Species Act, 119–20
Energy Information Agency, 130–32, 131*t*
Environmental Protection Agency (EPA), 27, 69, 87–88, 103–4, 119–21, 127–29, 128*t*

192

INDEX

Environment and Public Works
    Committee, 125–26
EPA. *See* Environmental Protection Agency
Equal Rights Amendment, 88
Europe, 51–52
European People's Party, 51–52

Fagan, E. J., 52, 93–94. *See also specific topics*
Federal Reserve, 133
Feulner, Ed
    DeMint and, 137
    for Heritage Foundation, 50, 137, 146
    reputation of, 32–33, 43
    Weyrich and, 76–77
Field Foundation, 38
Flake, Jeff, 100
Food Nutrition Service, 38
Ford, Gerald, 30, 32, 34–35, 36, 87–88, 119–20
Ford, Henry, 27
foreign aid nongovernmental organizations, 15
Four Corners of Deceit (Limbaugh), 24–25
free-markets, 137–39
Friedman, Milton, 30, 31*f*, 31
Furman, Jason, 11

Gaspard, Patrick, 50
GDP. *See* Gross Domestic Product
Germany, 5, 51–52
Gingrich, Newt, 6, 7, 71–72, 82–83
Global Financial Integrity, 15
global warming, 122*f*, 122. *See also* climate change
God and Men at Yale (Buckley), 31*f*, 31–32, 43,
    139–40, 142–43
Goldwater, Barry, 30
Google Books, 122*f*, 122
Graham, Lindsey, 57, 100, 129
Graham-Cassidy amendment, 56–57
Great Depression, 19–20
Great Recession, 19–20, 134
Green, Andy, 133
green jobs, 9, 119–21, 133–34
"Green Recovery" (CAP), 11
Greenstein, Robert
    American Recovery and Reinvestment Act
        and, 50
    career of, 38
    for CBPP, 4, 11, 12, 48–49, 146
    Clinton, B., and, 38–39
    in interviews, 168n.1
    Obama and, 11
    with White House National Economic
        Council, 11
Gross Domestic Product (GDP)
    to Charles Rivers Associates, 128–29
    economics of, 108
    to nonpartisan experts, 114–17, 116*t*, 117*t*

projections, 116–17, 117*t*
real, 113, 116*t*, 127, 128*t*
think tanks and, 170n.12
Grossman, Matt, 41–42, 105

Haislmaier, Edmund, 2
Hammond, Samuel, 136
Harrington, Scott, 111
Harris, Kamala, 86, 115–17
Hayek, Friedrich, 30–31, 31*f*
healthcare, 1–4, 54–57, 55*f*, 168n.12. *See also*
    Affordable Care Act
Health Equity and Access Improvement Act, 2
hearing witnesses. *See* witness testimony
Heartland Institute, 137–38
Heritage Action, 40
Heritage Foundation. *See also* data collection
    AEI and, 8, 58, 63, 111–12, 112*t*, 114–15, 130–
        31, 131*t*
    CAP and, 4, 7, 117–18, 131–32
    Carter to, 120
    CBPP and, 5, 38–39, 50
    Center for Data Analysis, 109
    climate change to, 126–27, 126*f*, 132
    to Democratic Party, 38
    EPA to, 120
    Feulner for, 50, 137, 146
    growth of, 76–77
    history of, 7, 25, 32–34, 43, 69, 84, 139–42
    ideology to, 35
    IHS Global Insight to, 128–29
    immigration reform to, 101–2
    influence of, 74
    in information wars, 139–40
    issue attention to, 64*f*, 65–66
    leadership at, 33
    Meese for, 51–52
    modern conservatives to, 7
    to Podesta, 39
    policy agenda of, 67
    Reagan to, 34–35
    Republican Party and, 36, 111, 134, 142–43
    research by, 33
    revenue of, 76–77, 77*f*–78*f*
    success of, 35, 67
    Tax Foundation and, 116–17, 117*t*
    think tanks and, 67–68
    Trump and, 46–47, 46*f*
Higher Education Act (1965), 110
histograms, 157–58, 159*f*, 160*f*
Hogan, Larry, 137
Honest Numbers (Williams), 36
Hoover, Herbert, 19–20
Hopkins, David, 41–42, 105
Horney, James, 4
Human Diversity (Murray), 104–5

INDEX

IHS Global Insight, 128–29
immigration reform, 99–102
Inflation Reduction Act (2022), 146
information
  democracy and, 139–40
  elite, 142–44
  Energy Information Agency, 130–32, 131*t*
  legislative, 82
  misinformation, 21–22
  polarization, 145
  from think tanks, 74
information wars
  democracy and, 9, 135–39, 140–42, 144–46
  elite information in, 142–44
  Heritage Foundation in, 139–40
  think tanks in, 58
Infrastructure Investment and Jobs Act, 86
Inhofe, Jim, 125–26
intense policy demanders, 16
international Comparative Agendas Project
    system, 168n.5
International Panel on Climate Change, 121–22
intratopic correlation between voice-vote adjusted
    and unadjusted party disagreement scores,
    160, 162*t*
"IQ and Immigration Policy" (Richwine), 102
Iraq, 10, 61, 61*f*
IRS forms, 74
Israel, 142
issues
  to Congressional Research Office, 90, 97
  issue attention, 64*f*, 65–66, 66*t*, 67
  issue ownership, 93–95, 97*t*
  issue salience, 63–65, 65*t*
  partisan think tanks across, 86–87, 97–98
  polarization across, 86–95, 97–98, 97*t*, 153–61
  polarization across issues, 153–61
  scholarship on, 87
  white papers and, 90

Jim Crow laws, 30
Jimmy Kimmel Live, 56–57
Johnson, Lyndon, 1, 36, 71
Joint Committee on Taxation, 107, 109, 113
Jones, Bryan D., 27, 72–73

Kaczynski, Ted, 137–38
Kennedy, John F., 50–51
Kennedy, Ted, 3
Kimmel, Jimmy, 56–57
Klobuchar, Amy, 40
knowledge regimes. *See also* partisan knowledge
    regimes
  CAP to, 7
  partisan think tanks and, 7
  to policymakers, 25–26, 26*f*

politics of, 43
scholarship on, 25
technocratic, 26–38
think tanks and, 41–42
in U.S., 52
Koch, Charles, 35, 135
Koch brothers, 84–85
Kohelet Policy Forum, 142
Konrad Adenauer Stiftung Foundation, 5, 51–52
Krupp, Fred, 120–21

laissez-faire capitalism, 30–31
laissez-faire libertarianism, 19
Lane, Lee, 128–29
Lapinski, John, 156–57
laws passed without roll call votes in the House and
    Senate, 156–57, 157*f*
Lee, Francis, 71–72
Lee, Mike, 137
legislative information, 82
Legislative Reference Service, 29–30
Legislative Reorganization Act (1970), 28*f*
Lehman Brothers, 10
Lehrer, Eli, 137–38
Lewis, Peter, 39, 73–74
libertarianism, 19, 30
Lieberman, Joe, 123
Lieberman-Warner Climate Security Act
    (2008), 123
Limbaugh, Rush, 24–25, 100
Lindsey, Brinks, 135–36
lobbying
  attention to policy in bills disclosed in lobbying
    disclosure relative to bills, 151–52, 153*f*
  bills, 164*t*
  disclosure reports, 89, 91, 91*f*, 151–52
  distribution of attention to policy in bills named
    in lobbying disclosures, 151–52, 152*f*
  economics of, 106
  Lobbying Disclosure Act, 151
  think tanks, 18
  in U.S., 17–18
Losing Ground (Murray), 35, 104–5

macroeconomics, 62–63, 113–14
Mandate (Heritage Foundation), 34–35, 40, 50, 120
The Man Show (TV show), 56–57
markets, 123–24
marriage penalty, 77–79
Matthews, Dylan, 102
McCain, John, 56, 100, 123
McConnell, Mitch, 137
McGann, James, 34
McNamara, Robert, 50–51
mean annual voice-vote adjusted party
    disagreement score by policy topic, 161, 164*f*

media organizations, 168n.4
Medicaid
    ACA and, 54
    to Democratic Party, 168n.12
    expansion of, 55–56, 110
    history of, 1, 30, 40, 49, 69
    support for, 141–42
Medicare, 1, 30, 40, 49, 69, 110, 168n.12
Meese, Edwin, 51–52
misinformation, 21–22
modern conservatives, 7, 139–40
money laundering, 15
most important problems, 63–67
Murkowski, Lisa, 56
Murray, Charles, 35, 104–5

National Bureau of Economic Research, 28
National Economic Council, 40
National Health Interview Survey, 55
National Parks System, 87–88
National Press Club, 33–34
Nelson, Ben, 3
Neustadt, Richard, 50–51
neutral experts, 6–7, 18, 20, 47–48, 143–44
New Deal, 26–27
newspaper citations, 79–80, 80f
Nigeria, 15
Niskanen Center, 135–38, 140
Nixon, Richard
    Clean Air Act by, 119–20
    Democratic Party and, 76–77, 169n.9
    economics to, 30
    Eisenhower and, 36
    Ford, G., and, 30, 32, 87–88
    Reagan and, 35, 71, 82–83
    Train and, 119–20
Noel, Hans, 31–32
nomination contests, 16–17
nonaligned think tanks, 140
nongovernmental organizations, 15
nonneutral experts, 6–7
nonpartisan experts, 52–53, 111–12, 112t–17t, 114–17
nonpartisan witnesses, 83–84, 83f
Nozick, Robert, 30–31

Obama, Barack
    ACA to, 1, 2–3
    Biden and, 109
    to CAP, 50
    CBPP to, 4
    election of, 71
    in elections, 45–46
    Emanuel and, 10
    Greenstein and, 11
    Lehman Brothers to, 10
    Trump and, 54

Office of Management and Budget, 45–46
Office of Technology Assessment, 29–30, 80–
    81, 81f
Oliver, John, 56–57
Omnibus Budget Appropriations Act (1993), 3–4
Ordinary Least Squares, 93–95, 97t
Orr, Robert, 136

Page, Benjamin, 113
Palmieri, Jennifer, 40
Paltsev, Sergey, 127
panel models, 95–97
partisan knowledge regimes
    to Democratic Party, 38–42
    history of, 24–26, 26f
    politics of, 42–44
    to Republican Party, 30–38
    technocratic knowledge regimes and, 26–38
partisan policy demanders, 16–18
partisanship, 42, 43–44, 61, 61f, 84
partisan think tanks
    agenda setting and, 54–57, 55f, 58–59, 67–68
    budgets of, 41, 41t
    to CBO, 108–9
    climate change denial in, 125–27
    in Congress, 75–80
    cuts to congressional capacity and, 80–84
    data and methods of, 59–63
    distribution of citation policy attention relative
        to hearings, 150–51, 151f
    distribution of partisan think tank citation policy
        attention, 150f, 150–51
    dynamic agenda setting in, 63–67
    economics of, 41, 41t
    issue polarization and, 88–95
    across issues, 86–87, 97–98
    networking by, 17
    newspaper citations of, 79–80, 80f
    polarization and, 6, 8, 69, 73–75, 84–85, 95–
        97, 140–42
    political parties and, 5–6
    politics in, 145–46
    for presidents, 49
    scholarship on, 6–9
    strategy of, 103
    white paper policy attention and, 61f–64f,
        61–63
    witnesses, 77–79, 78f, 83f, 83–84
partisan witnesses, 81–82, 82f
party competition, 51
party disagreement
    comparison between party disagreement
        scores, voice-vote adjusted scores, and DW-
        NOMINATE, 157, 158f
    scholarship on, 95t, 96–97
    score formula, 155

INDEX

voice-vote adjusted party disagreement, 89, 157, 158*f*, 159*t*, 161, 162*t*, 163*f*–64*f*
party organizations, 7–8, 9, 45, 46*f*, 47–53
Patient Protection and Affordable Care Act. *See* Affordable Care Act
Pederson, Ove, 25
Pelosi, Nancy, 146
Penn Wharton Budget Model, 113, 115–17, 117*t*
Podesta, John, 11, 39, 43, 45, 146
polarization
  asymmetric, 142–44
  in Congress, 75–80
  Congressional Record citations and, 91, 92*f*
  in COVID-19, 21
  information, 145
  across issues, 86–95, 97–98, 97*t*, 153–61
  lobbying disclosure reports and, 91*f*, 91
  partisan think tanks and, 6, 8, 69, 73–75, 84–85, 95–97, 140–42
  policy analysis and, 8–9, 99–102, 117–18
  policy debates in, 22–23
  of political parties, 6
  of problem-solving, 20–23
  research on, 70–73
  of roll call votes, 168n.1
  trends, 125
  in U.S., 3–4
  witness testimony and, 92–93, 93*f*
policy analysis
  of ACA, 109–12
  alternatives in, 1–2
  bad, 145
  biased, 102–5
  of Biden-Harris tax plan, 115–17
  Center for Economic and Policy Research, 5
  comparing, 107–9
  polarization and, 8–9, 99–102, 117–18
  problem-solving and, 6–7
  of renewable portfolio standards, 129–32, 131*t*
  of TCJA, 105–7, 112–15
policy attention, 61–63, 61*f*–64*f*
policy debates, 22–23, 40
policy demanders, 16–18, 19–20, 22, 46–47
policymakers
  advisers of, 48
  attention dynamics to, 13–14
  in COVID-19, 21
  democracy to, 14
  Emanuel and, 14
  goals of, 102–3
  knowledge regimes to, 25–26, 26*f*
  policy entrepreneurs, 14, 15–16
  politics of, 21–22
  in Republican Party, 25
  think tanks and, 28–29, 59
  U.S., 25

political entrepreneurs, 87
political parties
  ideology of, 22
  neutral experts to, 47–48
  nomination contests in, 16–17
  partisanship in, 43–44
  partisan think tanks and, 5–6
  party disagreement, 95*t*, 96–97
  party organizations and, 7–8
  polarization of, 6
  policy decisions by, 7–8
  positivism to, 37
  problem-solving to, 13–16
  scholarship on, 16
  U.S., 5, 7–8, 47, 53
politics. *See specific topics*
Poole, Keith T., 70, 73–74
Porter, Roger, 36
positivism, 37
The Power of Ideas (Edwards), 50
primary elections, 70–71
privately controlled party organizations, 45, 46*f*, 47–53
problem-solving
  to partisan policy demanders, 16–18
  polarization of, 20–23
  policy analysis and, 6–7
  to political parties, 13–16
  politics of, 10–13, 18–20
Progressive Era, 26–38
Progressive Policy Institute, 39
progressives. *See* Democratic Party
ProPublica, 46, 74
ProQuest Congressional database, 74
public preferences, 14

Rand, Ayn, 30–31, 31*f*
RAND Corporation, 29, 107, 110, 111–12, 112*t*
Reagan, Ronald, 7, 34–35, 38, 50, 71, 82–83
real GDP, 113, 116*t*, 127, 128*t*
Rector, Robert, 101–2
redistributive economic policy, 97–98
renewable energy, 11–13, 129–32, 131*t*, 170n.3
Republican Party. *See also specific topics*
  ACA to, 1–4
  AEI and, 84, 116–17, 117*t*
  climate change to, 119–20
  Clinton, B., to, 76
  compromise to, 21
  conservatism in, 82–83
  Democratic Party and, 9, 19, 24, 30, 51, 69, 84–85, 111–12, 112*t*, 119, 123
  economic conservatives in, 19
  elites in, 88
  gridlock to, 144–45
  Heritage Foundation and, 36, 111, 134, 142–43

INDEX

Republican Party (*cont.*)
history of, 31*f*, 87–88, 139–40
ideology of, 42
McCain for, 123
modern, 7
neutral experts to, 143
partisan knowledge regimes to, 30–38
polarization to, 73
policymakers in, 25
TCJA to, 170n.12
think tanks for, 103–4, 134
in U.S., 2
welfare reform to, 104–5
research universities, 83–84, 83*f*
Rich, Andrew, 35–36
Richwine, Jason, 101–2
The Road to Serfdom (Hayek), 31*f*, 139–40, 141
Roberts, James M., 138
Romney, Mitt, 2, 136
Roosevelt, Franklin Delano, 75–76, 75*f*
Roosevelt, Theodore, 87–88
Rosenthal, Howard, 70, 73–74
R Street Institute, 137–38
Rubin, Meir, 142
Rubio, Marco, 100
Ruckelshaus, William, 119–20

salience, 93–95, 97*t*
Samuelsson, Robert, 50–51
Sanders, Bernie, 45–46
Sandler, Herb, 39
Sandler, Marion, 39
Schlafly, Andrew, 36–37
Schlafly, Phyllis, 36–37
Sebelius, Kathleen, 45–46
"The SEC's Time to Act" (Thorn and Green), 133
Security and Exchange Commission, 133
Shakir, Faiz, 45–46
Social Security reform, 75–76
Soros, George, 39
South Africa, 75–76
State Policy Network, 84
Suskind, Ron, 37

Tanden, Neera, 45–47, 50
Tax Cuts and Jobs Act (TCJA)
Biden-Harris tax plan compared to, 115–16
to Corker, 105–7
economics of, 169n.4
impact of, 8–9
politics of, 105–7, 112–15
to Republican Party, 170n.12
to Trump, 106, 109
Tax Foundation, 5, 107, 116–17, 117*t*
Tax Policy Center, 113, 115–17, 117*t*
Taylor, Fredrick, 27

Taylor, Jerry, 135
TCJA. *See* Tax Cuts and Jobs Act
technocratic knowledge regimes, 26–38
technology, 123–24
Teixeira, Ruy, 137
Theriault, Sean M., 27, 71–73
Thiel, Peter, 19–20
think tanks. *See also* partisan think tanks
analytical bureaucracy formation and, 27, 28*f*
in Cold War, 29
Congressional Research Office and, 63–66, 65*t*, 66*t*
correlations between relative think tank attention across outputs, 164*t*
to Democratic Party, 35–36, 105, 111
expansion of, 41, 41*t*
GDP and, 170n.12
Heritage Foundation and, 67–68
information from, 74
in information wars, 58
in Israel, 142
issue attention in, 65–66, 66*t*, 67
issue salience in, 63–65, 65*t*
knowledge regimes and, 41–42
lobbying, 18
nonaligned, 140
policymakers and, 28–29, 59
prioritization in, 48
for Republican Party, 103–4, 134
speaking engagements with, 168n.1
systems at, 52
think tank witnesses, 81*f*
in U.S., 5, 39
Thorn, Alexandra, 133
Title IX, 18
total laws passed by voice vote and total roll call votes in Congress, 158–60, 161*f*
Toxic Substances Control Act, 119–20
Train, Russell, 119–20
Truman, Harry, 1
Trump, Donald, 46–47, 46*f*, 54, 106, 109, 137, 143
Trumpka, Richard, 48

unconscious bias, 169n.7
United States (U.S.)
advocacy models in, 34
CARES Act in, 21
climate change denial in, 121–25
conservatives in, 2
democracy in, 14
economics in, 19–20
elites in, 84–85
healthcare in, 54–57, 55*f*
insurance companies in, 1–2
international Comparative Agendas Project system to, 168n.5

INDEX

Israel and, 142
knowledge regimes in, 52
libertarianism in, 30
lobbying in, 17–18
National Parks System, 87–88
Nigeria and, 15
nonpartisan experts in, 52–53
partisanship in, 84
party organizations in, 9
polarization in, 3–4
Policy Agendas Project, 8, 25–26, 59–61, 60t, 89, 93–94, 152–53, 156–57
policymakers, 25
political parties, 5, 7–8, 47, 53
Progressive Era in, 26–38
think tanks in, 5, 39
Urban Institute, 29, 55, 107, 113
Urban Jobs and Enterprise Zone Act, 34–35
U.S. *See* United States

Values Voter summit (2012), 37
Van de Water, Paul, 4
voice-vote adjusted party disagreement scores, unadjusted party disagreement scores compared to, 160, 163f
voice-votes. *See* data collection
Voting Rights Act, 69, 140–41

Weber, Max, 17–18
welfare reform (1996), 39, 104–5
Weyrich, Paul, 32–33, 43, 76–77
"What Will the Climate Bill Cost?" (Lane), 128–29

White House National Economic Council, 11
white papers
    at AEI, 59
    data collection from, 147–49
    distribution of white paper policy attention, 147–49, 148f, 149f
    issues and, 90
    lobbying disclosure reports and, 89
    policy attention, 61f–64f, 61–63, 90f, 90
    scholarship on, 148f, 164t
Whyman, Michelle, 27, 72–73
Williams, Walter, 36
Win Ben Stein's Money (TV show), 56–57
witness testimony
    distribution of relative testimony policy attention relative to hearings, 153, 154f
    distribution of testimony attention to policy, 153, 154f
    hearing witnesses, 81f–83f, 81–82, 83–84, 92–93, 93f, 152–53, 164t
    nonpartisan witnesses, 83f, 83–84
    partisan think tanks witnesses, 77–79, 78f, 83f, 83–84
    partisan witnesses, 81–82, 82f
    revenue and, 168n.4
    scholarship from, 79, 79f, 92–93, 93f
    think tank witnesses, 81f
Wolbrecht, Christina, 88
women's rights, 88

Zients, Jeffrey, 50
Zycher, Benjamin, 130–31